T0211503

Lecture Notes in Artificial Intelligence   9935

Subseries of Lecture Notes in Computer Science

More information about this series at http://www.springer.com/series/1244

Matteo Baldoni · Cristina Baroglio
Floris Bex · Floriana Grasso
Nancy Green · Mohammad-Reza Namazi-Rad
Masayuki Numao · Merlin Teodosia Suarez (Eds.)

Principles and Practice of Multi-Agent Systems

International Workshops:
IWEC 2014, Gold Coast, QLD, Australia, December 1–5, 2014, and
CMNA XV and IWEC 2015, Bertinoro, Italy, October 26, 2015
Revised Selected Papers

 Springer

Editors

Matteo Baldoni
Università degli Studi di Torino
Turin
Italy

Cristina Baroglio
Università degli Studi di Torino
Turin
Italy

Floris Bex
Utrecht University
Utrecht
The Netherlands

Floriana Grasso
University of Liverpool
Liverpool
UK

Nancy Green
University of North Carolina Greensboro
Greensboro, NC
USA

Mohammad-Reza Namazi-Rad
University of Wollongong
Wollongong, NSW
Australia

Masayuki Numao
Osaka University
Osaka
Japan

Merlin Teodosia Suarez
De La Salle University
Manila
Philippines

ISSN 0302-9743   ISSN 1611-3349   (electronic)
Lecture Notes in Artificial Intelligence
ISBN 978-3-319-46217-2   ISBN 978-3-319-46218-9   (eBook)
DOI 10.1007/978-3-319-46218-9

Library of Congress Control Number: 2016958993

LNCS Sublibrary: SL7 – Artificial Intelligence

Printed on acid-free paper

This Springer imprint is published by Springer Nature
The registered company is Springer International Publishing AG
The registered company address is: Gewerbestrasse 11, 6330 Cham, Switzerland

Preface

This volume contains selected and revised versions of papers that were presented at the 15th Workshop on Computational Models of Natural Argument (CMNA XV), at the 5th International Workshop on Empathic Computing (IWEC-14), and at the 6th International Workshop on Empathic Computing (IWEC-15).

While IWEC-14 was co-located with the 13th Pacific Rim International Conference on Artificial Intelligence (Gold Coast, Australia, December 1–5, 2014), the other two workshops were held with the 14th International Conference on Principles and Practice of Multi-Agent Systems (PRIMA 2015) on October 26, 2015, in Bertinoro (Forlí-Cesena), Italy. PRIMA is one of the oldest active agent computing forums, beginning in 1998 as a regional agent workshop (the Pacific Rim International Workshop on Multi-Agents). Alongside the main conference, PRIMA includes workshops that are intended to facilitate active exchange, interaction, and comparison of approaches, methods, and various ideas in specific areas related to intelligent agent systems and multi-agent systems. PRIMA started as an Asia-Pacific workshop in 1998 and has been running as a full conference since 2009 to become one of the leading and influential scientific conferences for research on multi-agent systems. Each year, PRIMA brings together researchers, developers, and practitioners from academia and industry to showcase research in several domains, ranging from foundations of agent theory and engineering aspects of agent systems, to emerging interdisciplinary areas of agent-based research. Previous successful editions were held in Nagoya, Japan (2009), Kolkata, India (2010), Wollongong, Australia (2011), Kuching, Malaysia (2012), Dunedin, New Zealand (2013), Gold Coast, Australia (2014), and Bertinoro, Italy (2015).

The CMNA workshop series attracts high-quality submissions from researchers around the world since its inception in 2001. CMNA acts to nurture and provide succor to the ever-growing community working on argument and computation, a field developed in recent years overlapping argumentation theory and artificial intelligence. AI has witnessed a prodigious growth in uses of argumentation throughout many of its subdisciplines: agent system negotiation protocols that demonstrate higher levels of sophistication and robustness; argumentation-based models of evidential relations and legal processes that are more expressive; groupwork tools that use argument to structure interaction and debate; computer-based learning tools that exploit monological and dialogical argument structures in designing pedagogic environments; decision support systems that build upon argumentation theoretic models of deliberation to better integrate with human reasoning; and models of knowledge engineering structured around core concepts of argument to simplify knowledge elicitation and representation problems. Furthermore, benefits have not been unilateral for AI, as demonstrated by the increasing presence of AI scholars in classic argumentation theory events and journals, and AI implementations of argument finding application in both research and pedagogic practice within philosophy and argumentation theory. The longest standing event on argument and computation, the CMNA series forms a complement to more recent series, like ArgMAS, which began in 2004, COMMA, which held its first meeting in 2006, and the more recent ArgMining, which started in 2014.

The IWEC workshop series started in 2010 (in conjunction with the HumanCom 2010 conference, in the Philippines), and was subsequently held in 2011 in Vietnam, in 2012 in Malaysia along with PRICAI, in 2013 in China along with IJCAI, in 2014 in Australia along with PRICAI, and in 2015 in Italy along with the PRIMA conference. It is a well-known venue for researchers interested in technologies that bring emotional and social intelligence into computing systems. Empathic computing systems are software or physical context-aware computing systems capable of building user models and provide richer, naturalistic, system-initiated empathic responses with the objective of providing intelligent assistance and support. Empathy is viewed as a cognitive act that involves the perception of the user's thought, affect (i.e., emotional feeling or mood), intention or goal, activity, and/or situation and a response due to this perception that is supportive of the user. An empathic computing system is ambient intelligent, i.e., it consists of seamlessly integrated ubiquitous networked sensors, microprocessors, and software for it to perceive the various user behavioral patterns from multimodal inputs. Empathic computing systems may be applied to various areas such as e-health, geriatric domestic support, empathic home/space, productivity systems, entertainment, and e-learning. Lastly, this approach draws upon the expertise in, and theories of, ubiquitous sensor-rich computing, embedded systems, affective computing, user-adaptive interfaces, image processing, digital signal processing, and machine learning in artificial intelligence.

Papers submitted to these workshops were reviewed by at least three reviewers, and the accepted papers were included in the informal workshop proceedings and presented at the workshops. Selected papers were then invited to be revised and submitted for consideration for inclusion in this volume after further review by the workshop program chairs. CMNA XV had 12 submissions. Four were selected for inclusion in this volume. IWEC-14 had 11 submissions, and four were selected for this volume. IWEC-15 had eight submisisons, of which five were selected for this volume.

We thank the members of the workshop Program Committees who produced timely reviews under tight time constraints, and hope you enjoy the proceedings!

July 2016

Matteo Baldoni
Cristina Baroglio
Floris Bex
Floriana Grasso
Nancy Green
Mohammad-Reza Namazi-Rad
Masayuki Numao
Merlin Teodosia Suarez

Organization

PRIMA 2015 Workshop Chairs

Matteo Baldoni   University of Turin, Italy
Mohammad-Reza   University of Wollongong, Australia
  Namazi-Rad

PRIMA 2015 Tutorial Chair

Cristina Baroglio   University of Turin, Italy

CMNA XV Workshop Organizers

Floris Bex   University of Utrecht, The Netherlands
Floriana Grasso   University of Liverpool, UK
Nancy Green   University of North Carolina Greensboro, NC, USA

IWEC 2014 and IWEC 2015 Workshop Organizers

Masayuki Numao   Osaka University, Japan
Merlin Teodosia Suarez De La Salle University, Philippines
The Duy Bui   Vietnam National University - Hanoi, Vietnam
Ma. Mercedes Rodrigo Ateneo de Manila University, Philippines

CMNA XV Program Committee

Andrew Aberdein   Florida Institute of Technology, USA
Michał Araszkiewicz   Jagiellonian University, Poland
Kevin Ashley   University of Pittsburgh, USA
Katarzyna Budzynska   Polish Academy of Sciences, Poland,
                      and University of Dundee, UK
Tim Bickmore   Northeastern University, Boston, USA
Guido Boella   University of Turin, Italy
Elena Cabrio   Inria, France
Claire Cardie   Cornell University, USA
Chrysanne Di Marco   University of Waterloo, Ontario, Canada
Reva Freedman   Northern Illinois University, USA
Anne Gardner   Atherton, CA, USA
Massimiliano Giacomin University of Brescia, Italy
Tom Gordon   Fraunhofer FOKUS, Berlin, Germany
Davide Grossi   University of Liverpool, UK

Stella Heras	Universitat Politecnica de Valencia, Spain
Helmut Horacek	Universität des Saarlandes, Saarbrücken Germany
Fabrizio Macagno	Universidade Nova de Lisboa, Portugal
Fabio Paglieri	ISTC-CNR, Rome, Italy
Vincenzo Pallotta	University of Fribourg, Switzerland
Paul Piwek	Open University, UK
Chris Reed	University of Dundee, UK
Sara Rubinelli	University of Lugano, Switzerland
Patrick Saint-Dizier	IRIT-CNRS, Toulouse, France
Serena Villata	Inria, France
Doug Walton	University of Windsor, Ontario, Canada
Simon Wells	Edinburgh Napier University, UK
Adam Wyner	University of Aberdeen, UK
Tangming Yuan	University of York, UK

IWEC-14 and IWEC-15 Program Committee

Eriko Aiba	Japan Advanced Industrial Science and Technology, Japan
Arnulfo Azcarraga	De La Salle University, Philippines
Judith Azcarraga	De La Salle University, Philippines
Ryan Baker	Columbia University, USA
Nigel Bosh	University of Notre Dame, USA
Rafael Cabredo	Osaka University, Japan
Nick Campbell	Trinity College, Dublin
Scotty Craig	Arizona State University, USA
Jocelynn Cu	De La Salle University, Philippines
Akihiro Kashihara	University of Electro-Communications, Japan
Masashi Inoue	Yamagata University, Japan
Paul Salvador Inventado	Carnegie Mellon University, USA
Syaheerah Lebai Lutfi	Universiti Sains, Malaysia
Nelson Marcos	De La Salle University, Philippines
Radoslaw Niewiadomski	University of Genoa, Italy
Jaclyn Ocumpaugh	Columbia University, USA
Noriko Otani	Tokyo City University, Japan
Michael Sao Pedro	Worcester Polytechnic Institute and Apprendis, USA
Raymund Sison	De La Salle University, Philippines
Kaoru Sumi	Future University, Japan
Tran Minh Triet	Vietnam National University, Vietnam
Khiet Truong	University of Twente, The Netherlands
Luc Paquette	Columbia University, USA
Peerapon Vateekul	Chulalongkorn University, Thailand

Contents

X   Contents

CMNA XV Papers

A Cognitive Approach to Relevant Argument Generation

Jean-Louis Dessalles[✉]

Telecom ParisTech – Université Paris-Saclay,
46 rue Barrault, 75013 Paris, France
jl@dessalles.fr
http://www.dessalles.fr/

Abstract. Acceptable arguments must be logically relevant. This paper describes an attempt to retro-engineer the human argumentative competence. The aim is to produce a minimal cognitive procedure that generates logically relevant arguments at the right time. Such a procedure is proposed as a proof of principle. It relies on a very small number of operations that are systematically performed: logical conflict detection, abduction and negation. Its eventual validation however depends on the quality of the available domain knowledge.

Keywords: Argumentation · Relevance · Cognition · Minimalism

1 Introduction

Argumentative dialogues constitute the major part of the human language performance. Human beings spend about 6 h a day in verbal interactions (Mehl and Pennebaker 2003), uttering 16 000 words on average (Mehl *et al.* 2007). The two major types of verbal interactions are conversational narratives and argumentative dialogues (Bruner 1986; Dessalles 2007).

Argumentative dialogues are produced spontaneously and effortlessly in any group of healthy adult individuals. The ability to generate argumentative moves in spontaneous conversation is crucial to social life, as judgments of rationality and of social competence depend on it. Moreover, various cognitive processes seem to be common to argumentation and to deliberative reasoning (Dessalles 2008). Modeling the human argumentative ability should therefore be one of the main ambitions in Cognitive Science.

The previous statement relies on the implicit hypothesis that argumentation is a unitary phenomenon. There is no consensus on this. For instance, Walton considers various types of argumentative dialogues as governed by different rules: persuasion, inquiry, negotiation, information-seeking, deliberation and eristic (strife) dialogue (Walton 1982; Walton and Macagno 2007). Other authors build on the idea that interacting individuals choose which "dialogue game" they agree to play, among a set of conventional dialogue games available to them (Hulstijn 2000; Maudet 2001). The present paper makes the strong assumption that there is a cognitive core that is common to all argumentative dialogues, regardless of the category they fall into.

© Springer International Publishing Switzerland 2016
M. Baldoni et al. (Eds.): IWEC 2014/IWEC 2015/CMNA 2015, LNAI 9935, pp. 3–15, 2016.
DOI: 10.1007/978-3-319-46218-9_1

It may seem quite natural to see argumentative dialogues as a process involving people, as arguments are often described in terms of challenge, commitment, withdrawal or support. As a consequence, the social level is rarely separated from the logical (or knowledge) level. The difference between social aspects and logical aspects is however crucial for the present study. In this paper, we pay attention only to the conceptual and logical structure of argumentation. The challenge is to show that logical relevance can be computed in a phase relying on knowledge and preferences that can be kept separate from other computations based on social roles and social goals. We regard logical relevance as a prerequisite for any other computation regarding argumentation, as no valid argument can be logically irrelevant. The extreme version of our hypothesis consists in saying that the propositional content of argumentative moves follows a definite mechanical procedure, regardless of who makes them. At the knowledge level, it is not possible to tell whether a given argumentative sequence involved three people, two people or was a soliloquy. If this hypothesis is valid, we can study the logical organization of argumentative dialogues while ignoring other issues, independently from their importance in further computations, such as pragmatic goals (convince, influence, gain the upper hand) or saving/losing face. At the knowledge level, it is more urgent to concentrate on the logical relationships between utterances (Quilici *et al.* 1988). This, of course, amounts to supposing that the logical level has some form of autonomy.

Even if we limit our study of argumentation to computations performed at the logical (or knowledge) level, we must still determine which entities are processed by these computations. In most approaches to argument generation, a pre-computed set of arguments is supposed to be available. Arguments may be propositions that are known for instance to be in relation of support or of attack with another argument (Dung 1995). Such a set may be given or be computed through a planning module (Amgoud and Prade 2007). Various questions are then asked, such as finding 'acceptable' arguments (Dung 1995), or finding best argumentative strategies following rhetorical principles (van Eemeren et al. 2007, 2012). Postulating a graph of pre-existing arguments with attack/support weighted relations may be appropriate in task-oriented dialogues, in which at least some participants are expert not only in the domain of the task, but also in conducting dialogues about the task. Pre-established argument graphs may also be natural to study professional debating behavior, as in political debates. In spontaneous everyday dialogues, however, people are not expected to be experts. They are not even supposed to have any awareness about the possible existence of pre-existing argument collections to choose from. We must assume that every argumentative move is computed on the fly instead of being selected or retrieved. We do not postulate static graphs of arguments; we do not postulate complex procedures such as the search for minimal acyclic paths in such graphs either. It would not be parsimonious to grant such powers to brains. At the other extreme, a purely structural approach that would look exclusively at the surface of the arguments (Rips 1998) is unlikely to predict the content of utterances.

We choose to settle for the kind of computation considered in BDI approaches, *i.e.* computations about propositions (or predicates), about beliefs and about desires. We must, however, put further restrictions about the kind of computations that can be regarded as cognitively plausible. Since cognitive systems are "embedded systems", we cannot postulate any access to external oracles of truth. We cannot make use of notions such as possible worlds, as long as these "worlds" are supposed to be external entities. And as in any modeling enterprise, we must seek for minimal procedures.

We present here a tentative minimalist model of logically relevant argument generation. Following (Reed and Grasso 2007), this approach is an attempt of modeling *of* argument (rather that *with* argument). The purpose is to understand the human argumentative *competence* (as opposed to *performance*), rather than using argumentation processes to develop artificial reasoning. In what follows, we will first provide a definition of 'logical relevance'. Then we will introduce the notion of 'necessity', which usefully subsumes attitudes such as beliefs and desires. We then present the conflict-abduction-negation model, before discussing its scope and its limits.

2 Logical Relevance

Logical relevance is what makes the difference between acceptable dialogue moves and unacceptable ones, or more generally between rationality and pathological discourse. Logical relevance predicts the conditions in which saying that the carpet is grey is appropriate or, on the contrary, would lead to an expression of incomprehension like "So what?" (Labov 1997). Note that sentences may be meaningful (*e.g.* "the carpet is grey") and yet be fully logically irrelevant. Philosophical definitions of relevance that rely on the quantity and the cost of inferred information (Sperber and Wilson 1986) are of little help here, as they are too permissive and do not predict irrelevance. For instance, new knowledge may be easily inferred from "the carpet is grey" (*e.g.* it is not green, it differs from the one in the other room) without conferring any bit of relevance to the sentence in most contexts (*e.g.* during a dialogue about the death of a cousin). Conversely, any sentence can be relevant in an appropriate context (*e.g.* "I asked for a red carpet" or "It doesn't show the dirt"). The point is to discover the kind of logical relationship that an utterance must have with the context to be relevant.

Many task-oriented approaches to argumentation (often implicitly) rely on definitions of relevance or acceptability that refer to *goals*. A move is relevant in these contexts if it helps in achieving one of the speaker's goals. Many spontaneous dialogues, however, occur in the absence of any definite task to be fulfilled. For instance, when people discuss about the recent death of a cousin, they may exchanges arguments about the suddenness or the unexpectedness of the death without trying to achieve anything concrete. Another problem with 'goals' is that there is no way to circumscribe the set from which they would be drawn. Do people who are talking and reasoning about their cousin's sudden death have zero, one, ten or hundreds of goals?

The observation of spontaneous conversation (Dessalles 1985; 2007) suggests that *problems*, *i.e.* contradictions between beliefs and/or desires, are more basic and more systematic than the existence of goals. For instance, the cousin's sudden deadly stroke contradicts the belief that she was perfectly healthy. The definition of logical relevance that will be used here is straightforward:

> *A statement is logically relevant*
> *if it is involved in a contradiction*
> *or solves a contradiction.*

(for a more precise definition, see (Dessalles 2013)). It has long been recognized that aspects of argumentation have to do with incompatible beliefs and desires, and with belief revision. "Practical reasoning is a matter of weighing conflicting considerations for and against competing options, where the relevant considerations are provided by what the agent desires about and what the agent believes" (Bratman 1990). The above definition of logical relevance puts a tight constraint on the kind of move that is admissible in argumentation.

Suppose that the sky is clear and you want to go hiking. Your friend could make a relevant argumentative move by saying "They announce heavy rains this afternoon" because her move creates a contradiction between two desires (hiking and not getting wet). By contrast, saying "They announce heavy rains this afternoon in Kuala Lumpur" would have been irrelevant as long as the argument cannot be related to any contradiction (*e.g.* if you are hiking in the Alps). A further argument from you or your friend such as "I can see some clouds over there" may be argumentatively relevant, for instance by negating one term in the contradiction between 'observing clear sky' and 'having heavy rain soon'. Describing such a move (clouds) as merely 'strengthening' the preceding argument (heavy rains) is problematic as long as there is no way to compute such a 'strengthening' relation. Fortunately, this is unnecessary: as soon as the intermediary contradiction (clear sky *vs.* rain) is taken into account, the relevance of negating 'clear sky' by mentioning clouds becomes evident.

To be logically relevant, people or artificial systems must abide by the constraint above (create or solve a contradiction), or be at risk of being perceived as socially inept. Note that while some models seek for conflict-free arguments (Dung 1995), we must consider arguments as logically relevant precisely because they create a logical contradiction. Conversely, it is not enough for an argument to be logically consistent with the current state of knowledge. To be logically relevant, an argument that does not create or highlight a contradiction should *restore* logical consistency. In our framework, the only admissible 'goals' are prospective situations in which logical consistency is restored (which comes with the strong presupposition that the current situation is regarded as inconsistent for the goal to be considered).

3   Conflicting Necessities

Basic attitudes such as *true* and *false* have long been recognized to be insufficient to model argumentation. In line with the BDI approach, we consider that propositional attitudes can be gradual and may include both beliefs and desires. As we experience beliefs and desires as very different mental attitudes, we may expect them to be processed through two radically different mechanisms, one for beliefs and one for desires. We found that, surprisingly, both mechanisms can be naturally merged into a single one[1]. As far as the computation of logical relevance is concerned, the distinction between beliefs and desires can be (momentarily) ignored. To describe the argumentation procedure, we use a single notion, called *necessity* (note that the word 'necessity' is close here to the naïve notion and does not refer to a modality). Distinguishing desires from beliefs remains of course essential when it comes to argument wording. The claim is that it plays no role in the computation of logically relevant arguments.

We call *necessity* the intensity with which an aspect of a given situation is believed or wished[2]. Necessities are negative in case of disbelief or avoidance. For the sake of simplicity, we consider that necessity values are only assigned to (possibly negated) instantiated or uninstantiated predicates. We will still use the word 'predicate' to designate them. At each step t of the planning procedure, a function $v_t(T)$ is supposed to provide the necessity of any predicate T on demand. The necessity of T may be unknown at time t (we will omit subscripts t to improve readability). We suppose that necessities are consistent with negation: $v(\neg T) = -v(T)$. The main purpose of considering necessities is that they propagate through logical and causal links.

We say that a predicate is *realized* if it is regarded as being true in the current state of the world. Note that this notion is not supposed to be "objective". Moreover, in the case of contrefactuals, a predicate is realized as long as it is supposed to be true. A predicate T is said to be *conflicting* if $v(T) > 0$ when it is not realized, or if $v(T) < 0$ in a situation in which it is realized. We say that T creates a *logical conflict* $(T, v(T))$ of intensity $|v(T)|$. We will consider logical conflicts (T, N) in which N is not necessary equal to $v(T)$. Note that logical conflicts (also called *cognitive conflicts*) are internal to agents; they are not supposed to be "objective". More important, *logical conflicts do not oppose individuals*, but beliefs and/or desires. The point of the argumentative procedure is to modify beliefs or to change the state of the world until the current logical conflict is solved. In many situations, solving one logical conflict may create a new one. Argumentation emerges from the repeated application of the argumentative procedure. Within the present framework, argumentative dialogues can be seen as the *trace of a sequential multi-valued logical satisfaction procedure*. One could think of designing a problem solving device that would help people find out optimal plans or beliefs sets. This is not our concern here. The point is rather to discover a procedure that matches human argumentative behavior while remaining cognitively plausible. Our proposal is that such a procedure proceeds by solving logical conflicts sequentially, one at a time.

---

[1] This result was unexpected. Our initial attempts to capture argumentative competence involved separate procedures for epistemic moves (beliefs) and for epithymic moves (desires) (Dessalles 1985). Gradual simplification in both procedures led them to converge and eventually to merge into a single one.

[2] In (Dessalles 2008; 2013) we show how the notion of complexity (*i.e.* minimal description length) can be used to measure beliefs and desires on a same intensity scale.

4 The Conflict–Abduction–Negation Model

Our attempts to design a cognitively plausible model of spontaneous argumentation led to a minimal procedure that we describe below. In a nutshell, the procedure tries to detect a logical conflict, and then explores various ways to solve it. Solutions can be found by revising default assumptions, or by revising beliefs and preferences, or by proposing actions that change the state of the world. Our past efforts to design such a procedure involved intricate operations and an external planner. These developments were unsatisfactory due to their cognitive implausibility. To remain cognitively plausible, we stick to the following restrictions.

R1. Arguments can be potentially any predicate. Their effect on consistency is *computed* (rather than retrieved from pre-stored relations such as 'support' or 'attack').

R2. The knowledge base is addressed by content. We exclude the possibility of scanning the entire knowledge. Queries for rules must have at least one term instantiated.

R3. The procedure is supposed to be sequential, considering one problem (conflict) and one tentative solution at a time.

R4. The procedure should be kept minimal. A cognitive model of natural argument processing cannot consist in a general-purpose theorem prover with the power of a universal Turing machine that derives arguments from complex axioms.

The purpose of R1 and R2 is to avoid making any strong assumption about the nature of the available knowledge. From a cognitive perspective, representing knowledge using rules (as we do in our implementation) is just a commodity, as minds are not supposed to keep thousands of rules expressed in explicit form in their memory (Ghadakpour 2003). The purpose of R2 is also to make the model scalable. R3 aims at reflecting the reality of human argumentation which, contrary to artificial planning, is bound to be sequential. R4 is not only motivated by cognitive plausibility, but also by scientific parsimony concerns.

Finding a procedure that respects constraints R1-4 while being able to reproduce human performance, even in simple dialogues, proved significantly more challenging than anticipated. After a series of refinements, we succeeded in designing a procedure, named CAN (for Conflict–Abduction–Negation) that we consider for now as minimal (Fig. 1). This means that we could not find a more concise procedure than CAN that generates only logically relevant arguments and that generates all logically relevant arguments.

Figure 2 shows the sequence of operations in CAN. The first step consists in detecting a logical *conflict*. This captures the fact that no argumentation is supposed to occur in the absence of an explicit or underlying logical conflict. The *solution* phase allows actions to be performed and therefore lose there necessity. This phase is where decisions are taken, after weighing pros and cons. For predicates that are not actions, a solution attempt consists in considering them as realized. The next phase is *abduction*. It consists in finding out a cause for a state of affairs. The abduction procedure itself can be considered as external to the model. Necessity propagation occurs in this abduction

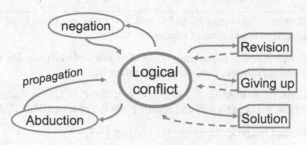

Fig. 1. CAN operations

phase. The effect of *negation* is to present the mirror image of the logical conflict: if (T, N) represents a conflict, so does $(\neg T, -N)$. Note that thanks to negation, positive and negative necessities play symmetrical roles. The *give-up* phase is crucial: by setting the necessity of T to $-N$, the procedure memorizes the fact that T resisted a mutation of intensity N. Lastly, the *revision* phase consists in reconsidering the necessity of T. This operation represents the fact that when considering a situation anew, people may change the strength of their belief or their desire (the situation may appear not so sure, less desirable or less unpleasant after all).

The different phases of the procedure are executed as a "or-else" sequence. This means that if a phase succeeds, the whole procedure starts anew. The solution phase is considered to fail if the intended action fails. The negation phase is executed only once for a given predicate T. The procedure introduces the notion of mutability. C is *mutable* with intensity N if $v(T)$ and N have opposite signs and if $|v(T)| < N$.

Note that the procedure is not following standard deductive reasoning, presumably reflecting the way human beings reason. The abduction phase implements contraposition by propagating negative necessity to the cause. When the propagated necessity is positive, however, the operation is no longer deductive. It can be interpreted as the search for a cause that will be presented as 'necessary'. Since the procedure constitutes a greedy algorithm, each solution is unique by the time it is found, so the distinction between 'necessary' and 'sufficient' gets blurred.

5 Implementing the CAN Procedure

The CAN procedure has been designed by successive simplifications of its implementation in Prolog. As suggested by Fig. 2, the core of the program is now quite short, as we managed to reduce the procedure to a very limited set of operations. Besides this CAN module, the program quite naturally includes two other modules: a domain knowledge and a module named 'world'. For testing purposes, we implemented the domain knowledge as a set of causal and logical rules with default assumptions. We adopted the usual and convenient technique which consists in using the same knowledge to simulate the world (*e.g.* rules are used in forward propagation to update the world when an action has been performed) and to perform abductive

Conflict:	If there is no current conflict, look for a new conflict (T, N) where T is a recently visited state of affairs.
Solution:	If $N > 0$ and T is *possible* (*i.e.* $\neg T$ is not realized), decide that T is the case (if T is an action, do it or simulate it).
Abduction:	Look for a cause C of T or a reason C for T. If C is *mutable* with intensity N, make $v(C) = N$ and restart from the new conflict (C, N).
Negation:	Restart the procedure with the conflict $(\neg T, -N)$.
Give up:	Make $v(T) = -N$.
Revision:	Reconsider the value of $v(T)$.

Fig. 2. The sequence of operations in the CAN procedure.

reasoning. Moreover, we made the simplifying assumption that the predicates included in the arguments are present in the domain knowledge. These easy options are by no means cognitively plausible. Both the management of the world and the kind of knowledge used for abduction could be implemented in radically different ways (*e.g.* using finer grain representations or even analogue devices) without the CAN procedure being affected.

We tested the model by reconstructing the production of arguments in real conversational excerpts. Below is an example of conversation.

[Context: A is repainting doors. He decided to remove the old paint first, which proves to be a hard work (adapted from French)]
A1- I have to repaint my doors. I've burned off the old paint. It worked OK, but not everywhere. It's really tough work! […] In the corners, all this, the moldings, it's not feasible!
[…]
B1- You should use a wire brush.
A2- Yes, but that wrecks the wood.
B2- It wrecks the wood…
[pause 5 seconds]
A3- It's crazy! It's more trouble than buying a new door.
B3- Oh, that's why you'd do better just sanding and repainting them.
A4- Yes, but if we are the fifteenth ones to think of that!
B4- Oh, yeah…
A5- There are already three layers of paint.
B5- If the old remaining paint sticks well, you can fill in the peeled spots with filler compound.
A6- Yeah, but the surface won't look great. It'll look like an old door.

If we just keep the argumentative skeleton, we get:

A1- repaint, burn-off, moldings, tough work
B1- wire brush

A2- wood wrecked
A3- tough work
B3- sanding
A5- several layers
B5- filler compound
A6- not nice surface

The challenge is to predict the dynamic unfolding of this argumentative dialogue using a static set of rules representing the domain knowledge. Despite the simplifying assumptions mentioned above, reconstructing the dialogue is a challenging task. The relevant predicates must be selected in the right order and with the right sign (positive or negated) from a (potentially vast) background knowledge base that has ideally been developed independently. For illustrative purposes, we used the following domain knowledge (the sign $\rightarrow$ stands for causal consequence). Since the program is written in Prolog, it accepts knowledge expressed in first-order logic (*i.e.* with variables). For this simple example, propositions are however sufficient.

```
(C1) burn_off & -wood_wrecked → nice_surface
(C2) filler_compound & -wood_wrecked → nice_surface
(C3) sanding & -several_layers & -wood_wrecked → nice_surface
(C4) burn_off & moldings & -wire_brush → tough_work
(C5) wire_brush & wood_soft → wood_wrecked
(C6) wood_wrecked → -nice_surface
(C7) repaint & nice_surface → nice_doors

actions([repaint, burn_off, wire_brush,
         sanding,filler_compound]).

default([-wood_soft, -several_layers, -wood_wrecked]).

initial_situation([moldings, -nice_surface, -nice_doors,
                   -wood_soft, -several_layers]).
```

The program needs a few attitudes in addition. These attitudes are represented as numerical values. Only the hierarchy of values is relevant, not the values themselves.

```
desirable(tough_work, -10)
desirable(nice_doors, 20)
```

With this knowledge, the CAN procedure is able to generate exactly the arguments of this conversation excerpt in the right order. The program starts by detecting a *conflict* on 'nice_doors', which is desirable with intensity 20 and yet is not realized. *Abduction* propagates the conflict back to 'repaint' through (C7). 'repaint' is decided as a *solution*, but the conflict is not solved. It is propagated to 'nice_surface' again through (C7), and then to 'burn_off' through (C1). 'burn_off' is performed, but then forward propagation through (C4) generates a new conflict of intensity 10 on 'tough_work'. The trace below illustrates what happens then.

```
** Restart.
 Conflict of intensity -10 with  tough_work
 Propagating conflict to cause: -wire_brush
 ------> Decision :  wire_brush
 inferring wood_wrecked from wire_brush
 ** Restart.
 Conflict of intensity 20 with  nice_doors
 Propagating conflict to cause: nice_surface
 Propagating conflict to cause: -wood_wrecked
 Negating -wood_wrecked , considering wood_wrecked
 Propagating conflict to cause: wire_brush
 ------> Decision :  -wire_brush
 inferring tough_work from -wire_brush
 inferring nice_surface from burn_off
 inferring nice_doors from nice_surface
 ** Restart.
 Conflict of intensity -10 with  tough_work
 Negating tough_work , considering -tough_work
 Giving up:  tough_work is stored with necessity 10
 We are about to live with tough_work ( -10 )!
 Do you want to change preference for tough_work ( -10 )?
 ?-  -30.
 ** Restart.
 Conflict of intensity -30 with  tough_work
 Propagating conflict to cause: burn_off
 ------> Decision :  -burn_off
 ** Restart.
 Conflict of intensity 20 with  nice_doors
 Propagating conflict to cause: nice_surface
 Propagating conflict to cause: sanding
 ------> Decision :  sanding
 ...
```

The trace shows how the system is able to go back on its decision twice, when it decides that 'wire_brush' and 'burn_off' are bad ideas after all. Note the *give-up* phase in which it keeps a memory of the fact that 'tough_work' resisted a mutating attempt of intensity 10. The *revision* phase is implemented as a question to the user, who sets the preference of 'tough_work' to −30. This triggers a new search for further solutions.

6 Discussion

CAN proceeds by detecting inconsistencies and then by propagating logical conflict to causes. Other systems rely on consistency checking to model argumentation (*e.g.* Thagard 1989; Pasquier *et al.* 2006). The present model has several qualities that make it more plausible cognitively.

- Locality: All operations are performed locally or through content addressing. There is no scanning of knowledge.
- Minimalism: The procedure is meant to be the most concise one.
- CAN is recursive, but not centrally recursive. This means that memory requirements do not grow during execution.
- CAN does not loop. The *give-up* phase, by changing necessity values: $v(T) = −N$, prevents abduction from being performed twice identically with the same input.

However, repeated revisions may simulate the fact that some human argumentation dialogues go around in circles.

- Despite the fact that CAN ignores people and argument ownership, it captures the dialectical nature of argumentation. Every decision made by CAN represents a move that could be taken on by the same speaker or by another one.

One merit of the CAN procedure is to separate logical relevance processing from the creative part of argumentation. The latter is captured by the abduction procedure. This procedure is external to the model. Thanks to this modularity, CAN may be used as an "argumentative module" in any system that is able to simulate the execution of actions and to perform abduction. The interface between those systems and CAN should involve predicates, but this does not mean that they should use predicates in their internal implementation[3].

At this point, we got little more than a proof of principle. We wanted to prove that part of the human argumentation competence could be plausibly modeled as a fixed procedure. The CAN procedure aims at capturing the rational aspect of argumentation. It does not take any notion of strategy, such as defeating the opponent's counterarguments, into account. It does not even consider the subjective nature of the social game (convincing game, dispute, counseling…) in which argumentation takes place. However, by enforcing logical relevance, it guarantees the well-formedness of reasoning.

Conversely, it is hard to imagine how logical relevance could be computed without a procedure like CAN. Even during a quarrel, arguments must be logically relevant, *i.e.* point to inconsistencies or restore consistency. Of course, a general-purpose satisfaction algorithm could produce an optimal solution to restore consistency with minimal attitude change. There is no guarantee, however, that such a solution would be perceived as relevant by human users. People make attempts to restore consistency step by step, following a local procedure like CAN. Logical relevance is checked at each step, changing one attitude at a time. A constraint satisfaction system that would propose a new set of attitudes is likely to be considered irrelevant, as it would be unable to justify the solution stepwise.

Some work remains to be done to turn CAN (or a better version of it) into an operational reasoning module for argumentation systems. Much progress should be made on the abduction procedure, which is currently crudely implemented. The challenge is to find a plausible abduction procedure that would scale up when the size of the knowledge base increases. There are also issues with the accuracy of the available knowledge. This paper shows that the problem of designing argumentative systems can be split in two main tasks: relevance and abduction. Our suggestion is that the CAN procedure captures the relevance part, and that systems based on CAN may produce convincing argumentative dialogues whenever an adequate abduction operation is available.

---

[3] (Dessalles 2015) shows how predicates can be generated by systems that use perceptual representations.

References

Amgoud, L., Prade, H.: Practical reasoning as a generalized decision making problem. In: Lang, J., Lespérance, Y., Sadek, D., Maudet, N.: (eds.). Actes des journées francophones 'Modèles formels de l'interaction' (MFI 2007), pp. 15–24. Annales du LAMSADE, Université Paris Dauphine, Paris (2007)

Bratman, M.E.: What is intention? In: Cohen, P.R., Morgan, J.L., Pollack, M.E. (eds.) Intentions in Communication, pp. 15–32. MIT Press, Cambridge (1990)

Bruner, J.: Actual Minds, Possible Worlds. Harvard University Press, Cambridge (1986)

Dessalles, J.-L.: Stratégies naturelles d'acquisition des concepts. In: Actes du colloque Cognitiva 1985, pp. 713–719. CESTA, Paris (1985)

Dessalles, J.-L.: Why We Talk - The Evolutionary Origins of Language. Oxford University Press, Oxford (2007)

Dessalles, J.-L.: La pertinence et ses origines cognitives - Nouvelles théories. Hermes-Science Publications, Paris (2008)

Dessalles, J.-L.: Algorithmic simplicity and relevance. In: Dowe, D.L. (ed.) LNCS, vol. 7070, pp. 119–130. Springer, Heidelberg (2013). doi:10.1007/978-3-642-44958-1_9

Dessalles, J.-L.: From conceptual spaces to predicates. In: Zenker, F., Gärdenfors, P. (eds.) SL, vol. 359, pp. 17–31. Springer, Heidelberg (2015). doi:10.1007/978-3-319-15021-5_2

Dung, P.M.: On the acceptability of arguments and its fundamental role in nonmonotonic reasoning, logic programming and n-person games. Artif. Intell. **77**, 321–357 (1995)

Ghadakpour, L.: Le système conceptuel, à l'interface entre le langage, le raisonnement et l'espace qualitatif: vers un modèle de représentations éphémères. Thèse de doctorat, Ecole Polytechnique, Paris (2003)

Hulstijn, J.: Dialogue games are recipe for joint action. In: 4th Workshop on Formal Semantics and Pragmatics of Dialogue (Gotalog 2000), pp. 99–106. Gothenburg Papers in Computational Linguistics 00-5, Göteborg (2000)

Labov, W.: Some further steps in narrative analysis. J. Narrat. Life Hist. **7**, 395–415 (1997)

Maudet, N.: Modéliser l'aspect conventionnel des interactions langagières: la contribution des jeux de dialogue. Thèse de doctorat en informatique, Univ. P. Sabatier, Toulouse (2001)

Mehl, M.R., Pennebaker, J.W.: The sounds of social life: a psychometric analysis of students' daily social environments and natural conversations. J. Pers. Soc. Psychol. **84**(4), 857–870 (2003)

Mehl, M.R., Vazire, S., Ramírez-Esparza, N., Slatcher, R.B., Pennebaker, J.W.: Are women really more talkative than men? Science **317**, 82 (2007)

Pasquier, P., Rahwan, I., Dignum, F.P.M., Sonenberg, L.: Argumentation and persuasion in the cognitive coherence theory. In: Dunne, P., Bench-Capon, T. (eds.) 1st International Conference on Computational Models of Argumentation (COMMA), pp. 223–234. IOS Press (2006)

Quilici, A., Dyer, M.G., Flowers, M.: Recognizing and responding to plan-oriented misconceptions. Comput. Linguist. **14**(3), 38–51 (1988)

Reed, C., Grasso, F.: Recent advances in computational models of natural argument. Int. J. Intell. Syst. **22**, 1–15 (2007)

Rips, L.J.: Reasoning and conversation. Psychol. Rev. **105**(3), 411–441 (1998)

Sperber, D., Wilson, D.: Relevance: Communication and Cognition. Blackwell Ed (1986, 1995)

Thagard, P.: Explanatory coherence. Behav. Brain Sci. **12**, 435–502 (1989) van Eemeren, F.H., Garssen, B., Meuffels, B.: The extended pragma-dialectical argumentation theory empirically interpreted. In: van Eemeren, F.H., Garssen, B., Godden, D., Mitchell, G. (eds.) 7th Conference of the International Society for the Study of Argumentation. Rozenberg/Sic Sat, Amsterdam (2007)

van Eemeren, F.H., Garssen, B., Meuffels, B.: Effectiveness through reasonableness - preliminary steps to pragma-dialectical effectiveness research. Argumentation **26**, 33–53 (2012)

Walton, D.N.: Topical relevance in argumentation. Pragmat. Beyond **3**(8), 1–81 (1982)

Walton, D.N., Macagno, F.: Types of dialogue, dialectical relevance, and textual congruity. Anthropol. Philos. **8**, 101–119 (2007)

Argumentation Mining in Parliamentary Discourse

Nona Naderi[✉] and Graeme Hirst

University of Toronto, Toronto, Canada
{nona,gh}@cs.toronto.edu

Abstract. We examine whether using frame choices in forum statements can help us identify framing strategies in parliamentary discourse. In this analysis, we show how features based on embedding representations can improve the discovery of various frames in argumentative political speech. Given the complex nature of the parliamentary discourse, the initial results that are presented here are promising. We further present a manually annotated corpus for frame recognition in parliamentary discourse.

1 Introduction

In parliamentary discourse, politicians expound their beliefs and ideas through argumentation, and to persuade the audience, they highlight some aspect of an issue, which is commonly known as framing [5]. Consider the following example[1]:

Example 1. *There was no need to change the definition of marriage in order for gays and lesbians to establish meaningful, long term relationships that are recognized in law.*

The speaker is framing his/her argument to promote the idea that the same-sex marriage is not necessary because the long-term relationships are already recognized in law.

While a deep understanding and analysis of beliefs and ideas remains a challenge, a relatively simpler task of argument tagging based on pre-existing frames has recently been proposed [1,6].

In this paper, we introduce our supervised model trained on user-generated Web content for classifying parliamentary discourse by its use of various frames. We use vector representations of words and sentences to capture their semantic information, and compute semantic similarity metrics across argumentative discourse-pairs. We further present our corpus of argumentative parliamentary discourse. These argumentative speeches are annotated with known frames.

---

[1] An example from our manually annotated corpus of parliamentary statements.

© Springer International Publishing Switzerland 2016
M. Baldoni et al. (Eds.): IWEC 2014/IWEC 2015/CMNA 2015, LNAI 9935, pp. 16–25, 2016.
DOI: 10.1007/978-3-319-46218-9_2

2   Related Work

We briefly summarize prior work on argument analysis of user postings. Cabrio and Villata [3] used a textual entailment approach to find pro and con arguments in a set of debates selected from Debatepedia[2]. Boltužić and Šnajder [1] proposed a categorization task of tagging user postings with a pre-existing set of frames. Their supervised classification model made use of entailment and semantic similarity features. To generalize their earlier work for various topics, Boltužić and Šnajder [2] presented an unsupervised model to recognize frames by means of textual similarity. In a similar task, Hasan and Ng [6] employed a probabilistic approach for stance and reason classification of user postings. Misra et al. [9] took a supervised approach to classify dialogue postings by "argument facets" using lexical and semantic similarity features. These approaches focused on user-generated content on online forums. In contrast, we explore framing strategies in parliamentary discourse.

3   Corpus and Annotation

For our frame prediction task, we use user-postings manually annotated with known frames (ComArg corpus) as a training set and argumentative parliamentary speeches as a test set. The corpora that we conducted our study on are described in the following sections.

3.1   The ComArg Corpus

ComArg[3], developed by Boltužić and Šnajder [1], is a corpus of user statements manually annotated with users' positions towards a specific topic (pro or con stance), and a set of pre-existing "arguments". These arguments are, in effect, *frames* in the sense that we introduced above, as each highlights certain aspects of the issue. The authors chose two different sources for collecting their data; the user statements are compiled from ProCon.org, where the statements are associated with a labeled *pro* or *con* stance, and the frames are taken from Idebate.org. The corpus covers two topics of *gay marriage (GM)* and *Under God in Pledge (UGIP)*. Since the latter (regarding the Pledge of Allegiance) is an issue specific to the United States, we focused solely on the GM part of the corpus, which contains 198 statements and 7 pre-existing frames, shown in Table 1[4]. In this corpus, the pairs of statements and frames are annotated as *explicit attack, implicit attack, no mention, explicit support,* and *implicit support;* that is the statements *for* gay marriage can support the *pro* frames, and attack the *con* frames, and vice versa for statements opposing gay marriage. In this work, we only used the statements that explicitly (176 instances) and implicitly (98 instances) *supported* the pre-existing frames.

---

[2] http://idebate.org/debatabase.
[3] http://takelab.fer.hr/data/comarg/.
[4] The third frame is modified to accommodate frames in our current corpus.

Table 1. ComArg pre-defined frames on gay marriage

Frame	Stance	Description
1	Con	Gay couples can declare their union without resort to marriage
2	Pro	Gay couples should be able to take advantage of the fiscal and legal benefits of marriage
3	Con	Gay marriage undermines the institution of marriage
4	Pro	It is discriminatory to refuse gay couples the right to marry
5	Con	Major world religions are against gay marriages
6	Pro	Marriage is about more than procreation; therefore gay couples should not be denied the right to marry due to their biology
7	Con	Marriage should be between a man and a woman

3.2 Argumentative Parliamentary Statements

For our test set, we focused on debates regarding same-sex marriage in the Canadian Parliament. In 2005, Bill C-38, *An act respecting certain aspects of legal capacity for marriage for civil purposes*, to legalize same-sex marriage in Canada, was introduced in the Parliament. Later that year, the bill was passed and the legal definition of marriage was expanded under the then-Liberal government to include conjugal couples of the same sex. After the Conservative Party of Canada gained power, the debate on same-sex marriage was re-opened in the Parliament in 2006; therefore, the issue was debated extensively in the Parliament in two different periods of time (same-sex marriage was debated briefly in 1999).

We selected speeches regarding same-sex marriage made by the members of the Canadian Parliament from both periods. The corpus described here consists of two sets of debate speeches. The first set consisted of 136 *sentences* of the debate speeches and the second set consisted of 400 *paragraphs* of the debate speeches with an average of 70 words. We asked three annotators to examine the statements in the first set with respect to the position of the speaker towards same-sex marriage, and assign *pro, con,* or *no* stance. We further asked them to examine which of the pre-existing frames (described in Sect. 3.1) support the statements, and manually annotate them with one of the frames or none; Table 4 shows a few examples from our corpus. To measure inter-annotator agreement, we adopted Weighted Kappa metric. Table 2 shows the achieved agreement for both stance and frames. For almost 90% of the statements, at least two annotators were in agreement. These statements were kept as the final dataset. Some

Table 2. Inter-annotator agreement on parliamentary discourse corpus

	Sentences	Paragraphs
Stance	0.54	-
Frame	0.46	0.70

Table 3. Corpus statistics

Frame	ComArg annotations		Parliamentary annotations	
	Explicit	Implicit	Sentences	Paragraphs
1	16	18	14	16
2	12	18	1	14
3	1	4	0	37
4	50	81	33	55
5	28	52	10	56
6	13	17	2	2
7	56	84	27	63
None	0	0	34	123

statements cannot be judged without their context, and annotators did not agree on the stance or the frame. After discarding the statements for which the annotators were not in agreement, the final set has 121 statements. 87 of these remaining statements are supported by one of the ComArg pre-existing frames.

Unlike the first set, for the paragraph set, we asked the annotators to examine the speeches with respect to only the ComArg frames and ignore the stance. The annotation task for this set was carried out by two annotators, and to check the

Table 4. Examples of frame and stance annotations from parliamentary discourse corpus

Stance	Frame	Parliamentary statements
Pro	4	In my opinion, the answer is clear and simple: two people who want to live together within a civil marriage, regardless of their sexual orientation, must be able to do so without the interference of the State.
Con	7	I urge all members who have even the slightest idea that they want to maintain the definition of marriage that we have known and understood for so long to vote in favour of this so that the government can act on it.
–	1	Let me give an example. When we put something in a category, we are discriminating against everything else that is not in that category. If we have a category of things that are blue, then we are leaving out all the yellows, but that does not mean that blue is better or worse than yellow. It just means that they are different.
–	2	If someone puts a lot into a relationship, into a couple, if someone invests in a house and property, that property has to be protected and we must ensure that if both of them invested, both of them reap the benefits. If one of them dies, at a minimum the inheritance must go to the other or be handled in accordance with the person's wishes. It should not be possible to deprive someone of what he or she has built up over the years along with his or her spouse. That is not all. There is not only the legal aspect, of course, but also the emotional aspect. We have to change and progress.

reliability, we computed Weighted Kappa (Table 2). The disagreements arose in cases where the speaker used anecdotes or examples. These ambiguous speeches were discarded to create the final dataset. The statistics of the annotated corpora are presented in Table 3.

4 Methods

Distributed word representations are used efficiently in various NLP tasks including sentiment analysis [11]. Recently, embedding models such as those of Mikolov et al. [8], Wang et al. [13], and Kiros et al. [7] have provided an effective and easy way to employ word and sentence representations. These distributed representations are real-valued vectors that capture semantic and syntactic content of words and sentences. Here, we use word and sentence vector representations to measure the semantic textual similarity (STS) between the statements and the frames. Our models then use these similarity measures as features to predict a frame that supports a given statement. We used word2vec embeddings [8] (300-dimensional vectors) trained on Google news articles, and syntactic embeddings [13] (300-dimensional vectors) trained on the Annotated English Gigaword, to compute sentence vectors, and further compare them to skip-thought sentence vectors (4800-dimensional vectors) [7]. Different composition measures are proposed in literature; one of the simplest measures is additive models (Mitchell and Lapata [10]), where word vectors are added together to represent a phrase or sentence representation. Here, we used additive models with word2vec and syntactic vectors to represent the statements (sentences or paragraphs) and we compared them with more complex composition functions based on neural language models. After computing the sentence vectors, we measured the similarity of the statement vector representation with the frame representation. We computed two similarity scores between statements and frames: (1) the cosine similarity of the two vectors, (2) the similarity score represented by a concatenation of the component-wise product of two vectors and their absolute difference (P&D) [12]. We further studied the impact of adding the stance feature (*pro/con*) to the similarity scores as suggested by Boltužić and Šnajder [1]. In addition to the semantic textual similarity and stance features, we also extracted POS-tags, typed dependencies [4], and distributed representations of the statements. Dependency relation features are extracted using the Stanford parser and they represent relationships between pairs of words. For example, for the sentence *We are abandoning traditional liberalism*, the following triples are extracted:

nsubj(abandoning-3, We-1)
aux(abandoning-3, are-2)
root(ROOT-0, abandoning-3)
amod(liberalism-5, traditional-4)
dobj(abandoning-3, liberalism-5)

Our supervised model then takes these features as input, and learns to identify the frames. For supervised learning, we use SVM^{light} and $SVM^{multiclass}$ by Joachims.[5,6]

5   Experiment and Results

In the first experiment, we use the statements from ComArg as a training set and the Canadian parliamentary statements on GM as a test set for our classification task. We first remove the stop-words, and then sum the vector representations of the remaining words in the sentences to compute the sentence vectors. For syntactic embeddings, we only used the noun, adjective, and verb embeddings. In case the vector representation for a given word is not found in the embeddings, the lemma of the word is searched and retrieved.

After representing the statements and frames using word2vec, the syntactic-based embedding model, and the skip-thought model, we computed the semantic similarity of each pair with the similarity measures described in Sect. 4.

Our baselines are the majority class and bag-of-words (with TF-IDF vectors and rare words removed) classifiers. Table 5 summarizes our results. We observe that almost all models that use STS features outperform the baselines. We also observe that the P&D similarity score provides a better measure for capturing the meaning of the statement-frame pairs. Furthermore, adding the stance feature to the cosine similarity scores improves the accuracy of the classifiers; however, adding it to P&D has no impact on the accuracy of the classifiers. Although the training set of explicit statements is smaller than the training set of explicit and implicit statements, the best results are mostly achieved by training the classifier on explicit instances. Furthermore, adding the stance feature to the cosine similarity scores gives an improvement of about 20 to 40 percentage points in accuracy above the baseline.

Without using the stance feature, the best score was obtained by training the classifier on explicit and implicit instances with the P&D similarity score of word2vec vectors. While we expected to achieve better accuracy with injecting syntactic information through syntactic embeddings and skip-thought vectors, the results do not show such improvements. This can be due to multiple reasons. First, syntactic embeddings were trained on a smaller set compared to word2vec embeddings. Furthermore, we only rely on three categories of syntactic embeddings (nouns, verbs, and adjectives), whereas even prepositions, such as *against* and *between* are informative features for predicting some frames. Skip-thought models are moreover trained on a dataset with a different genre. One of the challenges of using forum posts as a training set is that they are filled with spelling errors, and in our experiments, we did not correct any of these errors. For our paragraph corpus, since our training corpus based on ComArg is very small, we focused on the two dominant frames in ComArg corpus, frames 4 and 7, and used both explicit and implicit statements for training our models. The

---

[5] http://svmlight.joachims.org/.
[6] https://www.cs.cornell.edu/people/tj/svm_light/svm_multiclass.html.

Table 5. Frame prediction results on parliamentary sentences

Train	Features	Accuracy (%)
–	Majority class (argument 4)	33.0
ComArg (Explicit + Implicit)	Bag of words (BoW)	48.2
ComArg (Explicit + Implicit)	STS (Sum of vectors, word2vec, cosine)	54.0
ComArg (Explicit + Implicit)	STS (Sum of vectors, word2vec, cosine) + stance	**72.4**
ComArg (Explicit + Implicit)	STS (Sum of vectors, word2vec, P&D)	58.6
ComArg (Explicit + Implicit)	STS (Sum of vectors, word2vec, P&D) + stance	58.6
ComArg (Explicit + Implicit)	STS (Sum of vectors, syntactic embeddings, cosine)	49.4
ComArg (Explicit + Implicit)	STS (Sum of vectors, syntactic embeddings, cosine) + stance	**68.9**
ComArg (Explicit + Implicit)	STS (Sum of vectors, syntactic embeddings, P&D)	50.5
ComArg (Explicit + Implicit)	STS (Skip-thought vectors, cosine)	48.2
ComArg (Explicit + Implicit)	STS (Skip-thought vectors, cosine) + stance	**68.9**
ComArg (Explicit + Implicit)	STS (Skip-thought vectors, P&D)	51.7
ComArg (Explicit)	Bag of words (BoW)	52.8
ComArg (Explicit)	STS (Sum of vectors, word2vec, cosine)	55.1
ComArg (Explicit)	STS (Sum of vectors, word2vec, cosine) + stance	**73.5**
ComArg (Explicit)	STS (Sum of vectors, word2vec, P&D)	57.4
ComArg (Explicit)	STS (Sum of vectors, word2vec, P&D) + stance	57.4
ComArg (Explicit)	STS (Sum of vectors, syntactic embeddings, cosine)	54.0
ComArg (Explicit)	STS (Sum of vectors, syntactic embeddings, cosine) + stance	**68.9**
ComArg (Explicit)	STS (Sum of vectors, syntactic embeddings, P&D)	56.3
ComArg (Explicit)	STS (Skip-thought vectors, cosine)	52.8
ComArg (Explicit)	STS (Skip-thought vectors, cosine) + stance	**68.9**
ComArg (Explicit)	STS (Skip-thought vectors, P&D)	57.4

paragraph vectors were constructed by adding sentence vectors. For this set, in addition to STS features, we explored features based on POS-tags, the typed dependencies, and the vector representation of the statements. Despite the usefulness of the stance feature as we have seen in the first set, we decided to ignore this feature for our second experiment. The reason for this is that we believe some frames can be used with either positions, for example:

Example 2. *Earlier this year France rejected the marriage of same sex couples because of the effect that same sex marriages have on children.*

Example 3. *Are we going to divide this country into those children who are children of certain couples and children who are not? If we truly value children in the House, then we must understand, as one of the members spoke about children, that this is about the rights of the child, regardless of what their parents do, do not do or who they are.*

Both examples are supported by the frame, *impact on children*; however, the position of the speaker in the first example is against gay marriages, whereas the second speaker supports them.

Similar to the first set, most of the models using STS features outperform the baselines in the paragraph corpus (shown in Table 6). The best results were achieved by the P&D similarity score of word2vec features, followed by the word2vec features extracted from the statements, and typed dependencies. Another observation is that the models based on features extracted from the statements perform better than the models based on cosine similarity features.

Table 6. Frame prediction results on debate paragraph corpus using ComArg corpus (Explicit + Implicit)

Features	Accuracy (%)
Majority class (argument 7)	53.3
Bag of words (BoW)	71.0
Dependency features	72.0
Sum of vectors, word2vec	72.9
Sum of vectors, syntactic embeddings	64.4
STS (Sum of vectors, cosine, word2vec)	61.8
STS (Sum of vectors, P&D, word2vec)	**75.4**
STS (Sum of vectors, cosine, syntactic embeddings)	61.4
STS (Sum of vectors, P&D, syntactic embeddings)	62.7
STS (Skip-thought vectors, cosine)	53.3
STS (Skip-thought vectors, P&D)	59.3

Table 7. Five-fold cross-validation (4 frames)

Features	Accuracy (%)
Majority class (argument 7)	29.8
Bag of words (BoW)	65.0
POS tags	63.0
Dependency features	53.8
Sum of vectors, word2vec	**70.4**
Dependency features + word2vec	69.0
Sum of vectors, syntactic embeddings	62.8
Sum of vectors, skip-thought	54.7
STS (Sum of vectors, cosine, word2vec)	42.3
STS (Sum of vectors, P&D, word2vec)	**67.6**
STS (Sum of vectors, cosine, syntactic embeddings)	39.7
STS (Sum of vectors, P&D, syntactic embeddings)	60.9
STS (Skip-thought vectors, cosine)	41.8
STS (Skip-thought vectors, P&D)	58.6

We further report our results on five-fold cross-validation of four frames (frames 3, 4, 5, and 7) in our paragraph corpus (shown in Table 7). The best results were achieved by the model based on features extracted from the statements, followed by the P&D similarity measure. BOW achieves better performance compared to the other models.

Since the members of the parliament usually refer to the opposing viewpoints and their frames during the debates, relying on all the statements in the paragraphs for extracting features for the models causes errors. The following example was not successfully tagged with the frame due to treating all the statements in the paragraph in the same way.

Example 4. *Peace River constituents are not opposed to equal rights. In fact, the majority support the legal extension of rights and benefits to same sex couples. However, most are opposed to changing the historical term 'marriage' to include these unions. Many have strongly held religious views and are extremely worried that their long-held beliefs are being threatened by the same-sex marriage act. I do not think these views are limited to my riding; I believe they are shared by a majority of Canadians.*

6   Conclusion and Future Work

In this preliminary study, we examined recognizing frames in political argumentative discourse. Many directions have yet to be explored, including (1) discovering frames for various issues, (2) devising a method to deal with larger texts (3) exploring semi-supervised or unsupervised approaches due to the scarcity of human-annotated data for supervised approaches.

Acknowledgements. This work is supported by the Natural Sciences and Engineering Research Council of Canada and by the Social Sciences and Humanities Research Council. We thank Patricia Araujo Thaine, Krish Perumal, and Sara Scharf for their contributions to the annotation of parliamentary statements, and Tong Wang for sharing the syntactic embeddings. We also thank Tong Wang and Ryan Kiros for fruitful discussions, and Christopher Cochrane for insightful comments.

References

1. Boltužić, F., Šnajder, J.: Back up your stance: recognizing arguments in online discussions. In: Proceedings of the First Workshop on Argumentation Mining, pp. 49–58 (2014)
2. Boltužić, F., Šnajder, J.: Identifying prominent arguments in online debates using semantic textual similarity. In: Proceedings of the 2nd Workshop on Argumentation Mining, pp. 110–115. Association for Computational Linguistics, Denver, June 2015
3. Cabrio, E., Villata, S.: Combining textual entailment and argumentation theory for supporting online debates interactions. In: Proceedings of the 50th Annual Meeting of the Association for Computational Linguistics: Short Papers, pp. 208–212. Association for Computational Linguistics (2012)
4. De Marneffe, M.C., Manning, C.D.: The stanford typed dependencies representation. In: Proceedings of the Workshop on Cross-Framework and Cross-Domain Parser Evaluation, COLING 2008, pp. 1–8. Association for Computational Linguistics (2008)
5. Entman, R.M.: Framing: toward clarification of a fractured paradigm. J. Commun. **43**(4), 51–58 (1993)

6. Hasan, K.S., Ng, V.: Why are you taking this stance? Identifying and classifying reasons in ideological debates. In: Proceedings of the 2014 Conference on Empirical Methods in Natural Language Processing (EMNLP), pp. 751–762. Association for Computational Linguistics, Doha, October 2014
7. Kiros, R., Zhu, Y., Salakhutdinov, R., Zemel, R.S., Torralba, A., Urtasun, R., Fidler, S.: Skip-thought vectors. arXiv preprint arXiv:1506.06726 (2015)
8. Mikolov, T., Chen, K., Corrado, G., Dean, J.: Efficient estimation of word representations in vector space. arXiv preprint arXiv:1301.3781 (2013)
9. Misra, A., Anand, P., Tree, J.E.F., Walker, M.A.: Using summarization to discover argument facets in online idealogical [sic] dialog. In: The 2015 Conference of the North American Chapter of the Association for Computational Linguistics: Human Language Technologies, NAACL HLT 2015, Denver, Colorado, USA, May 31–June 5, 2015, pp. 430–440 (2015)
10. Mitchell, J., Lapata, M.: Vector-based models of semantic composition. In: Association for Computational Linguistics, pp. 236–244 (2008)
11. Socher, R., Pennington, J., Huang, E.H., Ng, A.Y., Manning, C.D.: Semi-supervised recursive autoencoders for predicting sentiment distributions. In: Proceedings of the Conference on Empirical Methods in Natural Language Processing, pp. 151–161. Association for Computational Linguistics (2011)
12. Tai, K.S., Socher, R., Manning, C.D.: Improved semantic representations from tree-structured long short-term memory networks. arXiv preprint arXiv:1503.00075 (2015)
13. Wang, T., Mohamed, A., Hirst, G.: Learning lexical embeddings with syntactic and lexicographic knowledge. In: Proceedings of the 53rd Annual Meeting of the Association for Computational Linguistics and the 7th International Joint Conference on Natural Language Processing (vol. 2: Short Papers), pp. 458–463. Association for Computational Linguistics, Beijing, July 2015

Modelling Argumentative Behaviour in Parliamentary Debates: Data Collection, Analysis and Test Case

Volha Petukhova[1]([⊠]), Andrei Malchanau[1], and Harry Bunt[2]

[1] Spoken Language Systems Group, Saarland University, Saarbrücken, Germany
{v.petukhova,andrei.malchanau}@lsv.uni-saarland.de
[2] Tilburg Centre for Communication and Cognition,
Tilburg University, Tilburg, The Netherlands
harry.bunt@uvt.nl

Abstract. In this paper we apply the information state update (ISU) machinery to tracking and understanding the argumentative behaviour of participants in a parliamentary debate in order to predict its outcome. We propose to use the ISU approach to model the arguments of the debaters and the support/attack links between them as part of the formal representations of a participant's information state. We first consider the identification of claims and evidence relations to their premises as an argument mining task. It is not sufficient, however, to indicate what relations occur without establishing how these relations are created and verified during the interaction. For this purpose the model requires a detailed specification of the creation, maintenance and use of shared beliefs. The ISU model provides procedures for incorporating beliefs and expectations shared between speaker and hearers in the tracking model. To evaluate the content of the tracked information states, we compare them to those of the human 'concluder' who wraps up a debate, stating the claims which the majority of the debaters have agreed on.

1 Introduction

Argumentation constitutes a major component of human intelligence. Many domains, including philosophy, politics, journalism, law, and theology rely on the use of arguments. Argumentation is used to justify solutions to many problems. The problem of understanding argumentation has been addressed by many researchers in different fields including philosophy, logic and artificial intelligence. In natural language processing, a surge of interest in argumentation mining tasks has recently been observed. Much successful work has been done to extract arguments and analyse their structure. Argumentation mining methods are mostly focused on the identification and classification of argument components.

The argument detection task is generally defined as a binary task by separating argumentative and non-argumentative units. Based on a domain-independent theory of argumentation schemes [1,2] an accuracy was obtained of 73.75% in identifying argumentative sentences in the Araucaria corpus [3], using features

M. Baldoni et al. (Eds.): IWEC 2014/IWEC 2015/CMNA 2015, LNAI 9935, pp. 26–46, 2016.
DOI: 10.1007/978-3-319-46218-9_3

such as word pairs, verbs, and keywords indicative for argumentative discourse, e.g. discourse markers.

Argumentative structures have been well understood and modelled for argumentative texts and to a certain extent also for two-party argumentative dialogues, see e.g. [5,11–13]. In order to identify arguments and relations between their constituents, discourse relations are often considered, inspired by Rhetorical Structure Theory, see [14]. Discourse relations help to identify to which other propositions a proposition serves as evidence and from which other propositions it receives support. One of the first studies on argument component classification is *Argumentative Zoning* [4]. In this study, sentences within one argument and texts as a whole are classified as having one of the rhetorical relations such as result, purpose, background, solution, and scope. When applied to scientific articles, this prediction method achieved an F-score of 0.46.

Although being very important, these methods are insufficient for many applications such as for example argumentative multi-agent multimodal interactions. For instance, it is not sufficient to indicate what claims and relations do occur without indicating how these relations are established and verified during a debate session. For a computer system to be engaged in the exchange of arguments, either as a direct participant or as side-participant like an observer, understanding the strength and sustainability of arguments along with the understanding of their structure is essential. The beliefs of a rational agent engaged in argumentation should be characterized not only by beliefs concerning his own supporting arguments but also by the beliefs concerning his partners' beliefs and relations between them. Cohen (1987), who provided an in-depth analysis of argument structures, emphasized that a tracking model of mutual beliefs between speakers and addressees is required, see [18]. The information state update (ISU) approach, see [19,20], applied successfully in a variety of dialogue tasks, provides a computational model for the creation of shared beliefs and specifies mechanisms for their transfer.

In this paper we present an approach to modelling the interaction in parliamentary debates. We present a debate model based on an analysis of the tasks of the participants, of the structure of their contributions, and of the relations between them. In this analysis, an argument structure is defined in terms of claims and evidence and the connections between them.

This paper is structured as follows. In Sect. 2 we discuss the application domain, specifying participant roles and tasks, and highlighting important interactive phenomena to be modelled. Sections 3 and 4 describe and analyse our data and discuss ways to segment and annotate debates. Section 5 presents the semantic framework within which we model debate interactions; it describes the information state update process in debates, leading to the creation of mutual beliefs. Section 6 proposes an evaluation method to validate to what extent the system's understanding of debate arguments corresponds to that of human understanding and can be used to predict debate outcomes. Section 7 summarizes our conclusions and indicates perspectives for further research.

2   Application Domain: The Nature of Parliamentary Debates

A parliamentary debate is a communication process in which participants argue *for* or *against* a *motion*. A debate is thus a type of dialogue, but it differs from the well-studied task-oriented dialogue in the number and roles of its participants, their tasks and the form of interaction. A debate *session* is motivated by a motion which is concerned either with a general topic, e.g. health, or with a proposed law (legislation). The so-called 'closure motion' is a special motion which ends the debate and leads to voting. The motion is announced by a *Moderator* (or Speaker in the UK). The Moderator chairs the session, opens and closes it, and regulates the turn-taking. The actual debate starts by the *Proponent* presenting the motion and arguments in favor of it. An *Opponent* attacks the proponent's arguments. There is a number of *Proponent's Seconders* and *Opponent's Seconders* whose task is to counter-attack either the opponent's or the proponent's arguments, respectively, or those of their seconders.

There are different debate types depending on type of motion and status of participating parliamentarians: debate on legislation, general debate and short debate. In this study we considered general parliamentary debates - plenary

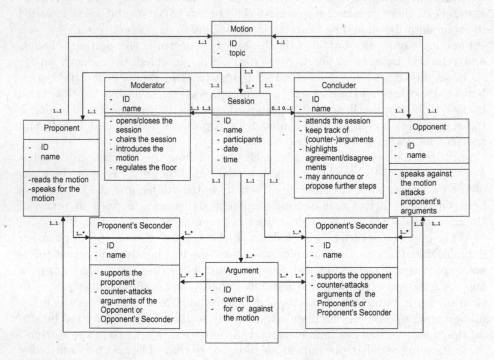

Fig. 1. Conceptual model of a parliamentary debate session.

sessions in the UK Youth Parliament (YP)[1]. Members of the Youth Parliament (MYPs) are elected to represent their constituency and do not belong to any political party. The YP does not decide on legislation, but simulates the environment of the actual Parliament plenary sessions discussing youth-specific current affairs issues. The results of YP debates are recorded in a publication called 'manifesto' which is available for the members of the actual Parliament. The general debate discussion is closed by the *Concluder* who wraps up the debate summarizing commonly agreed points and the most evident disagreements. Figure 1 shows a conceptual model of YP debates.

A YP debate is a formal interaction with certain rules, traditions and even rituals. Speakers present their positions by arguments that may take the form of quite lengthy verbal contributions with an articulate internal structure. Other MYPs listen to arguments and as a rule do not interrupt the current speaker. The right to have a turn is regulated by the Moderator. The Moderator nominates the next speaker. Participants who want to take the next turn, rise or half-rise from their seats in a bid to get the Moderator's attention.

3   Debate Data: Segmentation and Annotations

The data that we analysed forms three UK YP[2] sessions. These sessions are video recorded and available on Youtube[3]. The YP members, aged 11–18, debate issues addressing three different motions: (1) sex and relationship education (SRE); (2) university tuition fees and (3) job opportunities for young people in the UK. The corpus is provided with automatically generated subtitles which are corrected manually.

First, segmentation has been performed together with dialogue act annotations into functional segments according to guidelines provided in ISO 24617-2 [21]. To each segment a communicative function has been assigned in one or more of the nine ISO dimensions (Task, Auto- and Allo-Feedback, Discourse Structuring, Time and Turn Management, Own and Partner Communication Management, and Social Obligation Management). The annotated corpus consists of 1388 functional segments from 35 different speakers. Table 1 provides in the last column an overview of the relative frequencies of functional tags per ISO-dimension.

3.1   Task Acts

In our data, just over 41.4% of the dialogue acts performed by the debaters are Inform acts, which are often connected by discourse relations. For example,

---

[1] Youth Parliaments have been founded in many European countries and all over the world, e.g. in Greece, South Africa, Columbia. The European Youth Parliament is also active since 1987.

[2] http://www.ukyouthparliament.org.uk/.

[3] See as example http://www.youtube.com/watch?v=g2Fg-LJHPA4.

(1) $D1_{21}$[4]: Sex education covers a wide range of issues affecting young people [*Inform*]
$D1_{22}$: These include safe sex practices, STIs and legal issues surrounding consent and abuse [*Inform Elaboration* $D1_{21}$]

We observed a small portion of set questions (3.4%) that are rhetorical in the sense they are not intended to get an answer but rather to emphasise an important issue. For example,

(2) $D3_{72}$: This is not a question of morality [*Inform*]
$D3_{73}$: But a question of equality [*Inform Contrast* $D3_{72}$]
$D3_{74}$: Why should some children have sex education when others do not [*SetQuestion*]

About 1.7% of all task-related acts are explicit Agreements or Disagreements with previous speakers. For example,

(3) $D2_{37}$: it makes sense to teach a young person the basics of what a healthy relationship is before they want to have sex [*Inform*]
$D3_{62}$: we need a policy to reduce STDs [...] and address relationships aspects [*Inform*]
$D6_{153}$: I defend and I completely wholeheartedly agree that relationships are more important [*Agreement* $D2_{37}$; $D3_{62}$]

3.2 Dialogue Control Acts in Debates

There are other utterances concerned mostly with Turn Management from the side of the Moderator; Time Management acts like Stallings; Own Communication Management acts like Self Corrections; Social Obligation Management acts like Thankings; and Discourse Structuring acts for signalling that the debater has finished his speech. Consider the following example:

(4) $D7_{20}$: The government needs to keep up with the media in speed and in terms of sexual imaging [*Inform*]
$D7_{21}$: Thank you [*Thanking; Closing*]
Audience: *applause* [*Positive Auto/Allo-Feedback* $D7_1$ - $D7_{21}$; *Thanking*]
$D8_1$: *stands up* [*Turn Take*]
M_{212}: Let's hear this young gentleman [*Turn Assign*]
M_{213}: Who I think is from London [*CheckQuestion*]
$D8_2$: *head nod* [*Confirmation* M_{213}]
M_{214}: Good [*Positive Auto/Allo-Feedback* $D8_2$]
$D8_3$: My name's Landry Adelard, MYP of London [*Turn Accept* M_{212}; *SelfIntroduction; Confirmation* M_{213}]

---

[4] Here and henceforth Dk stands for Debater k; the subscript is the index of the identified functional segment.

3.3   Automatic Dialogue Act Recognition

For the automatic dialogue act recognition various machine learning techniques have been applied successfully for task oriented and free two-party conversations, e.g. Hidden Markov Models (HMM) by Stolcke et al. [9] with an accuracy of 71%; Bayesian Networks by Keizer [7] achieving an average accuracy of 81%; and a memory-based approach, based on the k-nearest-neighbour algorithm, by Lendvai et al. [8] with a tagging accuracy of 73.8%.

Debate data, however, has certain properties that are different from the data used in classification experiments reported in the above mentioned studies. The differences become apparent if we compare dialogue act distributions in different collected dialogue data such as, for example, HCRC MapTask corpus[5] consisting of human-human two-party instructing dialogues where one participant plays the role of an instruction-giver and another participant, the instruction-follower, navigates through the map, and AMI[6] corpus containing human-human multi-party face-to-face meeting interactions of remote control design teams, with the debate data. Table 1 presents relative frequencies of dialogue act tags across ISO dimensions for 3 compared corpora. It can be observed that both AMI and HCRC MapTask contain more interactive phenomena related to explicit feedback providing indication of the speaker's and partner's processing state, as well as related to turn and time management interactive aspects. Debate participants, along with the task-related acts, were more often concerned with structuring their contributions, see Sect. 4.

We conducted series of machine-learning experiments using different features both automatically extracted from the corpora and computed using available for English linguistic parsers. In order to train classifiers that are able to operate on data collected from various domains, along with frequently used n-grams and bag-of-words models we used part-of-speech (POS) information and shallow syntactic parsing features, and combinations of those. Linguistic features are expected to contribute to higher cross-domain portability of trained prediction models. For POS tagging Stanford CoreNLP[7] tagger was used and chunking was performed using Illinois shallow parser [10].

Support Vector Machine (SVM) classifier has been trained using scikit-learn implementation[8]. Training task has been defined as joined segmentation and classification task as proposed in [6]. To evaluate the classifiers' performance, the most commonly used performance metrics such accuracy, precision, recall and F-scores (harmonic mean) were computed. For the sake of simplicity, in this paper we report the best F-scores obtained in different classification experiments, see Table 2. As baseline the majority class, namely, `Task;Inform` of 0.41 has been used.

As for features, the best results were obtained on the complex features combining word bigrams, POS tags (unigrams) and chunking (bigrams) information.

---

[5] http://groups.inf.ed.ac.uk/maptask/.
[6] http://groups.inf.ed.ac.uk/ami/corpus/.
[7] http://nlp.stanford.edu/software/corenlp.shtml.
[8] http://scikit-learn.org/stable/.

Table 1. Distribution of dialogue act tags across ISO-dimensions in terms of their relative frequency in the AMI, HCRC MapTask and YP debate corpora.

Dimension	Relative frequency (in %)		
	AMI meetings	HCRC MapTask	YP debates
Task	31.8	52.4	54.9
Auto feedback	20.5	15.7	2.9
Allo feedback	0.7	4.7	1.0
Turn management	50.2	24.3	22.7
Time management	26.7	13.4	21.1
Discourse structuring	2.8	0.5	10.0
Own communication management	10.3	2.8	7.3
Partner communication management	0.3	0.3	0.0
Social obligation management	0.5	0.1	1.2

Table 2. Dialogue act classification results in terms of F-score on different feature set and with n-gram range computed for YP debate corpus.

Features set	unigrams	bi-grams	tri-grams
Chunks	0.45	0.71	0.41
Chunks, POS	0.63	0.75	0.55
Chunks, word tokens	0.66	0.68	0.60
Chunks, POS, word tokens	0.79	**0.84**	0.74
POS	0.62	0.58	0.64
POS, word tokens	**0.82**	0.79	0.76
Word tokens	0.74	**0.81**	0.67

For indication, when trained on unigram language models only we observed the decrease in performance of about 10% compared to the performance on features combination; trained on POS tags - 20% on average, trained on chunking information - 40%. Thus, wording of an utterance is still very important, but when supplied with linguistic information the performance of the classifier improves. The general conclusion is that dialogue acts can be successfully learned from linguistically processed debate transcripts in data-oriented supervised way.

4 Detection of Arguments and Their Structure

For our further analysis and modelling, arguments need to be identified. Toulmin [5] proposed a scheme with six functional roles to describe the structure of an argument (see Fig. 2). Based on evidence (*data*) and a generalization (*warrant*), which is possibly implicit and defeasible, a conclusion is derived. The conclusion can be *qualified*, e.g. by a modal operator indicating the strength of the inferential link between data and *conclusion*. A *rebuttal* specifies exceptional conditions that undermine this inference. A warrant can be supported by *backing*, e.g. reason, justification or motivation.

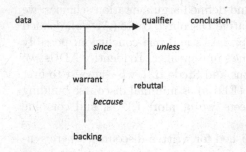

Fig. 2. Toulmin's argumentation diagram.

Toulmin's theory inspired many other argumentation schemes (see e.g. [11,12]). A recently proposed argumentation scheme is that of [13], where several previous approaches and theories are synthesized. It makes use of proponent and opponent moves as defined in [12]. The authors distinguish between *basic* elements of an argument which consists of a non-empty set of premises and a conclusion. Different patterns are observed linking premises and a conclusion. A premise supporting a conclusion form a basic argument.

Several premises may either jointly (*linked support*) or independently (*multiple support*) support one conclusion. A premise may provide support for another premise, and indirectly support a conclusion (*serial support*). A special form of lending support to a claim is that of providing examples (*example support*).

Further, arguments can be either attacked by the opponent, anticipated by the opponent (temporal role with proponent vs opponent, e.g. express awareness of exceptions), or counter-attacked by the opponent. There are two possible ways to attack an argument: one is to present an argument against a conclusion or a premise (*rebutting*), the other is to diminish their supporting force (*undercutting*). When *counter-attacking*, it is possible to rebut the rebutter of a conclusion; to rebut an undercutter of a support link; to undercut an undercutter; and to undercut a rebutter.

Good debaters are distinguished by concise clear arguments and try to make their arguments understandable for others. In other words, if a debater wants to be successfully interpreted, he needs to signal his intentions as unambiguously as possible, e.g. by using markers or cues, unless he wants to be deliberately vague or deceptive. This is applicable not only to arguments, but also to the supporting or undermining links between them. To achieve this, debaters often use linguistic cues such as discourse markers and dialogue act announcement acts. For example, 'I will talk in favour of ... Because ... Since international research shows...'. Thus, *discourse* relations are often marked explicitly by means of discourse markers. Discourse relations can be of various types. For example, to signal linked support of two or more premises for a conclusion, two premises can be connected by Elaboration or Sequence relations. Supporting links between premises and conclusion can be of Justification, Motivation, Cause/Result, Background/Evaluation, Evidence and Circumstance type, and many others. Rebuttal or undercutting links are often enabled by presenting Contrast, Exception and other Comparatives. Discourse relations have been proposed as an explanation for the construction of coherence in discourse or at least as crucial modelling tools for capturing this coherence, see e.g. Hobbs [16]; Mann and Thompson [14]; Sanders et al. [15]; Asher and Lascarides [17]. Discourse relations are learnable in a data-oriented way, using machine-learning techniques (see [22,23]). Figure 3 depicts the general analysed argument structure.

Based on discussed previous findings and defined argumentation schemes, we further segmented debates into Argumentative Discourse Units (ADUs), defined as a unit which consists of one or more premises and one conclusion, possibly restated or paraphrased several times by the same speaker. To identify ADUs, we followed the approach proposed by Peldszus and Stede [13], who suggest to first segment into Elementary Discourse Units (EDUs) as minimal discourse building blocks, then establish relationships between two or more EDUs, and combine those into ADUs.

Segmentation into EDUs is well established for written discourse, where syntactic clauses are considered as such units. For spoken discourse prosodic units [24], speaking turns [25], and intentionally defined discourse segments [26] have been proposed. For debates, turns are obviously too coarse to be considered, as

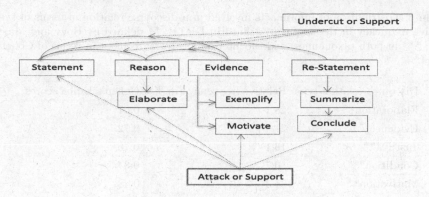

Fig. 3. Analysed argument structure.

they are too lengthy and may contain more then one argument. Prosodic units like interpausal units, e.g. bounded by at least 100 ms of silence [27], are too fine-grained since debaters often make pauses when emphasising a single word or phrase. EDUs in our data mostly coincide with intentionally defined units such as dialogue acts. The Task dialogue acts related to previous discourse by means of a discourse relation form the best-defined EDU for spoken discourse. In our corpus 1021 EDUs were identified meaning that about 73.6% of all dialogue acts constitute a part of an EDU.

Discourse relations were annotated using the annotation scheme designed for the Penn Discourse TreeBank (PDTB) corpus [28]), extended with discourse segment relations from the taxonomy proposed in [29]. Table 3 presents the types and frequencies of the relations along with the inter-annotator agreement reached annotating each relation type. It should be noted here that the inter-annotator agreement between three experienced annotators was moderate on this task (Cohen's kappa 0.54 on average), however on some relations like Elaboration, Evidence, Justification, Reason, Conclude and Restatement, which are important for our further processing, we obtained a substantial agreement (Cohen's kappa around 0.71).

Identifying ADUs, we observed a very frequent pattern[9]: an ADU will mostly start with a simple Inform act and end when an Inform Conclude or Restatement is identified, or before another Inform act which is not involved in any discourse relation. We assigned an index to each argument conclusion. Consider the following example:

(5) $D2_{30}$: Essentially we are experiencing a tragic loss of childhood [*Inform*]
$D2_{31}$: a walk down the high street reveals a depressing trend towards essentially adult's designs [*Inform Evidence $D2_{30}$*]
$D2_{32}$: children's pencil cases bearing playboy symbols [*Inform Evidence $D2_{30}$; Inform Motivate $D2_{31}$*]

---

[9] The inter-annotator agreement between three experienced annotators on this task was very high, 0.87 in terms of Cohen's kappa.

Table 3. Distribution of Inform acts involved in a discourse relation in terms of their relative frequency in the corpus (* defined in DPTB; ** defined by Hovy and Maier, 1995; *** in both taxonomies) and the inter-annotator agreement in terms of Cohen's kappa.)

Discourse relation type	Relative frequency (in %)	Cohen's kappa scores
Elaboration**	28.1	0.67
Evidence**	21.4	0.72
Justify***	16.1	0.76
Condition***	0.7	0.34
Motivation**	1.4	0.48
Background**	0.3	0.18
Cause***	3.4	0.37
Result***	2.2	0.26
Reason*	10.6	0.65
Conclude**	5.7	0.71
Restatement***	10.1	0.76

$D2_{33}$: our children being sexualized too young [*Inform Result* $D2_{30}$, $D2_{31}, D2_{32};$ *Cause* $D2_{34}$]

$D2_{34}$: we must aim to protect this short-lived innocence [*Inform Result* $D2_{33}$]

$D2_{35};D2\_2.1$[10]: SRE is simply inappropriate within a primary curriculum [*Inform Conclude* $D2_{30}$ - $D2_{34}$; *Conclusion* $D2\_2.1$]

In our data, 118 ADUs were identified in total, 37 to 40 per session.

The semantic content of an argument is incrementally constructed from its premises and conclusion using the representation formalism of DRSs [30, 31]. An example of the DRS representation for the argument exemplified in (5) is shown in Fig. 4, where the conclusion is marked in bold face. Computing semantic content for each conclusion, we observed that for instance in the session on SRE nine main claims (henceforth also called 'propositions') are identified:

(6) p_1: SRE should be compulsory
   p_2: SRE should be introduced in primary school
   p_3: SRE should be valued by parents
   p_4: SRE should be provided even in faith schools
   p_5: SRE should be counter-part for media images
   p_6: SRE should be about both sex and relationships education
   p_7: SRE should be provided in an appropriate context
   p_8: Government listens to the YP's campaign
   p_9: SRE should not be provided at school but in peer-education

---

[10] Here and henceforth _x.y is the index assigned to the conclusion of an ADU, where x indicates the debater index and y stands for the index of an ADU conclusion.

To incorporate support and attack links[11], we need the full specification of participants' information states. Only in this way can we establish beliefs concerning previously presented arguments that the current speaker either supports or attacks. We start with identified explicit and implicit agreement and disagreement dialogue acts signalling support or attack of arguments through the *functional dependence relations* defined in [21] between the detected argument conclusions. Consider the discussion on when SRE should be introduced at school.

(7) $D1_{47};D1_{1.2}$: Sex education needs to start early to stop the damage before it's too late [*Inform*]

$D2_5;D2_{2.1}$: SRE is simply inappropriate within a primary curriculum [*Inform&Disagreement* $D1_{47}$] - Attack 1.2

$D7_2;D7_{7.1}$: I think involving sex education in primary school is perfectly sensible [*Inform&Agreement* $D1_{47}$&*Disagreement* $D2_5$]- Support 1.2/Attack 2.1

Debater 1 (Proponent) states as his opinion that SRE needs to start early (read in primary school). Debater 2 thinks that SRE in primary school is inappropriate. Debater 7 supports SRE in primary school (argument 1.2) and thereby attacks the argument 2.1.

The proposed complete argument identification and processing flow is illustrated in Fig. 5. The process starts with segmenting a debater's turn into functional segments each of them having one or more communicative functions according to the ISO 24617-2 dialogue act annotation standard. Subsequently, we propose to identify discourse relations between dialogue acts that are mostly Informs and cluster them into EDU segments, and successively into ADUs as described in Sect. 4. The ADU's main statement can be then extracted which is either the opening Inform or the closing Conclusion or Re-statement. These

---

e1, x1, x2, e2, x3,x4,x5, e3, x6, x7 e4, x8, x2, e5,x9,x10, S1, x11, x12,

experience (e1) childhoood_loss (x1) we (x2) type(x2, person) type(x2, plural)
type(x2, collective) experiencer (e1, x2) stimulus(e1,x1)
reveal(e2) walk(x3_1) street(x3_2) path(x3_1, x3_2) trend(x4) adult-design (x5,)
theme (e2,x3_1) result (e2,x4)
evidence (e2,e1)
bear(e3) children_pencil_case (x6) type (x6, plural) playboy_symbol(x7) type (x7,
plural) pivot(e3, x6) theme(e3,x7)
evidence (e3,e1)
motivate(e3,e2)
sexualize (e4) child(x8) type(x8,plural) patient(e4,x8) attribute(x8,too_young)
result(e4,e1)
protect(e5) we(x9) type(x9, person) type(x9, plural) x9 = x2   innocence(x10)
agent (e5, x9) theme (e5, x10)
cause (e4,e5)
 result(e5,e4)
be_inappropriate (s1) SRE (x11) type (x11, abbreviation)
primary_curriculum (x12) setting(s1,x12) pivot(s1,x11) conclude (s1, e5)

Fig. 4. Example of DRS representation of the identified ADU presented in (5).

---

[11] Note we do not distinguish between rebuttals and undercutters in this study.

propositions can be linguistically processed using the state-of-the-art parsers of various types, e.g. syntactic parser and (shallow) semantic parsers. One of the tools that incorporates many of the required existing up-to-date semantic analyzers is Boxer[12]. It takes as input CCG (Combinatory Categorial Grammar) derivations and produces DRSs (Discourse Representation Structures). Further, in many cases the identification of attack/support links requires an additional step, since our analysis showed most of them are expressed by implicit (dis-)agreements. We suggest to check the selected propositions for semantic similarity combined with polarity detection. Similarity checking operation can be performed on proposition's exact wording or using obtained semantic representations like DRSs. Additionally, to achieve wider coverage of possible linguistic expressions, entities expansion steps may be needed, e.g. expansion through lists of synonyms, homonyms and/or entities with some ontological relations using available resources like, for example, WordNet[13]. Semantically similar propositions produced by different speakers are selected and functional dependence links are established between them. Finally, after polarity detection, similar positive propositions are linked as having support link, and similar negative ones as having an attack link. To make the picture complete, arguments represented by their main propositions and support/attack links between them are semantically modelled as part of the debaters' information states (see Sect. 5).

5 Computing Information States

Information state update approaches analyse dialogue utterances in terms of effects on the information states of the dialogue participants. An 'information state' (also called 'context') is the totality of a dialogue participant's beliefs, assumptions, expectations, goals, preferences and other attitudes that may influence the participant's interpretation and generation of communicative behaviour

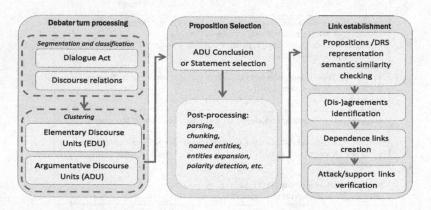

Fig. 5. Argument identification and processing flow.

---

[12] http://svn.ask.it.usyd.edu.au/trac/candc/wiki/boxer.
[13] http://wordnet.princeton.edu.

[21]. Dialogue acts are viewed as corresponding to update operations on the information states and consist of two main components: (1) the type of communicative act, expressed as its *communicative function*, e.g. Inform, Question, Request, etc., and (2) the *semantic content*, i.e. the objects, events, situations, relations, properties, etc. are addressed. Bunt (2014) provides a detailed specification of the update semantics of dialogue acts [32].

5.1 Mutual Belief Creation and Transfer in Debates

To be successful in debate, the participants have to coordinate their activities on many levels. In the speaker role, a participant produces utterances with the aim to be understood by others. In dialogue act theory, understanding that a certain dialogue act is performed means creating the belief that the preconditions hold which are characteristic for that dialogue act. As the ultimate goal of a debater is to convince his audience of the rightness of his position, he wants the addressees to incorporate his beliefs as beliefs of their own (belief *adoption*).

The coordination of the beliefs and assumptions of the participants is a central issue in any communication. A set of propositions that the dialogue participants mutually believe is called their *common ground*, and the process of establishing and updating the common ground is called *grounding*. The speaker expects under 'normal input-output' conditions [33] that what he is saying is perceived and understood as intended. These expectations may be strengthened when there is positive evidence from the audience, and if negative feedback occurs the expectations are canceled. Such evidence takes the form of explicit or implicit positive feedback; we observed instances of feedback on what was just said, such as laughter, applause, verbal 'yeah' and 'hear! hear!'. However, not all propositions are addressed immediately, and a debater may not get a chance to react to or correct misinterpretations or rejections of his contributions.

In parliamentary debates, where political confrontations and ideological convictions often play a significant role, the goals of a debater depend on the type of debate. In legislation debates the main goal is to gain the majority of supporters in terms of votes. A lot of preparatory work is done before the actual debate takes place, in committees and lobbies. To achieve their main goal parliamentarians may be ready to compromise on some points and negotiate on others. A governing party with a majority in the parliament has a bigger chance to get their beliefs adopted by the majority, therefore has stronger initial expectations. Parliamentarians also have certain knowledge about their opponents and their seconders, which should be modelled in the initial dialogue context together with knowledge about common and individual goals, and should be taken into consideration when computing the strength of expectations concerning the outcome of a debate. In HCI research it is common to incorporate user models where all available information about dialogue participants is specified [34]. This type of information is typically useful to design adaptive human-computer systems and can be profitably used when modelling interactive behaviour in dialogue, in particular related to grounding.

In general YP debates no strong political division is obvious a priori, and it is reasonable to assume that each debater expects that many of his partners will adopt his beliefs. At least, this is what he strives for, otherwise it would make little sense to participate in such a debate. With this goal in mind, a participant does his best to be convincing and persuasive, presenting his claims and evidence as convincingly as possible. Example (5) from our corpus can be used to illustrate this. Proponent D_1 presents arguments with the conclusion p_1: *'SRE should be introduced in the primary school curriculum'*. The debaters $D_2...D_n$ understand this proposition and make it part of their common ground. Following the computational model of grounding proposed by [35], beliefs are updated as follows:

(8) D1_1.2: Sex education needs to start in primary school to stop the damage before it's too late
preconditions: $Bel(D_1, p_2)$; $Want(D_1, Bel(\{A1, ..., An\}, p_2))$
expected understanding:$Bel(D_1, MBel(\{D_1, A1, ..., An\}, WBel(D_1, Bel(Ai, Bel(D_1, p_2)))))$ [for each addressee Ai];
$Bel(D_1, MBel(\{D_1, A1, ..., An\}, WBel(D_1, Bel(Ai, Want(D_1, Bel(Ai, p_2))))))$
expected adoption: $Bel(D_1, MBel(\{D_1, A1, ..., An\}, WBel(D_1, Bel(Ai, p_2))))$

D2_2.1: SRE is simply inappropriate within a primary curriculum
understanding: $MBel(\{D_1, D_2\}, Bel(D_1, p_2))$; $MBel(\{D_1, D_2\}, Want(D_1, Bel(D_2, p_2)))$
cancelled adoption: ~~$Bel(D_1, MBel(\{D_1, D_2\}, WBel(D_1, Bel(D_2, p_2))))$~~
preconditions: $Bel(D_2, \neg p_2)$; $Want(D_2, Bel(\{A1, ..., An\}, \neg p_2))$;
expected understanding: $Bel(D_2, MBel(\{D_2, A1, ..., An\}, WBel(D_2, Bel(Ai, Bel(D_2, \neg p_2)))))$; $Bel(D_2, MBel(\{D_2, A1, ..., An\}, WBel(D_2, Bel(Ai, Want(D_2, Bel(Ai, \neg p_2))))))$
expected adoption:$Bel(D_2, MBel(\{D_2, A1, ..., An\}, WBel(D_2, Bel(Ai, \neg p_2))))$

D7_7.1: I think involving sex education in primary school is perfectly sensible
understanding: $MBel(\{D_1, D_7\}, Bel(D_1, p_2))$; $MBel(\{D_1, D_7\}, Want(D_1, Bel(D_7, p_2)))$; $MBel(\{D_7, D_2\}, Bel(D_2, \neg p_2))$; $MBel(\{D_7, D_2\}, Want(D_3, Bel(D_2, \neg p_2)))$
adoption: $Bel(D_7, MBel(\{D_1, D_7\}, p_2))$
cancelled adoption: ~~$Bel(D_2, MBel(\{D_2, D_7\}, WBel(D_2, Bel(D_7, \neg p_2)))$~~
preconditions: $Bel(D_7, p_2)$; $Want(D_7, Bel(\{A1, ..., An\}, p_2))$;
expected understanding: $Bel(D_7, MBel(\{D_7, A1, ..., An\}, WBel(D_7, Bel(Ai, Bel(D_7, p_2)))))$; $Bel(D_7, MBel(\{D_7, A1, ..., An\}, WBel(D_7, Bel(Ai, Want(D_7, Bel(Ai, p_2))))))$
expected adoption:$Bel(D_7, MBel(\{D_7, A1, ..., An\}, WBel(D_7, Bel(Ai, p_2))))$

We implemented a system that keeps track of all created and adopted beliefs on the part of each debater as the debate proceeds. We used the conclusions identified in Sect. 4 to update the information states of participants and that of the system. This leads to the system's creation and adoption of beliefs concerning these propositions. For example, with regard to the proposition p_1 in (6) the following system's beliefs are created: $Bel(S, MBel(\{S, D_1, D_3, D_4, D_{12}\}, Bel(\{D_1, D_3, D_4, D_{12}\}, (p_1)))$, $Bel(S, MBel(\{S, D_1, D_3, D_4, D_{12}\}, Want(\{D_1, D_3, D_4, D_{12}\}, Bel$

$(S, p_1))))$, where S stands for System. In the final state, the system predicts that the belief $Bel(S, MBel(\{S, D_1, D_3, D_4, D_{12}\}, p_1))$ will be adopted.

6 Concluder Agent: Evaluation

A system operating as described in the previous section can form the basis of an artificial agent that could play different roles in a debate. It could for instance play the role of one of the Debaters or their Seconders by supporting or attacking certain arguments. In this study we consider the system in the role of Concluder, whose task is to understand the arguments of all the debaters and to conclude the debate by stating the opinion of the majority. We call the system playing this role the C-Concluder (Computational Concluder).

In order to assess the quality of the C-Concluder final information state, we need to evaluate against some form of 'ground truth'. For this purpose we use the final state of a human concluder (H-Concluder). The human concluder is called by the Moderator at the end of the session to wrap up the debate.

The H-Concluder provides a general assessment of what was discussed by emphasizing all major arguments brought up by debaters. It is mostly a summary of the arguments that the majority is in favour of, and of points of strong disagreement. The summary exemplified in (9) is the basis of the H-Concluder' final state. The H-Concluder wraps up his summary by announcing further steps, e.g. the motion needs more discussion.

(9) HC$_{15.1}$: Compulsory sex and relationships education is something the UKYP strives for [*Support 1.1, 3.1, 4.3, 12.2/Attack 2.2*]

HC$_{15.2}$: Many believe teaching children about relationships from a young age is vitally important [*Support 1.2, 6.1, 7.1, 9.2, 10.1, 11.1, 14.2/ Attack 2.1, 5.1, 8.1*]

HC$_{15.3}$: Also it is highlighted that SRE is strongly valued by parents [*Support 1.3, 12.5, 14.3/Attack 2.3*]

HC$_{15.4}$: Many schools work successfully to provide effective SRE, even in faith organizations [*Support 1.4*]

HC$_{15.5}$: Our generation have a much disfigured view on sex from things such as peer pressure, and as many mentioned, sexualized media formats. [*Support 2.5, 7.2, 10.3, 14.1*]

HC$_{15.6}$: As it has already been mentioned by Poppie and many others before her that this is not just sex and sex education or the anatomy of it. This is sex and relationships education [*Support 2.4, 4.2, 6.2, 8.2, 9.1, 10.2, 11.2, 12.3, 13.1*]

HC$_{15.7}$: Children should understand the meanings of a relationship, trust and respect [*Support 3.2, 6.3, 7.3, 10.4, 11.3, 12.4*]

HC$_{15.8}$: I believe as a unified organization we can make the government sit up and listen to our campaign [*Support 1.5, 4.1, 7.4, 12.1*]

The evaluation method is depicted in Fig. 6. Both C- and H-Concluders try to understand participants' arguments and links between them (strengthening, adoption and rejection effects). In the final state they have the beliefs of all participants resulting from their understanding of each other and adopting each others beliefs.

Table 4. Example of C-Concluder expected information state and H-Concluder actual information state. (pred.und = predicted understanding; und = understanding; pred.ad = predicted adoption; ad = adoption; pred.canc = predicted cancelling; canc = cancelling; Bel = believes; MBel = mutually believed; WBel = weakly believes)

source	C-Concluder (CC)	source	H-Concluder (HC)
pred.und	$Bel(CC, MBel(\{CC, D_1, D_3, D_4, D_{12}\},$ $Bel(\{D_1, D_3, D_4, D_{12}\}, p_1)))$ $Bel(CC, MBel(\{CC, D_1, D_3, D_4, D_{12}\},$ $Want(\{D_1, D_3, D_4, D_{12}\},$ $Bel(CC, p_1))))$	und	$Bel(HC, MBel(\{HC, D_1, D_3, D_4, D_{12}\},$ $Bel(\{D_1, D_3, D_4, D_{12}\}, p_1)))$ $Bel(HC, MBel(\{HC, D_1, D_3, D_4, D_{12}\},$ $Want(\{D_1, D_3, D_4, D_{12}\},$ $Bel(HC, p_1))))$
	$Bel(CC, MBel(\{CC, D_2\}, Bel(D_2, \neg p_1)))$ $Bel(CC, MBel(\{CC, D_2\},$ $Want(D_2, Bel(CC, \neg p_1))))$		
	$Bel(CC,$ $MBel(\{CC, D_1, D_6, D_7, D_9, D_{10}, D_{11}, D_{14}\}$ $Bel(\{D_1, D_6, D_7, D_9, D_{10}, D_{11}, D_{14}\}, p_2)))$ $Bel(CC, MBel(\{CC, D_1, D_6, D_7,$ $D_9, D_{10}, D_{11}, D_{14}\},$ $Want(\{D_1, D_3, D_4, D_{12}D_1, D_6, D_7, D_9,$ $D_{10}, D_{11}D_{14}\}, Bel(CC, p_2))))$		$Bel(HC,$ $MBel(\{HC, D_1, D_6, D_7, D_9, D_{10}, D_{11}, D_{14}\}$ $Bel(\{D_1, D_0, D_7, D_9, D_{10}, D_{11}, D_{14}\}, p_2)))$ $Bel(HC, MBel(\{HC, D_1, D_6, D_7,$ $D_9, D_{10}, D_{11}, D_{14}\},$ $Want(\{D_1, D_3, D_4, D_{12}D_1, D_6, D_7, D_9,$ $D_{10}, D_{11}, D_{14}\}, Bel(HC, p_2))))$
	$Bel(CC, MBel(\{CC, D_2, D_5, D_8\},$ $Bel(\{D_2, D_5, D_8\}, \neg p_2)))$ $Bel(CC, MBel(\{CC, D_2, D_5, D_8\},$ $Want(\{D_2, D_5, D_8\},$ $Bel(CC, \neg p_2))))$		
	$Bel(CC, MBel(\{CC, D_1, D_{12}, D_{14}\},$ $Bel(\{D_1, D_{12}, D_{14}\}, p_3)))$ $Bel(CC, MBel(\{CC, D_1, D_{12}, D_{14}\},$ $Want(\{D_1, D_{12}, D_{14}\}, Bel(CC, p_3))))$		$Bel(HC, MBel(\{HC, D_1, D_{12}, D_{14}\},$ $Bel(\{D_1, D_{12}, D_{14}\}, p_3)))$ $Bel(HC, MBel(\{HC, D_1, D_{12}, D_{14}\},$ $Want(\{D_1, D_{12}, D_{14}\}, Bel(HC, p_3))))$
	$Bel(CC, MBel(\{CC, D_2\}, Bel(D_2, \neg p_3)))$ $Bel(CC, MBel(\{CC, D_2\},$ $Want(D_2, Bel(CC, \neg p_3))))$		
	$Bel(CC, MBel(\{CC, D_1\}, Bel(D_1, p_4)))$ $Bel(CC, MBel(\{CC, D_1\},$ $Want(D_1, Bel(CC, p_4))))$		$Bel(HC, MBel(\{HC, D_1\}, Bel(D_1, p_4)))$ $Bel(HC, MBel(\{HC, D_1\},$ $Want(D_1, Bel(CC, p_4))))$
	$Bel(CC, MBel(\{CC, D_2, D_7, D_{10}, D_{14}\},$ $Bel(\{D_2, D_7, D_{10}, D_{14}\}, p_5)))$ $Bel(CC, MBel(\{CC, D_2, D_7, D_{10}, D_{14}\},$ $Want(\{D_2, D_7, D_{10}, D_{14}\}, Bel(CC, p_5))))$		$Bel(HC, MBel(\{HC, D_2, D_7, D_{10}, D_{14}\},$ $Bel(\{D_2, D_7, D_{10}, D_{14}\}, p_5)))$ $Bel(HC, MBel(\{HC, D_2, D_7, D_{10}, D_{14}\},$ $Want(\{D_2, D_7, D_{10}, D_{14}\}, Bel(HC, p_5))))$
	$Bel(CC, MBel(\{CC, D_2, D_4, D_6, D_8,$ $D_9, D_{10}, D_{11}, D_{12}, D_{13}\}$ $Bel(\{D_2, D_4, D_6, D_8,$ $D_9, D_{10}, D_{11}, D_{12}, D_{13}\}, p_6)))$ $Bel(CC, MBel(\{CC, D_2, D_4, D_6, D_8,$ $D_9, D_{10}, D_{11}, D_{12}, D_{13}\},$ $Want(\{CC, D_2, D_4, D_6, D_8,$ $D_9, D_{10}, D_{11}, D_{12}, D_{13}, \}, Bel(CC, p_6))))$		$Bel(HC, MBel(\{HC, D_2, D_4, D_6, D_8,$ $D_9, D_{10}, D_{11}, D_{12}, D_{13}\}$ $Bel(\{D_2, D_4, D_6, D_8,$ $D_9, D_{10}, D_{11}, D_{12}, D_{13}\}, p_6)))$ $Bel(HC, MBel(\{HC, D_2, D_4, D_6, D_8,$ $D_9, D_{10}, D_{11}, D_{12}, D_{13}\},$ $Want(\{HC, D_2, D_4, D_6, D_8,$ $D_9, D_{10}, D_{11}, D_{12}, D_{13}\}, Bel(CC, p_6))))$
	$Bel(CC, MBel(\{CC, D_3, D_6, D_7,$ $D_{10}, D_{11}, D_{12}\}$ $Bel(\{D_3, D_6, D_7,$ $D_{10}, D_{11}, D_{12}\}, p_7)))$ $Bel(CC, MBel(\{CC, D_3, D_6, D_7,$ $D_{10}, D_{11}, D_{12}\},$ $Want(\{D_3, D_6, D_7, D_9, D_{10}, D_{11}, D_{12}\},$ $Bel(CC, p_7))))$		$Bel(HD, MBel(\{HC, D_3, D_6, D_7,$ $D_{10}, D_{11}, D_{12}\}$ $Bel(\{D_3, D_6, D_7,$ $D_{10}, D_{11}, D_{12}\}, p_7)))$ $Bel(HC, MBel(\{HC, D_3, D_6, D_7,$ $D_{10}, D_{11}, D_{12}\},$ $Want(\{D_3, D_6, D_7, D_9, D_{10}, D_{11}, D_{12}\},$ $Bel(HC, p_7))))$
	$Bel(CC, MBel(\{CC, D_2, D_4, D_7, D_{12}\}$ $Bel(\{D_2, D_4, D_7, D_{12}\}, p_8)))$ $Bel(CC, MBel(\{CC, D_2, D_4, D_7, D_{12}\},$ $Want(\{D_2, D_4, D_7, D_{12}\}, Bel(CC, p_8))))$		$Bel(HC, MBel(\{HC, D_2, D_4, D_7, D_{12}\}$ $Bel(\{D_2, D_4, D_7, D_{12}\}, p_8)))$ $Bel(HC, MBel(\{HC, D_2, D_4, D_7, D_{12}\},$ $Want(\{D_2, D_4, D_7, D_{12}\}, Bel(HC, p_8))))$
	$Bel(CC, MBel(\{CC, D_{10}\}, Bel(D_{10}, p_9$ $Bel(CC, MBel(\{CC, D_{10}\},$ $Want(D_{10}, Bel(CC, p_9))))$		
pred.ad	$Bel(CC, MBel(\{CC, D_1, D_3, D_4, D_{12}\}, p_1))$ $Bel(CC, MBel(\{CC, D_1, D_6, D_7,$ $D_9, D_{10}, D_{11}, D_{14}\}, p_2))$ $Bel(CC, MBel(\{CC, D_1, D_{12}, D_{14}\}, p_3))$	ad	$Bel(HC, MBel(\{HC, D_1, D_3, D_4, D_{12}\}, p_1))$ $Bel(HC, MBel(\{HC, D_1, D_6, D_7,$ $D_9, D_{10}, D_{11}, D_{14}\}, p_2))$ $Bel(HC, MBel(\{HC, D_1, D_{12}, D_{14}\}, p_3))$ $Bel(HC, MBel(\{HC, D_1\}, p_4))$
	$Bel(CC, MBel(\{CC, D_2, D_7, D_{10}, D_{14}\}, p_5)$ $Bel(CC, MBel(\{CC, D_2, D_4, D_6, D_8,$ $D_9, D_{10}, D_{11}, D_{12}, D_{13}\}, p_6)$ $Bel(CC, MBel(\{CC, D_3, D_6, D_7,$ $D_{10}, D_{11}, D_{12}\}, p_7)$ $Bel(CC, MBel(\{CC, D_2, D_4, D_7, D_{12}\}, p_8)$		$Bel(HC, MBel(\{HC, D_2, D_7, D_{10}, D_{14}\}, p_5)$ $Bel(HC, MBel(\{HC, D_2, D_4, D_6, D_8,$ $D_9, D_{10}, D_{11}, D_{12}, D_{13}\}, p_6)$ $Bel(HC, MBel(\{HC, D_3, D_6, D_7,$ $D_{10}, D_{11}, D_{12}\}, p_7)$ $Bel(HC, MBel(\{HC, D_2, D_4, D_7, D_{12}\}, p_8)$
pred.canc	$Bel(CC, MBel(\{CC, D_2\},$ $WBel(CC, Bel(D_2, \neg p_1)))$ $Bel(CC, MBel(\{CC, D_2, D_5, D_8\},$ $WBel(CC, Bel(\{D_5, D_8\}, \neg p_2))))$ $Bel(CC, MBel(\{CC, D_2\},$ $WBel(CC, Bel(D_2, \neg p_3))))$ $Bel(CC, MBel(\{CC, D_1\},$ $WBel(CC, Bel(D_1, p_4))))$ $Bel(CC, MBel(\{CC, D_{10}\},$ $WBel(CC, Bel(D_{10}, p_9))))$	canc	$Bel(HC, MBel(\{HC, D_2\},$ $WBel(HC, Bel(D_2, \neg p_1)))$ $Bel(HC, MBel(\{HC, D_2, D_5, D_8\},$ $WBel(HC, Bel(\{D_5, D_8\}, \neg p_2))))$ $Bel(HC, MBel(\{HC, D_2\},$ $WBel(HC, Bel(D_2, \neg p_3))))$ $Bel(HC, MBel(\{HC, D_{10}\},$ $WBel(HC, Bel(D_{10}, p_9))))$

We compute the H-Concluder beliefs by applying the analysis exemplified in (8) to a summary given by a human concluder in (9). For the C-Concluder we compute the list of predicted beliefs resulting from understanding, grounding and the propositions supported by a 'winning' majority, as well as the negation of all rejected propositions that are not addressed by any of the debaters. The *predicted* final C-Concluder and computed *actual* H-Concluder states are compared.

Table 4 presents the predicted final information state of the C-Concluder and the actual final state of the H-Concluder. The representation of expected understanding effects has been omitted both for C- and H-Concluders, since they are identical. The proposition symbols p_1 to p_9 stand for conclusions.[14]

As we can observe, the predicted C-Concluder information state differs slightly from the actual H-Concluder state, but not significantly. The H-Concluder did not address the arguments concerning the propositions $\neg p_1$, $\neg p_2$, $\neg p_3$ and p_9, hence we do not find evidence in his final state for his understanding of the Inform and (Dis-)Agreement acts with that propositional content. As for the C-Concluder, we had taken the decision that in case of conflicting updates (e.g. $Bel(CC, p)$ and $Bel(CC, \neg p)$ we decide in favor of the majority, comparing the number of supporters. Thus, the adoption of beliefs concerning propositions $\neg p_1$, $\neg p_2$, $\neg p_3$ are cancelled for the C-Concluder state.

Closer inspection shows that of the two arguments that have not been supported or attacked, p_4 is addressed by the H-Concluder while p_9 is not. The H-Concluder considers p_4 as adopted and p_9 as cancelled. Our intuition says that human concluders may have personal considerations such as attitudes towards certain debaters or towards certain arguments, or maybe other factors play a role here. To model this computationally one would need to construct more sophisticated participant models which include their *a priori* beliefs and preferences.

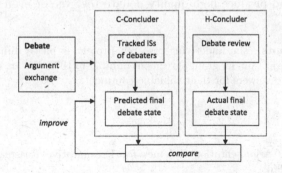

Fig. 6. Evaluation model for the C-Concluder role.

---

[14] For the sake of simplicity we do not spell out the semantic content of the propositions and leave out evidence links here.

7 Conclusions

In this study we showed how the ISU approach can be applied to modelling and managing argumentative multi-party discourse such as parliamentary debates. We argued that in order to model such complex interactions at least three models are needed. First, a domain model is required where the roles and tasks of the participants are specified. Second, we need a model for the analysis of their contributions. The identification of arguments and analysis of their internal structure (i.e. evidence relations from premises to conclusions) can be based on the identification and classification of discourse units and relations, and can be learned in a data-oriented way as shown by previous research [2,4,36]. Third, in order to identify support/attack links between arguments of different debaters, a computational model of belief creation and transfer is needed. An ISU model, where a dialogue is viewed as a sequential structure consisting of communicative acts that participants perform in order to change each other information states, is particularly suitable for this task. We showed how the participants' beliefs are created when a speaker's behaviour is understood and how it leads to the adoption or cancellation of beliefs when participants support or attack each other's arguments.

We evaluated the proposed approach against the debate review produced by a human who acts as a concluder. The system in the role of a concluder, having tracked the information states of the debaters, predicts which propositions will be adopted by the human concluder and which will be cancelled. The comparison shows that such predictions were fairly accurate.

In conclusion, we believe that this paper has addressed a very challenging and exciting research topic, even though it is obviously still a long way to a fully automatic and robust system that is able to understand debate arguments with high accuracy and produce high-quality debate reviews, or even to replace one of the debaters.

Acknowledgements. The underlying research project is partly funded by the EU FP7 Metalogue project, under grant agreement number 611073. We are also very thankful to anonymous reviewers for their valuable comments.

References

1. Walton, D.N.: Argumentation Schemes for Presumptive Reasoning. Routledge, Abingdon (1996)
2. Moens, M., Boiy, E., Mochales-Palau, R., Reed, C.: Automatic detection of arguments in legal texts. In: Proceedings of the ICAIL 2007, Stanford, California, pp. 225–230 (2007)
3. Reed, C., Mochales-Palau, R., Rowe, G., Moens, M.: Language resources for studying argument. In: Proceedings of the LREC 2008, Marrakech, Morocco, pp. 2613–2618 (2008)
4. Teufel, S.: Argumentative zoning: information extraction from scientific text. Ph.D. thesis, University of Edinburgh (1999)

5. Toulmin, S.: The Uses of Arguments. Cambridge University Press, Cambridge (1958)
6. Petukhova, V., Bunt, H.: Incremental recognition and prediction of dialogue acts. In: Bunt, H., Bos, J., Pulman, S. (eds.) Computing Meaning, vol. 4, pp. 235–256. Springer, Dordrecht (2014)
7. Keizer, S.: Reasoning under uncertainty in natural language dialogue using Bayesian networks. Ph.D. thesis, Twente University Press, The Netherlands (2003)
8. Lendvai, P., van den Bosch, A., Krahmer, E., Canisius, S.: Memory-based robust interpretation of recognised speech. In: Proceedings of the SPECOM 2004, St. Petersburgh, Russia, pp. 415–422 (2004)
9. Stolcke, A., Ries, K., Coccaro, K., Shriberg, E., Bates, R., Jurafsky, D., Taylor, P., Martin, R., van Ess-Dykema, C., Meteer, M.: Dialogue act modeling for automatic tagging and recognition of conversational speech. Comput. Linguist. **26**(3), 339–373 (2000)
10. Punyakanok, V., Roth, D.: The use of classifiers in sequential inference. In: NIPS, pp. 995–1001 (2001)
11. Klein, W.: Argumentation and argument. Zeitschrift für Literaturwissenschaft und Linguistik **10**(38/39), 9–56 (1980)
12. Freeman, J.B.: Argument Structure: Representation and Theory. Argumentation Library, vol. 18. Springer, Berlin (2011)
13. Peldszus, A., Stede, M.: From argument diagrams to argumentation mining in texts: a survey. Int. J. Cogn. Inf. Natural Intell. (IJCINI) **7**(1), 1–31 (2013)
14. Mann, W., Thompson, S.: Rhetorical Structure Theory: Toward a Functional Theory of Text Organisation. MIT Press, Cambridge (1988)
15. Sanders, T., Spooren, W., Noordman, L.: Toward a taxonomy of coherence relations. Discourse Process. **15**, 1–35 (1992)
16. Hobbs, J.: On the coherence and structure of discourse. Research report 85–37, CSLI, Stanford (1985)
17. Asher, N., Lascarides, A.: Logics of Conversation. Cambridge University Press, Cambridge (2003)
18. Cohen, R.: A computational theory of the function of clue words in argument understanding. In: Proceedings of the COLING-ACL 1984, Standford, pp. 251–258 (1984)
19. Poesio, M., Traum, D.: Towards an axiomatization of dialogue acts. In: Proceedings of the Twente Workshop on the Formal Semantics and Pragmatics of Dialogues, pp. 207–222 (1998)
20. Bunt, H.: Information dialogues as communicative action in relation to partner modelling and information processing. In: Taylor, M., Neel, F., Bouwhuis, D. (eds.) The Structure of Multimodal Dialogue, vol. 1, pp. 47–73. Elsevier, North Holland (1989)
21. ISO: Language resource management - Semantic annotation framework - Part 2: Dialogue acts. ISO 24617-2. ISO Central Secretariat, Geneva (2012)
22. Sporleder, C., Lascarides, A.: Using automatically labelled examples to classify rhetorical relations: an assessment. Nat. Lang. Eng. **14**(03), 369–416 (2008)
23. Marcu, D.: The rhetorical parsing of natural language texts. In: Proceedings of of Association for Computational Linguistics Annual Conference (ACL), pp. 96–103 (1997)
24. Hirschberg, J., Litman, D.: Empirical studies on the disambiguation of cue phrases. Comput. Linguist. **25**(4), 501–530 (1993)
25. Sacks, H., Schegloff, E., Jefferson, G.: A simplest systematics for the organization of turn-taking for conversation. Language **50**(4), 696–735 (1974)

26. Grosz, B.J., Sidner, C.L.: Attention, intentions, and the structure of discourse. Comput. Linguist. **12**, 175–204 (1986)
27. Ishimoto, Y., Tsuchiya, T., Koiso, H., Den, Y.: Towards automatic transformation between different transcription conventions: prediction of intonation markers from linguistic and acoustic features. In: Proceedings of the LREC 2014, Reykjavik, Iceland, pp. 311–315 (2014)
28. Prasad, R., Dinesh, N., Lee, A., Miltsakaki, E., Robaldo, L., Joshi, A., Webber, B.: The penn discourse treebank 2.0. In: Proceedings of the LREC 2008, Marrakech, Maroc, pp. 2961–2968 (2008)
29. Hovy, E., Maier, E.: Parsimonious of profligate: how many and which discourse structure relations? (1995, unpublished manuscript)
30. Bos, J.: Towards wide-coverage semantic interpretation. In: Proceedings of the 6th International Conference on Computational Semantics (IWCS-6), pp. 42–53 (2005)
31. Bunt, H.: Annotations that effectively contribute to semantic interpretation. In: Bunt, H., Bos, J., Pulman, S. (eds.) Computing Meaning, vol. 47, pp. 49–69. Springer, Dordrecht (2014)
32. Bunt, H.: A context-change semantics for dialogue acts. In: Bunt, H., Bos, J., Pulman, S. (eds.) Computing Meaning, vol. 4, pp. 177–201. Springer, Dordrecht (2014)
33. Searle, J.R.: Speech Acts. Cambridge University Press, Cambridge (1969)
34. Fischer, G.: User modeling in human-computer interaction. User Model. User-Adap. Inter. **11**, 65–68 (2001)
35. Bunt, H., Keizer, S., Morante, R.: A computational model of grounding in dialogue. In: Proceedings of SIGDIAL 2007, Antwerp, Belgium, pp. 283–290 (2007)
36. Florou, E., Konstantopoulos, S., Koukourikos, A., Karampiperis, P.: Argument extraction for supporting public policy formulation. In: Proceedings of the LAT-ECH Workshop, Sofia, Bulgaria (2013)

Automatically Detecting Fallacies in System Safety Arguments

Tangming Yuan[1], Suresh Manandhar[1], Tim Kelly[1], and Simon Wells[2](✉)

[1] University of York, York, UK
{tommy.yuan,suresh.manandhar,tim.kelly}@york.ac.uk
[2] Edinburgh Napier University, Edinburgh, UK
s.wells@napier.ac.uk

Abstract. Safety cases play a significant role in the development of safety-critical systems. The key components in a safety case are safety arguments, that are designated to demonstrate that the system is acceptably safe. Inappropriate reasoning with safety arguments could undermine a system's safety claims which in turn contribute to safety-related failures of the system. Currently, safety argument reviews are conducted manually, require expensive expertise and are often labour intensive. It would therefore be desirable if software can be employed to help with the detection of flaws in the arguments. A prerequisite for this approach is the need for a formal representation of safety arguments. This paper proposes a predicate logic based representation of safety arguments and a method to detect argument fallacies. It is anticipated that the work contributes to the field of the safety case development as well as to the area of computational fallacies.

1 Introduction

As technology advances, microprocessors and the software that runs on them have found their way into the heart of products that many of us routinely use as part of our daily lives. The presence of microprocessor-based electronic control units in devices that people lives depend upon, such as the braking systems of cars and radiation therapy machines in hospitals, justifies the importance of safety as a foremost requirement in the engineering of these crucial systems. Safety-critical systems include any system where failure could result in loss of life, significant property damage, or damage to the environment. Safety-critical systems are deployed in a wide range of sectors and industries, such as high-speed rail in the transport sector and nuclear power plants in the energy sector.

These systems have high dependability requirements. That is, they are frequently subjected to industrial, national, and international regulations that require compliance to rules or procedures in their design, deployment, operation, and decommission process, the attainment of one or more minimum standards in areas such as security, reliability, availability, or safety. The construction of a safety case, or functionally equivalent documentation, is mandated in many standards used to guide the development of software for safety-critical systems,

© Springer International Publishing Switzerland 2016
M. Baldoni et al. (Eds.): IWEC 2014/IWEC 2015/CMNA 2015, LNAI 9935, pp. 47–59, 2016.
DOI: 10.1007/978-3-319-46218-9_4

such as the UK Ministry of Defence standard DS 00-55 [1] and Part 3 of the International Electrotechnical Commission (IEC) standard 61508 [2]. A safety case is defined by Bishop and Bloomfield [3] as "A documented body of evidence that provides a convincing and valid argument that a system is adequately safe for a given application in a given environment". The approach is to support sophisticated engineering arguments, for example, by assuring a safety argument within a safety case. This approach aims to demonstrate clearly how the safety requirements are fulfilled by the presented evidence, and thus derive confidence in the system's dependability. A key strength of this approach is to make the set of arguments explicit and available for introspection. This in turn increases confidence that the form of argument and its conclusion are both sound. Arguments are by their nature subjective, and their robustness is not self-evident (e.g. confirmation bias [4]). To increase the soundness of the arguments, a review element is necessary for the assurance of safety cases. A review normally involves two parties: the proposing party, typically the system engineer, who asserts and defends the safety case, and the assessing party, e.g. an independent safety assessor, who represents the certification authority, and whose task is to scrutinise and attack the arguments to uncover any vulnerability. The objective of a review is for the two parties to form a mutual acceptance of their subjective positions [5]. A safety argument review model [6] and tool [7] have been developed to facilitate this process. Despite the usefulness of the review framework, the quality of review arguments is not guaranteed as this largely relies on the reviewers' strategic wisdom and expertise. A complementary approach, we argue, is to provide users with a software agent, which can assist the reviewers to detect argument flaws (e.g. conflict and circular arguments) on the fly so that the argument quality can be improved. This paper aims to investigate a suitable methods for the automatic detection of argument flaws leading to additional assurance regarding the dependability of the system. This is achieved by providing a formal underpinning for the Goal Structuring Notation [8,9], a graphical language for safety arguments, that is widely adopted for describing safety critical systems during the safety assurance process.

The rest of the paper is organized as follows. Section 2 discusses the current graphical representation of safety arguments and the need of a formal representation at sentence level. Section 3 proposes a predicate logic-based ontology via domain analysis of an existing safety case. Section 4 discusses how safety argument fallacies can be detected via the ontology. Section 6 concludes the paper and gives pointers for our planned future work in this area.

2   Safety Argument Representation

Graphical notations are often deployed to represent arguments in a more structured and transparent manner as exemplified by, e.g. Shum [10], Gordon and Walton [11], and Reed and Rowe [12]. In the safety-critical domain, there are two established, commonly used notations the Goal Structuring Notation (GSN) proposed by the University of York [8,9] and the Claims Argument Evidence notation proposed by Adelard LLP [13]. The GSN has been adopted by an increasing number of companies in safety-critical industries and government agencies, such as the London Underground and the UK MoD, as a standard presentation scheme for arguments within safety cases [14]. For example, 75% of UK military aircraft have a safety case with safety arguments expressed in GSN [13]. This paper will use GSN to represent arguments graphically unless stated otherwise.

The GSN uses standardised symbols to represent an argument:

- individual constituent elements (claims, evidence, and context)
- relationships between elements (e.g. how claims are supported by evidence).

In GSN, claims in an argument are shown as Goals (rectangles). They are often broken down into sub-goals further down a hierarchy. Alternatively they may be supported by evidence, presented in the GSN as Solutions (circles), and for an argument to be robust, all sub-goals must eventually be supported by solutions at the bottom. Strategies adopted (especially when breaking down goals) are shown in parallelograms, and they are related to argument schemes [15]. Contexts in which goals are stated appear as bubbles resembling race-tracks. If necessary, ovals are used in GSN to denote Assumptions and Justifications. They can be distinguished by an A or J at the lower right of the symbol. Two types of links are used to connect the constituent elements. A line with a solid arrowhead, representing a Supported by relation, declares an inferential or evidential relationship. Permitted connections are goal-to-goal, goal-to-strategy, goal-to-solution, strategy-to-goal. A line with a hollow arrowhead represents an In-context-of relation, that declares a contextual relationship. Permitted connections are goal-to-context, goal-to-assumption, goal-to-justification, strategy-to-context, strategy-to-assumption, and strategy-to-justification [8,9].

An example use of the key components of the GSN is shown in Fig. 1. The argument shows that in order to achieve the G1 both legs of evidence are collected and the arguing strategy is from diverse forms of evidence. For complex systems with many arguments, modular approaches [16] have been used to aid with argument abstraction and composition. There has been substantial experience of using graphical GSN-based arguments for a wide range of scales of safety argument (from single programmable devices to whole aircraft safety cases).

The graphical representation shown in Fig. 1 is more structured and transparent compared to free text representation, and software can help with the conformance of GSN syntax to ensure a valid safety argument is a connected diagraph with each path ending in, at least, one item of evidence. However, the representation treats the content inside each GSN node as black-box and as result any argument flaws related to the content of the element cannot be detected by an automatic means. A formal representation for the contents inside the nodes is necessary so as to make them machine processible. There are at least three possible approaches to formal representation of a sentence that can be found from the literature, namely, propositional logic, predicate logic and description logic. A predicate-based approach is chosen in this paper due to its expressive power than a proposition-based approach. We will cater for the description-based approach in the future. A predicate-based representation of GSN elements will be discussed next.

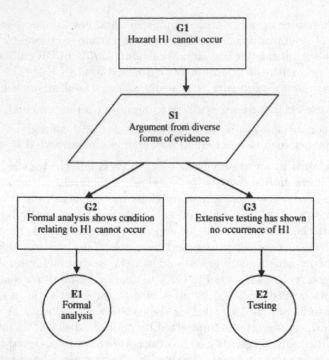

Fig. 1. An example showing the use of key components of the Goal Structuring Notation.

3   Safety Argument Ontology

For a predicate-based approach to formal representation of GSN elements, it is necessary to build an ontology that contains a set of constant symbols, function symbols and predicate symbols which form the vocabulary for the expressions of GSN nodes. To derive the ontology vocabulary, domain analysis of some existing safety cases has to be carried out. The preliminary study of the Europe Air Traffic Management (ATM) System Safety Case [17] was chosen to serve the domain analysis in order to form the first prototype of the ontology. The ATM study was conducted to evaluate the possibility of developing a whole airspace ATM system safety case for airspace belonging to EUROCONTROL member states.

Our domain analysis focuses on the GSN elements and their related documentation in the report. The report was read manually and the frequencies of relevant keywords were counted with the aid of the document search function. As a result of the analysis, the frequently used terms came into light and they are system, hazards, hardware, software, integrity level, probability and process. The frequently used relations or interactions among the terms are "meeting standards", "lower than" and "greater than". The actions normally placed on the objects are reviewed, analyzed, eliminated and mitigated. The subjective view is often safe. There are also patterns discovered when using these terms, for example, when hazards are used, the actions such as *eliminated* and *mitigated* will follow; when process is used, actions such as *implemented* and *meet certain standard* will be used; when an item of evidence is used, terms like *review* and *analysis* will be used. The analysis helps to build up the initial set of safety-argument vocabulary [18], for example:

Constant Symbols :
  System(Name), Standard(Name), Authority(Name), Hardware(Name),
  Software(Name),
  Process(Name), Condition(Content), Adv(Content), Hazard(Name).
Function Symbols :
  probabilityOf(Object), integrityOf(Object), hardwareOf(Object, namedAs),
  hazardOf(Object, namedAs), softwareOf(Object, namedAs),
  processOf(Object, namedAs), analysisOf(Software), reviewOf(Software)
Predicate Symbols :
  meetStandard(Object,Standard), greaterThan(Object1, Object2),
  lowerThan(Object1,Object2), hasBeenImplemeted(Object, adv), isSafe(Object, Condition), hasBeenReviewed(Object, adv.), isAlike(Object1, Object2).

The atomic level is the constant symbols. Constant symbols denote the entities or objects in the domain. Function symbols denote functions from tuples of objects to objects. In system safety argument, it is essential to represent the objects inside the sentence, such as "hardware of system x". In order to achieve this, function symbols are used to solve this problem, hardwareOf(system(x)) will present "hardware of system x". Function symbols will serve to identify the properties of certain objects. Based on the nature of the properties, they can be further divided into two categories: countable and uncountable. For the countable properties, each property needs to be distinguished and it is necessary to do so, and this can be formulated as: symbols (object, name). For example, hazardOf(system(x), h1) can be read as "hardware of system x named as h1". So the "name" parameter inside the functions symbol will help to distinguish the countable properties. On the other hand uncountable properties are not necessarily distinguished, for example, integrityOf(system(x)). Comparing to predicate symbols, function symbols donate objects instead of a complete sentence. We use content to distinguish function symbols since a function symbol is normally an argument inside a predicate symbol.

Predicate symbols are used to represent a sentence. A sentence normally provides an action on the object or a description of an object. Based on the nature of the sentence, the predicate symbols can be divided into two categories. The actions can be formulated as symbol (object, adv.), such as eliminated (hazardOf(system(x)), completely), implemented(processOf(system(x)), safely). There are other actions such as meeting certain standard and comparison objects (e.g. lower than, higher than). These predicates can be formed as symbols (object 1, object 2), such as meetingStandard(processOf(system(x), standard(y)) can be translated as "the process of system x meet the standard y", and lowerThan(probabilityOf(hadzardOf(x), probabilityOf(standardOf(x0)) means that the probability of hazard x happens is lower than the probability required by standard x. It is also essential to present the adjective words that describe the object, such as safe. However the adjective words to describe the object can only be valid in some conditions. In order to include the conditions in the predicate, the adjective predicate symbols can be formulated as: symbol (object, condition). For example: isSafe(system(x), Condition(hazards are avoided)) means that system x is safe when hazards are avoided.

4   Automatic Detection of Safety Argument Fallacies

A fallacy is defined by Damer [19] as a mistake in an argument that violates one or more of the five criteria of a good argument: (i) A well-formed structure, (ii) Premises that are relevant to the truth of the conclusion, (iii) Premises that are acceptable to a reasonable person, (iv) Premises that together constitute sufficient grounds for the truth of the conclusion, (v) Premises that provide an effective rebuttal to all anticipated criticisms of the argument. In safety arguments, fallacies exist in different forms. Greenwell *et al.* [20] studied a number of safety cases, such as EUR Reduced Vertical Separation Minimums (RVSM) and EUR Whole Airspace Preliminary and derived a number of fallacies in safety cases organized into three categories namely, relevance, acceptability and sufficiency fallacies. This paper examines a subset of these argument fallacies and how they can be detected in an automatic means via the predicate-based representation as outlined in Sect. 3 above. The fallacies e.g. appeal to improper authority, fallacious use of language, faulty analogy, circular argument, fallacious composition and confusion of necessary and sufficient condition, are discussed in turn below and each followed by means to detect them.

4.1   Appeal to Improper Authority

The fallacy of appeal to improper authority is a member of relevance fallacy family where arguments that violate the relevance criterion of a good argument. They employ irrelevant premises or make appeals to irrelevant factors to draw a conclusion. The fallacy of appeal to improper authority attempts to support a claim by appealing to the judgment of an authority which is actually not an authority in the field and likely to be biased [19]. The authorities cited in safety arguments could be individuals, committees, standard documents, "best practices", and system pedigree [20]. The fallacies occur mostly in the form of transferring one authority's competence into another field in which its competence is not valid. For example, an entertainer or athlete is appealed as an authority on marriage and family.

To automatically detect this fallacy, constant symbols such as standard() and Authority() should be used. A database can be built so that each authority can be checked against their field of expertise. For example, meetStandard(processOf(system(x)), standard(y)) => safe(system(x)). The standard(y) will be checked against the database to verify whether it is the correct one being applied.

4.2   Fallacious Use of Language

The fallacy of the use of language occurs when an argument violates the acceptability criterion for a good argument. There are five types of unacceptable premises: (i) A claim that contradicts credible evidence, a well-established claim, or a legitimated authority, (ii) A claim that is inconsistent with ones own experience or observations, (iii) A questionable claim that is not adequately defended in the context of the argument or not capable of being adequately defended by evidence in some other accessible source, (iv) A claim that is self-contradictory or linguistically confusing, (v) A claim that is based on another unstated but highly questionable assumption [19]. Fallacious use of language typically happens due to a lack of clarity in the meaning of a key word or phrase used in the premise. An ambiguous word, phrase, or sentence is the one that has more than one meaning. The inferential relationship between claims in argument should clearly define the exact meaning being used. A typical example is to describe the desirable system properties by using expressions such as safety, reliability and dependability interchangeably.

To detect this fallacy automatically, it is essential to know common misleading words, or phases. Since a sentence is represented by predicate symbols which are pre-defined, the fallacious use of language can be reduced significantly. For example: isSafe(), isReliable(), isDependent() will have different meaning in safety argument, and they are treated differently in the logical representation to avoid any confusion with their meanings.

4.3   Faulty Analogy

Faulty analogy is a type of acceptability fallacy. It assumes that because two things are alike in one or more respect, they are necessarily alike in some other important respect. This fallacy fails to distinguish the insignificance of their similarities and the significance of their dissimilarities [19]. In safety argument cases it could be that, using the argument for the development of the previous system to support current system without stating the differences between these two systems. There is a typical example, the Ariane 5 accident in 1996 could be the result from a faulty analogy within the rockets safety cases [21].

To enable a machine to detect such a fallacy, the predicate symbol isAlike() and isMinor() can be used. For example, isAlike(system(x), system(y)) ∧ isSafe(system(y)) => isSafe(system(x)) can be read as because system x and system y are alike, system y is safe, so system x is safe. When this situation happens, it is easy to identity the missing elements such as the justification on the difference. The expression "isAlike(system(x), system(y)) ∧ isSafe(system(y)) ∧ isMinor(differenceOf(system(x), system(y)) => isSafe(system(x))" seems to be more convincing than the one without such a justification.

4.4   Circular Argument

Circular argument is a type of acceptability fallacy that involves either explicitly or implicitly asserting in the premise of the argument is asserted in the conclusion of that argument [19]. Instead of providing supporting evidence, it simply brings up the conclusion as its evidence. In the standard form, it looks like: since A (premise), therefore, A (conclusion). And it also can be implicitly assuming the conclusion is true. For example, when people argue God exists because he does not want to go to the hell. By arguing that, he already assumes that God exists, which is the conclusion he want to draw. Sometimes it is hard to detect this kind of fallacy, since different words or different forms may be used in the premises or conclusion. The complexity of an argument also causes the difficulty to detect the kind of fallacy because the conclusion may be drawn far away after the premises.

   To automatically detect such a fallacy in safety arguments, it is necessary to find a similar argument that is in the circle, for example: isSafe(system(x)) => meetStandard(processOf(System(x)), Standard(y)), meetStandard(processOf(System(x)), Standard(y)) => isSafe(System(x)). Based on the predicate symbols used in the argument, it is feasible to trace the argument and identify similar arguments used as supporting arguments.

4.5   Fallacy of Composition

Fallacy of composition is a type of acceptability fallacy that assumes that every part is true therefore the whole is true, without taking the relations between the parts into account [19]. Typical example could be a football team with excellent players may not be a good team, because when gathering excellent players together, their skills may be compromised to team work. In safety cases, the example could be argument for the whole system is safe by supporting sub-system A, B, C are safe, which ignores the interactions between these sub-systems [20].

   The fallacy can be detected with aid of the predicate-based language. With such a representation, The pattern of argument from system decomposition [15], e.g. isSafe(hardwareOf(System(x), h1)) ∧ isSafe(hardwareOf(system(x), h2)) => isSafe(system(x)) can be identified. Upon the identification of the argument pattern, the predicate with regard to the component interaction can be searched for. As an example, the argument of isSafe(hardwareOf (system(x), h1)) ∧ isSafe(hardwareOf(system(x), h2)) ∧ isNone(interactionOf (hardwareOf(system(x))) => isSafe(system(x)) is a proper argument while missing the isNone will result in fallacy of composition.

4.6   Confusion of Necessary and Sufficient Conditions

This fallacy occurs when there is insufficient evidence is provided, e.g. no or little evidence, biased or week evidence, or omitting crucial types of evidence. When arguing for or against a position, relevant and acceptable reasons should be provided, together with justification of the sufficiency in number or weight to the acceptance of the conclusion.

Necessary condition of an event is a condition that must be present in order for an event to happen. Sufficient condition will trigger the occurrence of an event. In safety cases, a typical example argument is "hazards have been mitigated" with evidence showing the case that hazards have been mitigated. However, in order to mitigate hazards, the sufficient condition is to identify all the hazards. To better support the argument, the identification process should be included [15]. In the argument structure, it is often valid to say isSafe(System(x)) => isSafe(System(x), condition1), while it is invalid to say isSafe(system(x), condition1) => isSafe(system(x)) due to insufficient conditions for the whole system to be safe. The fallacy of distinction without a difference is opposite to faulty analogy and fallacy of division is the opposite of fallacy of composition. The means to detect these fallacies are similar. There are also other safety argument fallacies that are categorized in [20] but not examined in this paper, e.g. red herring, drawing the wrong conclusion, using the wrong reasons, false dichotomy, pseudo-precision, hasty inductive generalization, arguing from ignorance, omission of key evidence, ignoring the counter-evidence and gambler's fallacy. We are going to cater for these in the future in terms of the appropriate representations in order to detect them by an automatic means.

5 Implementation and Evaluation

In order to facilitate the evaluation of the fallacy detection approach and algorithms, the safety argument review tool, namely DiaSAR as reported in [22] has been extended by incorporating fallacy detection functionalities. DiaSAR operates a safety argument review model (SARM) which is a dialogue based model. The review process under the SARM encompasses three distinct phases: initiation, review, and revision. It starts with an initiation of a proposal of safety arguments followed by reviews conducted by independent reviewers. The proposer then responds and revises the initial proposal in light of the criticisms made by the reviewers. The revised version of the safety arguments will be further reviewed until reviewers reject or accept the arguments or the proposer withdraws. The number of iterations can be defined by mutual agreement of all participants if they wish to set such a limitation. However, the ultimate aim of the iterations is to reach a position where the safety arguments are mutually accepted by both proposer and reviewers.

DiaSAR has a graphical user-interface that supports multiple user access and a backend database storing the user profiles and the review sessions. There are three types of users of the system: system administrator, argument proposer, and reviewer. The system administrator manages all the users of the system and the review sessions. The argument proposers propose and subsequently defend their arguments. The reviewers criticise the arguments made by the proposer. An example system interface for the proposer can be seen in Fig. 2. A proposer can create a new review session which specifies a session name, a proposer, and

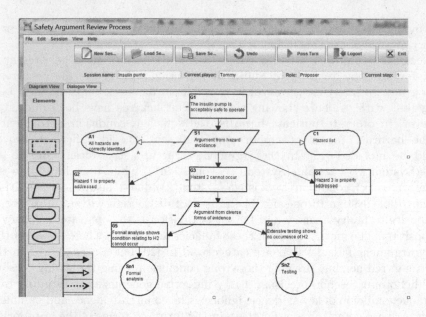

Fig. 2. An example user interface for the proposer.

a reviewer of the session. The interface displays the current status of the session, e.g. the current player, his/her role, and the current step of the review. A proposer can use provided tools (i.e. claim, strategy, evidence, context, assumption, and links) to construct safety arguments following GSN syntax as described in Sect. 2. A session can be saved and loaded for further editing. Once it has been done, the turn can be passed to the reviewer and a notification email will be sent to the reviewer. The session will then transit from the proposing state to the reviewing state.

A reviewer can log onto the system and load the sessions under review. By right clicking on any elements of the safety argument, a submenu will be available with items for the reviewer to accept, challenge, and question an argument element. A reviewer can also propose a counter-argument. Graphical notations have been developed for the set of the review tools alongside GSNs. Some of them can be seen in Fig. 3. For example, a rectangle with dashed borderline represents a counter-argument and a dashed line with an open arrow represents an 'attacked by' relation (e.g. the argument 'Extensive testing shows no occurrence of H2' is attacked by argument 'Accident database shows the occurrence of H2'). A question mark represents a question (e.g. Is the analyst experienced?) and an exclamation mark represents a challenge (Why is it the case that hazard 3 is properly addressed?) made by the reviewer. Accepted elements are coloured green and withdrawn elements red. A short vertical line with open arrow at both ends is used to mark the situation where a resolution demand is made to a conflict among two or more elements.

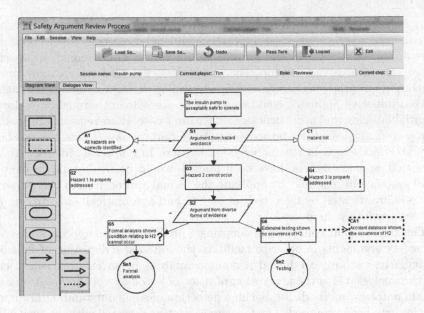

Fig. 3. An example user interface for the reviewer.

When the review is completed, the reviewer can pass the turn back to the proposer. The session will transit from the review state to the revision state and a notification email will be sent to the proposer. Upon receiving the notification, the proposer can respond to the criticisms and revise the arguments following SARM rules, e.g. to respond to a challenge with a withdrawal, claim, evidence, or strategy. These rules are implemented as submenus attached to a review element where the proposer can select a suitable response. The responses, e.g. newly made claims, strategies, evidence, context, or assumptions, are automatically displayed as part of the safety argument, and the symbol of the review being responded to is removed from the user-interface. Once all the reviews have been responded to and other necessary revisions are done, it can be passed back to the reviewer for a second review. The process goes on until the safety argument has been fully accepted.

6 Conclusions and Future Work

The work presented in this paper is but one stage within a wider program of research on analysis of existing safety cases in order to enrich the ontology vocabulary and automated analysis of safety arguments. Additionally, there are opportunities within other domains, such as security policy documents which utilise similar constrained and formalised domain specific languages to represent clauses within the policies. We also plan to incorporate the safety argument ontology into current safety argument software tools such as that from [7]. Additionally, a dialectical model of interaction between the engineer and a safety-system agent could support the elicitation of higher quality safety cases in the first instance. For example, such a dialectical approach could build existing educational dialogue approaches [23], existing knowledge elicitation interactional approaches [24] or else involve the development and description of a wholly new protocol using appropriate technologies [25]. A similar dialectical model, but using a mixed initiative approach could support the assessor in thoroughly exploring potential fallacies, and other deficiencies, within a case. However such approaches are reserved, at present, for future work. An important aspect that has not been adequately addressed in this paper is evaluation. In one sense, identifying fallacies that would otherwise have been missed, would be weakly indicative of a useful system. For example, by applying the formal approach from this paper to the cases investigated by Greenwell *et al.* [20] and automatically identifying the fallacies previously discovered.

This paper reports our work in adopting a predicate-based approach to represent safety arguments in order to facilitate the automatic detection of fallacies. Particularly, we have conducted a domain analysis of an existing safety case and the analysis helps the generation of a set of ontology vocabularies. Via the domain ontology, methods for machine detection of some outstanding argument fallacies have been proposed. The fallacies cannot be detected without such a formal representation. In terms of the contribution of the paper, the proposed safety argument representation goes further than the current graphical representation, e.g. GSN, and the new representation makes the GSN nodes from black-boxes to white-boxes and thus being machine processable. The work will contribute to both the field of the safety case development and the area of computational fallacies.

References

1. UK Ministry of Defence: Defence standard 00-55 the procurement of safety critical software in defence equipment (1997). http://www.dstan.mod.uk/. Accessed 20 May 2011
2. International Electrotechnical Commission: Functional safety of electrical/ electronic/programmable electronic safety-related systems (IEC 61508 ed2.0) (2010). http://www.iec.ch/. Accessed 20 May 2011
3. Bishop, P.G., Bloomfield, R.E.: A methodology for safety case development. In: Safety-Critical Systems Symposium (SSS 1998) (1998)
4. Leveson, N.: The use of safety cases in certification and regulation. J. Syst. Safety **47**(6), 1–5 (2011)
5. Kelly, T.P.: Reviewing assurance arguments a step-by-step approach. In: Proceedings of Workshop on Assurance Cases for Security: The Metrics Challenge, Dependable Systems and Networks (DSN), Edinburgh (2007)
6. Yuan, T., Kelly, T.: Argument-based approach to computer system safety engineering. Int. J. Crit. Comput. Based Syst. **3**(3), 151–167 (2012)
7. Yuan, T., Kelly, T., Xu, T.: Computer-assisted safety argument review a dialectics approach. Argum. Comput. **6**(2), 130–148 (2014)
8. Kelly, T.P.: Arguing safety - a systematic approach to safety case management. Ph.D. thesis, Department of Computer Science, University of York, York (1999)

9. Kelly, T., Weaver, R.: The goal structuring notation - a safety argument notation. In: Proceedings of the Dependable Systems and Networks 2004 Workshop on Assurance Cases, Florence (2004)

10. Shum, S.B.: Cohere: towards web 2.0 argumentation. In: Proceedings of the 2nd International Conference on Computational Models of Argument (COMMA 2008), Toulouse (2008)

11. Gordon, T., Walton, D.: The Carneades argumentation framework: using presumptions and exceptions to model critical questions. In: Proceedings of Computational Models of Argument (COMMA 2006), pp. 195–207. IOS Press (2006)

12. Reed, C.A., Rowe, G.W.A.: Araucaria: software for argument analysis, diagramming and representation. Int. J. AI Tools **13**(4), 961980 (2004)

13. Emmet, L., Cleland, G.: Graphical notations, narratives and persuasion: a pliant systems approach to hypertext tool design. In: Proceedings of the Thirteenth ACM Conference on Hypertext and Hypermedia, Conference on Hypertext and Hypermedia (2002)

14. Group, O.M: Argument metamodel (2010). http://www.omg.org/spec/ARM

15. Yuan, T., Kelly, T.: Argument schemes in computer system safety engineering. Informal Log. **31**(2), 89–109 (2011)

16. Kelly, T.P.: Using software architecture techniques to support the modular certification of safety critical systems. In: Proceedings of Eleventh Australian Workshop on Safety-Related Programmable Systems, Melbourne (2005)

17. Kinnersly, S.: Whole airspace ATM system safety case preliminary study. A report produced for EUROCONTROL by AEA technology, AEAT LD76008/2 Issue, 1 (2001)

18. Wan, F.: Auto-detecting fallacies in system safety arguments. Master's thesis, University of York, York (2013)

19. Damer, T.E.: Attacking Faulty Reasoning: A Practical Guide to Fallacy-Free Arguments, 6th edn. Wadsworth Cengage Learning, Boston (2009)

20. Greenwell, W.S., Holloway, C.M., Knight, J.C.: A taxonomy of fallacies in system safety arguments. In: Proceedings of the International Conference on Dependable Systems and Networks, Yokohama, Japan (2005)

21. Lions, J.L.: Ariane 501 failure: report by the inquiry board. European Space Agency, July 1996

22. Yuan, T., Kelly, T., Xu, T., Wang, H., Zhao, L.: A dialogue based safety argument review tool. In: Proceedings of the 1st International Workshop on Argument for Agreement and Assurance (AAA-2013), Kanagawa, Japan (2013)

23. Yuan, T., Moore, D., Grierson, A.: A human-computer dialogue system for educational debate, a computational dialectics approach. Int. J. Artif. Intell. Educ. **18**(1), 3–26 (2008)

24. Reed, C., Wells, S.: Dialogical argument as an interface to complex debates. IEEE Intell. Syst. J. Spec. Issue Argum. Technol. **22**(6), 60–65 (2007)

25. Wells, S., Reed, C.: A domain specific language for describing diverse systems of dialogue. J. Appl. Log. **10**(4), 309–329 (2012)

IWEC-14 and IWEC-15 Papers

Modeling User Music Preference Through Usage Scoring and User Listening Behavior for Generating Preferred Playlists

Arturo P. Caronongan III and Rafael A. Cabredo[✉]

College of Computer Studies, De La Salle University, Manila, Philippines
arturo.caronongan@delasalle.ph,
rafael.cabredo@dlsu.edu.ph

Abstract. Recommending the most appropriate music is one of the most studied fields in the context of Recommendation systems with the growing number of content available to users and consumers alike. As it is an important aspect in the use of multi-media systems and the music industry, it is important to note that the typical approach is through collaborative-filtering.

In this paper, the study considered a more personalized view and examined to which degree a user's music preference can be modeled using information gathered from the user with respect to their listening behavior and music selected. The study proposes an approach to modeling a user's music preference using a series of usage scores obtained from a user's listening behavior and to generate a playlist derived from the obtained model.

Using a novel data set, the proposed approach resulted to an average True-Positive rating of 54.43% in predicting music files that the user will select for the month given the previous month's data and an overall performance of 82.53% in producing entries to a preferred playlist, showing the possibility of more refinements and further study.

Keywords: Music preference · User modeling · Computational modeling · Recommendation

1 Introduction

One of the most important aspects of studies that involve recommending the proper music would be a proper approach for modeling a user's listening behavior. The main purpose of a music recommendation system is to estimate the user's preference and present them with items that may fit their preference [1].

In the standard setting, Music Recommendation is done by a collaborative filtering approach [10] where the basis come from other users providing absolute ratings to instances but not from the features of the music itself nor the users. Recommendations after a study conducted [6] emphasized the need to give a more thorough analysis on taking the user's interaction to the music player (referred to as "listening behavior" in this paper) as a parameter for recommendation or deriving a user's music preference. Preference on some contents or items can also be periodic [5] and user's music preferences can change through time, so there is a need to determine when a user's music preference has changed to keep recommendations up to date.

© Springer International Publishing Switzerland 2016
M. Baldoni et al. (Eds.): IWEC 2014/IWEC 2015/CMNA 2015, LNAI 9935, pp. 63–73, 2016.
DOI: 10.1007/978-3-319-46218-9_5

This study proposes an approach that can be used for modeling a user's music preference and deriving a playlist from the resulting model.

2   Related Work

A study conducted [10] created a predictive model of music preference through pairwise comparisons. In evaluating the model, the resulting performance of 76% showed potential for further refinement and evaluation. The study made use of a small-scale dataset [12] that consists of 10 test subjects, 30 audio tracks, and 10 audio tracks per genre, namely Classical, Heavy Metal, and Rock/Pop.

User experience and patterns of song listening in an online music community was defined using statistical models in another study [13]. An LDA model was adapted to capture music taste from listening activities across users and to identify the group of songs associated with those types of users who had a similar preference in music. Experiments concluded that the session model was better in terms of perplexity compared to the other models used in creating an inference with regards to grouping listeners with similar song preferences.

Due to the small scale data set in the first work mentioned and a generalized resulting model of a group of users, this study made use of a novel music corpus which contains a larger variety of audio tracks and 7 users which aims to create a user specific model with regards to their listening preference. The users were each provided with a developed music player module that recorded their interactions with the player. The module then produced a listening log for each user that was used as a basis for modeling their user listening behavior and music preference through a utility matrix.

3   Methodology

The procedure of the study was subdivided into three phases, namely building the music corpus to be used for the study, gathering user listening information, and modeling the user's music preference through the obtained data. Each phase is explained in a separate section respectively.

Due to the large music corpus and the music recommendation model being evaluated through a system, the resulting model will be compared with a random playlist generator and will have its performance evaluated using the "4 quadrant test" [3]. This is to ensure that the model outperforms a simulated behavior of users randomly selecting music from a collection that they are unfamiliar with.

4   Music Collection

The music corpus consisted of 427 WAV files and their extracted features using jAudio [7]. The collection originally consisted of varying file types and to ensure uniformity amongst the features extracted, all were normalized into WAV files using Audacity 2.0.3 [2].

4.1   Genre Distribution

The music collection consisted of 5 genres, namely Pop, Classical, Instrumental, Disco, and Techno [15]. They were eventually grouped according to three genres: Classical, Pop, and Techno music. The study made use of 120 classical music files, 133 pop music files, and 174 techno music files. Music that were of solo instrumental (i.e. piano) nature and instrumental music were grouped as classical music. Songs that were Metal, Rock, or Pop were grouped as Pop. Finally, Disco and Techno music were labelled as Techno. While unequal in distribution, this is to ensure that the users would have a large variety of music selections to choose from.

4.2   Feature Extraction

To take into consideration a music file's content in determining a user's music preference, the audio features had to be extracted. To extract the music file's audio features, jAudio 1.0.4 [7] was used. The "validate recordings" option was chosen to ensure that the audio files were valid for processing. These features were used to determine the validity of the genre labels given to the music files and as a basis for the similarity measure regarding music context when used as a basis for generating the resulting preferred playlist. The features extracted were Spectral Centroid, Spectral Rolloff Point, MFCC, Fraction of Low Energy Windows, Root Mean Square, Zero Crossings, Strongest Beat, Compactness, Beat Sum, LPC, Method of Moments, Peak Based Spectral Smoothness, Partial Based Spectral Flux, and the Strongest Frequencies.

4.3   Genre Label Validity

Using various experiments performed using University of Waikato's WEKA [11], Table 1 displays the models used in the said module with the highest performance.

Table 1. Models used in validating genre label

Model	Accuracy	Kappa	MAE
SVM + CFS	82.4	0.77	0.070
SVM + CFS + Merged	**91.3**	**0.87**	**0.058**
J48 + CFS + Merged	90.6	0.86	0.068

Using a Support Vector Machine with a 10 fold cross validation along with feature selection and merging the genre labels as indicated in Section IIIA, a 91.3% accuracy with a kappa statistic of 0.87 was achieved. The confusion matrix achieved is shown in Table 2.

The resulting confusion matrix indicated that the music files contained valid genre labels with respect to the attributes considered in Sect. 4.2. It is also because of this that the resulting audio features extracted were used as a basis in determining a music file's similarity measure for generating preferred playlists.

Table 2. Confusion matrix of SVM and CFS and Merged

	Classical	Pop	Techno
Classical	112	6	2
Pop	7	106	20
Techno	0	2	172

5   Gathering User Listening Information

The next part of the approach required the users (a total of 7, aged 18 to 30 years old) to undergo a music listening phase that lasted for a total of 7 months. This requires the user to make use of a music player that will allow the user to select music from the library, music that is either provided to them or provided by them. The user will listen to music and the system will take note of the user's listening activity [9]. The activities that will be considered are listening to the song up to the very end, how much of the song was listened to, the number of times the song is repeated, and how the song was selected.

5.1   Music Player

A music player was developed with the purpose of allowing listeners to listen to music from the collection. The system was developed in Java and made use of JavaZoom jlGUI [8], an open source music player as a basis. The developed module simulated operations available in a common music such as making a new playlist, adding music to the playlist, removing music from the playlist, playing music, or setting a music file to be repeated after it finishes playing.

5.2   Music Listening Activity Tracking

Attached to the Music Player developed was a module used for tracking the user's listening activity. The module ran in the background as the music application was active which produced the user's listening behavior and interaction with the system. The activity tracker identified the date and time when a user listened to music as well as an indication whether the player has been opened or closed. Following the date and time, an indication of the music file played as well as an indication on how it ended up being selected. The activities considered as "listening activity" and were tracked were limited into the following:

1. "MANUAL" – Manually selecting a music file (Clicking on it or selecting it manually)
2. "AUTOMATIC" – Allowing a music file to play automatically
3. "REPEAT" – Allowing a music file to repeat due to the repeat option being selected
4. "NEXT" – Proceeding to the next entry in the playlist (or to the first entry if at the last entry) without finishing the music file
5. "NEWPLAYLIST" – Loading music file via a new playlist

6. "ADDED" – Adding a music file to the playlist
7. "DELETE" – Removing a music file from the playlist

The produced output from the activity tracker is then preprocessed using a separate module which is shown in Fig. 1. The log is pre-processed into the following syntax:

<Month> <Day> <Activity>

<Activity> can have the following arguments:

– "CLOSED PLAYER" indicates the player was closed
– "OPENED PLAYER" indicates the player was opened
– <Listening Activity> indicates that the user listened to music. This indicates whether a user played a song, set it into repeat, loaded a song into the playlist, or removed it from the playlist.

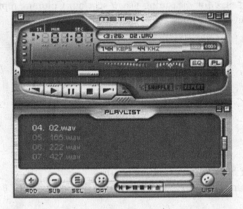

Fig. 1. Music player used for data gathering

Playing a song is followed by an integer which is the duration in seconds as to how long that song file was listened to. The resulting log is used as an input for the next phase of the research (Fig. 2).

```
2 24 394.wav AUTO 261
2 24 348.wav AUTO 232
2 24 CLOSED PLAYER
2 25 OPENED PLAYER
2 25 426.wav MANUAL 243
2 25 427.wav AUTO 220
2 25 374.wav AUTO 233
2 25 410.wav AUTO 205
2 25 349.wav AUTO 173
2 25 380.wav AUTO 303
2 25 394.wav AUTO 261
2 25 348.wav AUTO 232
2 25 426.wav MANUAL 243
2 25 427.wav AUTO 220
```

Fig. 2. Pre-processed listening log of each user

6 Modeling User Music Preference

The next phase of the research investigated the type of music a user liked. In order to determine whether a music file receives a positive reaction, the output from the previous phase will be needed.

6.1 Measuring Through Usage Scoring

Each user was provided with a $3 \times n$ matrix as indicated in Table 3. This was used to represent a user's usage scores for the song files, where:

$$n = (\text{no. of songs in the music library}) - 1 \qquad (1)$$

Table 3. User utility matrix for measuring usage scoring. Columns represent each WAV file from 1.wav to (n−1).wav, while rows are explained in the next page.

	0	1	2	...	n
0	w[0,0]	w[0,1]	w[0,2]	...	w[0,n]
1	w[1,0]	w[1,1]	w[1,2]	...	w[1,n]
2	w[2,0]	w[2,1]	w[2,2]	...	w[2,n]

Where:

w[0,i] = Usage Score for (i−1) wav file
w[1,i] = A binary value (0 or 1) which indicates that (i−1) wav has been played.
w[2,i] = A binary value (0 or 1) which indicates that (i−1) wav has been played for the day.

The utility matrix updated accordingly:

$$w[0,i] = w[0,i] + x \qquad (2)$$

Where:

x = E for manually selected, repeated, first music played upon opening player
  = E/2 for automatically selected music
  = −(E/2) for Skipped music or songs unplayed for the day (but played before)
  = |w[0,i]| + .01 for Added or Loaded into playlists
  = −2w[0,i] for Deleted music from the playlist if w[0,i] > 0
  = 0 for deleted music from the playlist if w[0,i] < 0

$$w[1,i] = a \qquad (3)$$

Where:

a = 1 for playing a song in any way or when w[0,n] is updated with a value
  = 0 otherwise as long as w[0,n] = 0

$$w[2,i] = z \tag{4}$$

Where:

$z = 1$ for playing a song in any way or when $w[0,n]$ is updated with a value for the day

    $= $ Refreshed value to 0 at the start of each day

Whereas the final usage score U is considered as:

$$U = w[0,i] * w[1,i] \tag{5}$$

Where:

$U > 0$ is considered a favorable rating

    < 0 is not considered a favorable rating

    $= 0$ is considered as unplayed

The resulting utility matrix indicates the usage scores of music files according to the user's music preference. The column with the highest $w[0,i]$ indicates the user's most preferred music.

As the research's limitation was that user preference was modeled on a per monthly basis, the values of all the utility matrix's rows for each user would refresh to 0 at the start of each month.

6.2 Measuring Through Usage Scoring

The resulting output from the said procedure is a user-specific utility matrix that consists of the usage scores of a particular music file derived from the user's listening behavior. The values in the utility matrix can be used as a basis for generating entries into the preferred playlist by determining which music files will be used as a basis for calculating music similarity with other music files in the data set.

6.3 Calculating Music Similarity

An experiment was conducted where the top 5 music files that received the highest utility values were used as a basis for music recommendation. The similarity measures used as a basis for playlist generation were based on the features extracted and labels from Sects. 4.2 and 4.3. The top 5 songs were referred to as base songs. Each base song is used for computing a maximum of 3 recommendation songs given the following equation:

$$RV = \sum_{i=1}^{n} w_i f_i \tag{6}$$

Where $n = $ number of functions, $w_i = $ weight of f_i and $f_i = $ computational function.

The approach made use of two computational functions. The first computational function f_0 (described in Eq. 7) was used to compute for the absolute difference among the acoustic values extracted using jAudio as explained in Sect. 4.2.

$$f_0 = \sum_{i=1}^{n} (|X_r - Y_i| * 1/n) \qquad (7)$$

$$X_r = \{baseSong_1 \ldots baseSong_5\} \qquad (8)$$

X_r (described in Eq. 8) is one of the 5 base songs whereas n is the number of attributes. The lower the value of f_0, the more similar the music file's contents are based on their attributes.

$$f_2 = floor((X_r - Y_i)/\alpha)/\theta \qquad (9)$$

The second computational function f_2 is the function used to calculate for the difference between BPM (Beats Per Minute). BPM is used to indicate how fast a particular music file is, thus it is important to keep track of a music file BPM in ensuring that only slow music will be added to a playlist where the user prefers slow music and fast music will be added to a playlist where the user prefers fast music. The α indicates an allowance amongst songs to be recommended, therefore if $\alpha = 20$, then a song that is 130 BPM will consider songs from 110 BPM to 150 BPM as similar songs. θ is the value determining (in %) distinguishing how much difference a music file with different BPMs will be considered.

6.4 Generating Preferred Playlists

The lower the value of RV indicates a higher similarity among the music file it has been compared with. A value of 0.000 indicates that the music files are exactly identical.

3 of the most similar music files were added to a playlist. If two music files produced the same playlist addition, then that music file was not added to the playlist. This made the generated playlist will contain a maximum of 20 music files (Top 5 preferred music files + 3 additional playlist entries stemming from each). The smaller the recommendation playlist generated indicated a closer similarity amongst the music listened to by the user while a larger playlist generated indicated a wider variety with the user's music selected.

7 Results and Analysis

The performance of the recommendation module was based on the "4 quadrant test" [3]. The concept (as shown in Table 4) involved grouping the set of music collected into either any of the four sections in a 2 × 2 matrix, where rows represent whether a song was recommended and rows indicate whether a song was used or not. The True-Positive rating for recommendation was determined by the amount of songs that received a favorable rating from the recommendations used.

Table 4. The 4-Quadrant test for recommendation systems as described in [3]

	Recommended	Not recommended
Used	True-Positive (TP)	False-Negative (FN)
Not used	False-Positive (FP)	True-Negative (TN)

An experiment was conducted to determine the feasibility of prediction, where the users were to match the songs they listened to (with favorable utility values) within the month based on the recommendations generated from their listening log in the previous month. The average prediction performance peaked at 57.99% while the average performance rating was at 54.43%. This indicated that given the user's listening behavior and usage scores their songs, the model was able to determine the music files the user would listen to with a 54.43% success rate on average during the next month. In determining the effectiveness of modeling the user's music preference using the approach stated in Sect. 6, the final usage score of each user's set of basis songs is considered and how much ended up having a negative value. The overall accuracy as to whether a user would select the base song ended up at 95.71% but this is without taking into consideration the resulting usage scores.

To evaluate the performance of the approach in generating playlists, the users were presented the playlists that were produced from three different models produced that were obtained in three different phases (After 3 months for the first, and 2 months each for the second and third phase for a total of 7 months) during the data gathering period. The users were then asked to indicate whether they found the generated playlists to be favorable to their modeled music preferences obtained from Sect. 6.1. In terms of producing preferred playlist entries that are suitable to the user's music preference, the approach achieved a mean true positive rate of 82.53% for the recommendations produced by the model, as indicated in Table 5. This indicates that although 87.23% of the generated playlist entries were received with favorable responses (including the base songs that were used to generate these playlists), 82.53% of the recommended music from these base songs were well received from the users. From the positive entries produced, an average of 54.06% was entries that the users were not familiar with.

This could possibly mean that this approach has the potential for allowing users to expand their music preference and to organize a large collection of music as well as expose the user to other music that they would prefer within the said collection that was previously unfamiliar to them.

To further evaluate the approach, a set of generated playlist entries were created randomly. The results were compared with the approach used for generating preferred playlist entries. For each user, a module which produced a random playlist was

Table 5. Performance of the recommendation module in recommending music

	Total playlist	Recommendations	New entries
Session 1	85.07%	79.79%	70.17%
Session 2	88.20%	83.68%	50.19%
Session 3	88.41%	84.11%	38.54%
Average	**87.23%**	**82.53%**	**54.06%**

Table 6. Comparison between model TP rate of generated and randomly generated playlists

	Model	Random playlist
Prediction	**54.43%**	8.12%
Preferred entries	**82.53%**	31.16%

executed 10 times and the average True-positive (TP) rate was calculated for each user. The combined average of all their TP rates was used as the value for the particular month. The users were also presented these playlists and were asked to evaluate how much of the playlist entries were favorable to them.

The results are shown in Table 6 where it is clearly shown that using the approach is more effective than generating a random playlist. The performance of the Random Playlist was extremely low due to the number of music files used to generate playlist entries (427 music files) and a similar result occurred with regards to adding entries to a user's preferred playlist. This further justifies the possibility that using the approach is effective in introducing the user to music that they will prefer within a very large collection of music files.

8   Conclusions and Future Work

The study proposed an approach to model a user's listening behavior using a series of usage scores and music features to generate a playlist that matches the user's music preference. The resulting approach garnered a True Positive Rating of 82.53% in contrast to a random playlist's 31.16% performance in creating a playlist that is suitable to the user's preference. The study was conducted on a new dataset that contained 427 music files and demonstrated promise with regards to introducing new music files that they are not familiar with in the collection to users at an average True Positive Rating of 54.06%. The resulting values indicated show promise with regards to generating music recommendation within a music dataset given the parameters presented by the user in this proposed approach.

This study can be used as a basis for future works that would go into music recommendation. Future studies may also wish to expand the approach by adding more computational functions specified in Section VIC by considering lyrics, affect, artist, and other contents of a music file. A different music collection that contains different genre to refine the approach should genre be included as a basis for one of the added computational functions may be used to refine the proposed approach. The approach may also be applied to a bigger data set. With the continuous growing commercial music streaming service [14], there is a need to make use of big data to produce better recommendations, predictions, and eventually more payouts to the rights holders. The proposed approach shows promise as a starting point for future works that wish to go further using big data for music recommendation and eventually more studies in the field of user modeling, big data processing, and machine learning.

References

1. Aquino, R.J., Battad, J.R., Ngo, C.F., Uy, G., Trogo, R., Suarez, M.: Towards empathic music provision for computer users. In: 2011 Third International Conference on Knowledge and Systems Engineering, pp. 245–251. IEEE (2011)
2. Audacity Team: Audacity 2.0.3 [Computer program] (2008). http://audacity.sourceforge.net/. Accessed 5 Jan 2013
3. Gunawardana, A., Shani, G.: Evaluating recommender systems. In: Ricci, F., Rokach, L., Shapira, B. (eds.) Recommender Systems Handbook, pp. 257–297. Springer, New York (2011)
4. Hu, Y., Ogihara, M.: NextOne player: a music recommendation system basedon user behavior. In: 12th International Society for Music Information Retrieval Conference (ISMIR), Miami, Florida, 24–28 October 2011
5. Kahng, M., Park, C.H.: Temporal dynamics in music listening behavior: a case study of online music service. In: 9th IEEE/ACIS International Conference on Computer and Information Science
6. Liu, N.-H., Hsieh, S.-J.: Intelligent music playlist recommendation based on user daily behavior and music content. In: Muneesawang, P., Wu, F., Kumazawa, I., Roeksabutr, A., Liao, M., Tang, X. (eds.) PCM 2009. LNCS, vol. 5879, pp. 671–683. Springer, Heidelberg (2009). doi:10.1007/978-3-642-10467-1_59
7. McEnnis, D., McKay, C., Fujinaga, I.: jAudio: additions and improvements. In: Proceedings of the International Conference on Music Information Retrieval, pp. 385–386 (2006)
8. jlGUI MP3 player for the Java Platform. http://www.javazoom.net/jlgui/jlgui.html. Accessed January 2013
9. Pampalk, E., Pohle, T., Widmer, G.: Dynamic playlist generation based on skipping behavior. In: Proceedings of 6th ISMIR, pp. 634–637 (2005)
10. Jensen, B.S., Gallego, J.S., Larsen, J.: A predictive model of music preference using pairwise comparisons. In: 2012 IEEE International Conference on Acoustics, Speech and Signal Processing (ICASSP), pp. 1977–1980, 25–30 March 2012
11. Hall, M., Frank, E., Holmes, G., Pfahringer, B., Reutemann, P., Witten, I.: The WEKA data mining software: an update. SIGKDD Explor. 11(1), 10–18 (2009)
12. Jensen, B.S., Gallego, J.S., Larsen, J.: A predictive model of music preference using pairwise comparisons - supporting material and dataset. www.imm.dtu.dk/pubdb/p.php?6143
13. Zheleva, E., Guiver, E., Mendes Rodrigues E., Milic-Frayling, N.: Statistical models of music-listening sessions in social media. In: The 19th International World Wide Web Conference (WWW2010), Raleigh, NC, USA, 26–30 April 2010
14. Van Rijmenam, M.: How Big Data Enabled Spotify To Change The Music Industry. DATAFLOQ Connecting Data and People (2013). https://datafloq.com/read/big-data-enabled-spotify-change-music-industry/391
15. Manalili, S.: i3DMO: an interactive 3D music organizer. MS thesis, College of Computer Studies, De La Salle University, Manila, Philippines (2010)

Neural Prediction of the User's Mood from Visual Input

Christina Katsimerou[✉] and Judith A. Redi

Multimedia Computing Group,
Delft University of Technology, Delft, The Netherlands
{C.Katsimerou, J.A.Redi}@tudelft.nl

Abstract. Affect-adaptive systems mutate their behavior according to the user's affective state. In many cases, such affective state is to be detected in a non-obtrusive way, i.e. through sensing that does not require the user to provide the system explicit input, e.g., video sensors. However, user affect recognition from video is frequently tuned to detect instantaneous emotional states, rather than longer term and more constant affective states such as mood. In this paper, we propose a non-linear computational model for bridging the gap between the recognized emotions of a person captured by a video and the overall mood of the person. For the experimental validation, emotions and mood are human annotations on an affective visual database that we created on purpose. Based on features describing peculiarities and changes in the user's emotional state, our system is able to predict the corresponding mood well above chance and more accurately than existing models.

Keywords: Mood recognition · Emotional signal · Neural networks · Affect-adaptive systems

1 Introduction

Smart environments, sensing the needs of the user and adapting with various actuators to assist him/her are soon to come. Modern technology allows imagining rooms equipped with colorful LEDs of fluctuating dynamics, orchestrating to maintain the occupant in a positive mood or to alleviate his/her burden, when his/her mood is systematically negative. System self-adjustment based on a person's mood, requires such mood to be detected in the first place. Ubiquitous unobtrusive sensors, such as cameras, can be deployed to this goal, specifically being tuned to recognize long-term, underlying affective states (i.e., moods) of users. The emphasis here is put on the long-term aspect of the affective state, since it is neither intuitive nor desirable to have a system adapting to rapid and abrupt emotional changes. Automated mood recognition is, therefore, key to implement such systems.

An abundance of affective computing research is conducted for recognizing the *emotions* from video, either via the channel of face (Cohen et al. 2003), or body (Kleinsmith and Bianchi-Berthouze 2013) or multi-modally (Gunes and Piccardi 2007). Affective state measurements based on instantaneously expressed *emotions* are then assimilated to mood, assuming one-to-one mapping between the two affective states.

M. Baldoni et al. (Eds.): IWEC 2014/IWEC 2015/CMNA 2015, LNAI 9935, pp. 74–85, 2016.
DOI: 10.1007/978-3-319-46218-9_6

To the best of our knowledge, little work has been done to study explicit mood detection, instead.

It is important to point out at this stage than e*motion* and *mood* are inherently different concepts in their construction and properties (Lane and Terry 2000, Jenkins et al. 1998, Thayer 1996). Emotion is defined as short-term, impulsive and sudden affective state; mood is instead indicated to be more long-term and less mutable. An actual, distinctive temporal duration of the two is hardly quantified in literature; in this research, we are going to consider that emotions are *instantaneously* expressed, whereas mood refers to the affective state felt (or deemed to be felt by an external observer) by the user over a certain *time period*. As a result, the one-to-one mapping between mood and emotion adopted by current mood recognition systems may be inaccurate.

On the other hand, it is known from psychology that mood and emotions are related, influencing each other and co-evolving. For example, Morris (2000) finds as potential sources of mood the onset or offset of an emotional episode. In turn, emotion elicitation is influenced by the underlying mood (Oatley and Johnson-Laird 1987). This dependence suggests that inferring the one affective state should be possible when the other is known, as long as we have a functional representation of this dependence. In other words, if we can recognize over time the emotions felt by a person, we could retrieve his mood over the same time period as a function of these emotions.

In (Katsimerou et al. 2014), the authors proposed a framework (Fig. 1), which predicts the mood from a sequence of emotions recognized punctually and over time. This concept allows employing automatic emotion recognition algorithms for assessing the user's mood: the automatically recognized emotional signal works as an intermediate layer in predicting mood from continuous sensor (e.g. video) data.

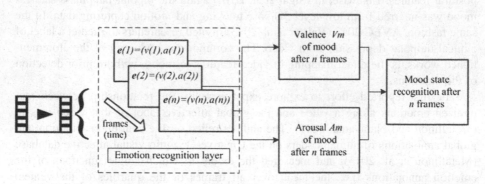

Fig. 1. Framework of automatic mood recognition module from a sequence of recognized emotions.

In this paper, we further explore the functional relationship between emotional signals and corresponding mood, and retrieve a robust non-linear model for the emotion-mood mapping. We define a set of features describing peculiarities of the emotional signal from which the mood is to be predicted, and then use an Extreme

Learning Machine (Huang et al. 2004) to map these features into a mood value estimation. To train our system, we employ a new affective database of our own craft, which includes videos of actors in different moods, all continuously annotated in terms of emotions and globally annotated in terms of mood. As a *proof of concept*, we use these human annotations of perceived affect to validate our model. We compare our multi-feature representation of the emotional signal, with baseline the a-priori explicit modelling of the emotion-mood function of (Katsimerou et al. 2014). Our results show that the increase in complexity has added value on the prediction ability when mapping emotions to mood.

2 Related Work

In psychology, emotion and mood are explicitly defined as different affective states in their construction (Russell 2003), yet they are highly associated, to the extent of being used interchangeably. Ekman (1999), for example, claims that we infer mood from the signals of the emotions we associate with the mood, at least in part: we might deduce that someone is in a cheerful mood because we observe joy. Typically, this is the approach adopted from the perspective of automatic mood recognition, especially in the case of visual input. In fact, the latest studies in the field have been geared towards recognizing continuously the emotions along videos rich in emotions and emotional fluctuations, e.g. in (Metallinou et al. 2012, Nicolaou et al. 2011). However, most commonly the decision on the affective state is made on frame-level, i.e., for punctual emotions, whereas no summarization into a mood prediction is attempted.

Explicit reference to user mood recognition we find in (Thrasher et al. 2011), where the authors predicted positive versus negative valence of mood from upper body postural features. Likewise, in (Sigal et al. 2010) again the bipolar happiness-sadness mood was inferred from low level 3D pose tracking and motion capturing data. In the same fashion, AVEC 2013 (Valstar et al. 2013) invited researchers to predict a label of clinical unipolar depression from video. The common methodology of the aforementioned works, is the direct mapping of video features to mood, without prior detection of the emotions.

The first reported effort to explore experimentally the relationship between recognized emotions along a video and the global affective label of that video was in (Metallinou and Narayanan 2013). The authors relied on the continuous emotion and global annotations of human coders on the Creative-IT audio-visual affective database (Metallinou et al. 2013), and measured the extent to which single functions of the emotion annotations (i.e., the mean over all frames or the quartiles of the values) predict the overall affective label. However, they did not take into account temporal information. Katsimerou et al. (2014) proposed instead a mood model from simple and time-aware functions of sequences of recognized emotions, and explored its temporal properties. The authors found that the mean of the exponentially discounted past emotions can predict the mood significantly better than chance; yet, for all the above mentioned systems the performance in mood prediction is far from optimal.

3 Mood as a Function of Emotional Signal: A Neural Approach

To define a model that maps a sequence of recognized emotions into a single mood, it is necessary to first define the domains in which emotion and mood will be expressed. We choose the dimensional representation of affect, rather than a discrete one such as (Ekman 1992), for both emotions and mood, as it allows continuous representation in value and time. Quite commonly in literature two dimensions are identified, valence and arousal, accounting for most of the variance of affect in its non-interactive form (Rusell 1980). Valence measures how pleasant the affective state is, and arousal is a measure of the physical activation the affect entails. For instance, sadness is a positive valence-low arousal emotion; likewise, depression is a positive valence-low arousal mood. We will consider these dimensions independent and able to characterize any affective state (Mehrabian 1996); therefore, we will investigate separately the mapping between emotional valence and mood valence and the mapping between emotional arousal and mood arousal.

Suppose we have a sensor (e.g., a camera), monitoring the state of a person in an emotionally colored (or neutral) affective state. The goal of our model is to find a function that, given the signal of such sensor, is able to detect the overall mood of the portrayed person, *as it would be perceived by a human observer*. We will assume here that another system (e.g. a facial expression recognition algorithm), recognized the emotion portrayed by the monitored person at a frequency of $1/n$, where n is the duration of the period in frames during which the person has been monitored. From this sequence of recognized emotions, we want to retrieve the overall mood m through a functional relationship.

For instance, if we have a video of n frames, at each frame k $(1 \le k \le n)$ the emotional state $e(k) = (v(k), a(k))$ of the person portrayed in the video has been recognized by an emotion recognition system and assigned a value of both emotional valence $v(k)$ and emotional arousal $a(k)$. Two (quasi)-continuous in time signals of emotional valence V and arousal A can be then defined, which evolve along the video, characterizing the sequence E of punctual emotions portrayed (felt) by the user in the video:

$$E = (V, A) = ((v(1), v(2), \ldots, v(n)), (a(1), a(2), \ldots, a(n))). \tag{1}$$

Our model uses this sequence to estimate the mood valence $\mathcal{V}_m$ and the arousal $\mathcal{A}_m$ of the mood vector $\boldsymbol{m} = (\mathcal{V}_m, \mathcal{A}_m)$ as

$$\mathcal{V}_m = F_V(V) \tag{2}$$

and

$$\mathcal{A}_m = F_A(A) \tag{3}$$

where F_v and F_A are the functions mapping the valence signal to the mood valence and the arousal signal to the mood arousal respectively.

In this work, we adopt a two-step strategy to retrieve the functions F_A and F_V. First, we extract meaningful features that summarize V and A over time. Then, we use a non-linear function γ to map this feature-based description of the emotional signal into an estimation of perceived mood m. Equation (2) can therefore be re-written as:

$$\mathcal{V}_m = \gamma_V(\varphi_V(V)),\qquad(4)$$

where $\varphi_V(V) = (\varphi_{V1}(V), \varphi_{V2}(V), \ldots, \varphi_{Vm}(V))$ is the feature vector characterizing the emotional valence signal V. Likewise, Eq. (3) can be re-written for arousal as:

$$\mathcal{A}_m = \gamma_A(\varphi_A(A)),\qquad(5)$$

with $\varphi_A(A) = (\varphi_{A1}(A), \varphi_{A2}(A), \ldots, \varphi_{Ap}(A))$ the feature vector characterizing the emotional signal of arousal A and in general $m \neq p$ and $\gamma_V \neq \gamma_A$. The feature vectors φ_V and φ_A will be further described in Sect. 3.1, whereas the specific implementation chosen for γ_V and γ_A is the object of Sect. 3.2. Figure 2 presents an overview of the emotion-mood mapping.

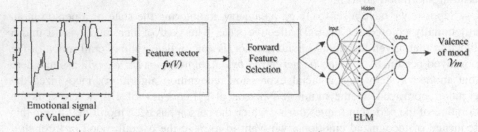

Fig. 2. Stages of mood estimation from the continuous emotion signal of valence. The same scheme holds for the arousal signal.

3.1 Features of the Emotional Signals

Due to the lack of previous research on the topic, the design of our feature sets started with the exploration of a large number of possible features of the valence and arousal signals. The feature pool was inspired by (Metallinou and Narayanan 2013, Valstar et al. 2013), and was extended with features we defined ourselves to capture salient properties of the emotional signals (see below φ_{11V}, φ_{12V}, φ_{16V}–φ_{20V}). Our initial feature pool consisted of 24 features computed from the V and A signals separately. In the following list we present these features, which can be categorized in:

a. **Statistical features** summarizing the signal magnitude. In essence, they give the first approximation of the signal and its shape. We denote by

- φ_{1V} the *arithmetic mean*;
- φ_{2V} the *root quadratic mean*;
- φ_{3V}, φ_{4V} and φ_{5V} the *standard deviation, skewness, kurtosis*;
- φ_{6V}, φ_{7V}, φ_{8V}, φ_{9V} and φ_{10V} the *25%, 50%, 75%, 1% and 99% percentiles* of V;
- φ_{11V} and φ_{12V} as the *percentage of values below -0.5 or above 0.5*, respectively;

- $\varphi_{13V} = \varphi_{8V} - \varphi_{6V}$ (*interquartile range*);
- $\varphi_{14V} = \varphi_{10V} - \varphi_{9V}$ (*inter-percentile range* between *1–99%* percentile);
- φ_{15V} as the *optimum with the highest absolute value*.

b. **Features from the occurrence frequency histogram** (bin size = 0.2), describing the distribution of the signal values. We denote by

- φ_{16V} the *value of the largest bin*, normalized to the number of samples of V;
- φ_{17V} the *center of the largest bin*.

c. **Temporal features,** describing values in important temporal positions and temporal properties of the emotional signal. We denote by

- $\varphi_{18V} = V(1)$, $\varphi_{19V} = V(n/2)$, $\varphi_{20V} = V(n)$;
- φ_{21V} the *zero-crossings rate*.

d. **Features of the signal derivative,** computed *as* $V'(k) = V(k) - V(k - 1)$, $2 \leq k \leq n$ representing changes in the emotional signal. We denote by

- φ_{22V}, φ_{23V} and φ_{24V} the *arithmetic mean*, *root quadratic mean* and *standard deviation of* V', respectively.

We then explored how these features would contribute in predicting mood, with the aim of narrowing down the number of features to be included in the vectors $\boldsymbol{\varphi}_V$ and $\boldsymbol{\varphi}_A$. To preserve the most meaningful features, we used forward subset feature selection. Eventually, $\boldsymbol{\varphi}_V$ included 10 features and $\boldsymbol{\varphi}_A$ included 7 features; in fact $\boldsymbol{\varphi}_A$ turned out to be a subset of $\boldsymbol{\varphi}_V$, with these 7 features in common: *mean (φ_1), last sample (φ_{20}), percentage of values above 0.5 (φ_{12}), first quartile (φ_6) third quartile (φ_8), 99% percentile (φ_{10}), mean of the signal derivative (φ_{22})*, and additionally for valence the *optimum with the largest absolute value (φ_{15}), 1% percentile (φ_9)* and the *second quartile (φ_7)*.

It is interesting to notice how the arithmetic mean is chosen as most important feature for both valence and arousal. *Mean* is often considered a representative summary of a signal, dampening the emotional extremes and preserving an emotional bias, which potentially reflects the overall mood. Time also seems to be an important factor in the mood function, and in particular the *last emotion*, probably because it is retained more vividly in the annotators' memory. Intuitively, the most "intense" sample of the signal (φ_{15}) is expected to have a high impact on the overall valence or arousal within a given timespan; however, it seemed to contribute only in valence, but not in arousal. For both valence and arousal, the percentage of samples with a value above *0.5* is rather discriminating, increasing the separation between the extreme positive mood class and the rest. Finally, from the domain of the derivatives, only the overall rising/falling trend was selected, represented by the *mean derivative*. Surprisingly, the most frequent emotion (φ_{17}), reflecting the intuition that mood gets fortified by the emotions that agree with it (Gebhard 2005), was not clustered in the set of important features.

3.2   Neural Mapping into Mood Values

To implement the functions γ_V and γ_A we chose to use the Extreme Learning Machine (ELM) (Huang et al. 2004), mainly due to its generally reported good performance in both classification and regression problems and its fast learning speed. The ELM algorithm is based on a multilayer perceptron architecture. Typically, a single hidden layer is used, with its neurons fully connected to the input and output layers. In a nutshell, the training of an ELM boils down to two essential steps: (1) the random assignment of the weights between input and hidden neurons (instead of iterative adjustment of the weights with the back-propagation algorithm) and (2) the computation of the weights between the hidden and output neurons as the least square solution that minimizes the error between predicted values, as computed through the randomly initialized network, and the targets. This procedure guarantees fast training, yet yielding high prediction accuracy, as shown for many applications (Huang et al. 2006).

4   Experimental Validation

4.1   Data

To check whether the model proposed in Sect. 3 can capture properly the relationship between emotional sequences and underlying mood, we were in need of ground truth that would couple, for a set of videos portraying people in different moods, both the punctually, continuously perceived emotions, and the corresponding overall perceived mood. Unfortunately, despite the wide amount of audio-visual affective databases (Douglas-Cowie et al. 2007, McKeown et al. 2010, Metallinou et al. 2013) available in literature, none reports continuous emotional annotations along with explicit mood annotations. Therefore, we created our own database, EMMA (Database with Emotion and Mood Annotations), which includes videos portraying single persons in a certain mood. For the creation of EMMA we employed actors, but to increase the naturalness of the recordings, we induced to them the desired mood with music (Västfjäll 2002). The actors performed daily non-interactive sequences of activities, such as sitting, standing, walking, eating and reading, while being under affective charge or affectively neutral. The scenes were captured simultaneously by two cameras, one focused on the face and one containing the whole face and body. The database consists of *364* clips in total (*182* for face and *182* for the combined face and body), each clip with average duration of 6 min (standard deviation 2 min). The simple daily scenarios, in combination with the long duration of each recording, resulted in a wide range of rather mild facial and bodily affective expressions. In this paper, we use *only the EMMA-face* subset.

Human annotators were then recruited to report both the emotions and the mood they perceived the actors in the video to be in. Emotions were annotated along the valence or arousal dimension continuously in time, using a modified version of G-Trace (Cowie and Sawey 2011). G-trace allows the user to rate one dimension at a time moving a slider, as seen in the interface snapshot in Fig. 3(a). The sampling rate of G-trace depends on the CPU, but it ranges between 0.3 and 0.5 s. To ensure uniform temporal sampling, we interpolated the annotations per second, as an economical

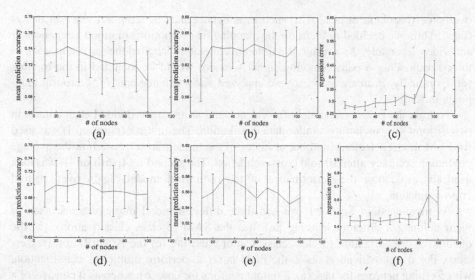

Fig. 3. Tuning of number of hidden nodes after 10-fold cross-validation on the partition I for valence (top row) and arousal (bottom row). From left to right: mean prediction for 3-classes, mean prediction for 5-classes and mean RMSE for regression. The error bars correspond to the 95% CI.

choice that practically preserves all the information of the emotional signal (Cowie and McKeown 2006). The range of the valence and arousal values of the raw data was [−1,1], so no further normalization was necessary. The first 10 s of annotation were discarded, to eliminate the transition from the initial random position of the slider in the beginning of the video.

At the end of each video, annotators had to report the overall perceived mood on a 5-point scale Self-Assessment Manikin (SAM (Bradley and Peter 1994), Fig. 3(b)). As a measure of self-consistency of each annotator, we also requested two alternative mood reports: (1) the Affect Button (Broekens and Brinkman 2009) (Fig. 3(c)), an emoticon which dynamically changes expression as the mouse scans its area, and records simultaneously valence-arousal with a click, and (2) a categorical description (positive/neutral/negative for valence, high/medium/low for arousal). This allowed us to obtain ground truth for mood in different levels of measurement, namely ordinal (SAM), nominal (descriptions) and interval (Affect Button). Every clip was annotated by 8 annotators on average.

4.2 Experimental Setup

To test the model described in Sect. 3, a common choice would be to study the relationship between emotions and mood at a clip level, i.e., learning the mapping between the aggregate emotional sequence (averaged per video across annotators) into the aggregate (e.g. mean) mood label for the same video. However, when fusing affective labels to obtain one ground truth per video, there are subjectivity issues to overcome (Nicolaou et al. 2012), such as annotator bias or temporal reaction delays (lags). Thus, we decided to focus on the mapping from emotions to mood per annotator and video separately. As a result, if *8* different annotators labelled the same clip, each of the corresponding *8* pairs (emotion signal – mood) would be included in the training set. Eventually, in this experiment we analyzed *1384* valence and *1358* arousal mappings in total.

To train the ELMs (separately for valence and arousal) we divided each dataset in two disjoint sets, including similar data distribution. The first set (partition I) was used for ELM model selection (number of nodes of the hidden layer), based on the average prediction accuracy after 10-fold cross-validation. The second set (partition II) was then used for evaluating the performance of the optimized model, again over 10-fold cross-validation.

As mentioned in Sect. 4.1, we had three different mood measurements, each of them defining a different learning task: (a) the SAM (5-class classification), (b) the qualitative categorization (3-class classification) and the (c) the AffectButton (regression). For the classification tasks, the ELM is set to perform multiclass classification, with 5 output neurons for task (a), 3 output neurons for task (b), whereas it consists of a single output in task (c). The performance is evaluated differently per learning task, as the correct prediction rate in classification (tasks (a) and (b)) and as the RMSE on the test set for the regression problem (c).

To the best of our knowledge, there is no published work which attempts to predict mood from visually expressed emotions. Even though there are a few papers mentioned in our related work that predict depression from video features, they do not follow the same experimental setup that would allow a direct comparison with our work, neither on the affective quantity to be predicted (*i.e.*, levels of one single mood, namely unipolar depression) nor on their methodology (*i.e.*, mapping directly video features to the depression label).

As a low baseline, we consider the naïve-chance predictor, which is *33%* in the case of 3-class classification and *20%* in the case of 5-class classification. For continuous value prediction, it is not as straightforward to define the random baseline analytically, since the calculation of RMSE becomes very complicated for vector sizes larger than one. In an approximation attempt, we computed this baseline for the particular case of our data, by assigning random values within the range [−1,1] and calculating the RMSE of the error. Iteratively this number converged to *0.82*. Since the chance predictor is a rather low benchmark, we also compared our data to the straightforward model proposed in (Katsimerou et al. 2014), namely the weighted average of the emotions with exponentially discounted value of the past emotions, defined for valence as

$$\mathcal{V}_m = F_V(V) = \sum_{k=n-w}^{n} v(k) \cdot \left(D_w(k) / \sum_{k=n-w}^{n} D_w(k) \right), \tag{6}$$

with

$$D_w(k) = e^{\frac{k-(n-w)}{n-w}}, k = n-w, .., n, \tag{7}$$

and w defined as the *30%* of the duration n of the video. Equation (6) can be modified accordingly for arousal. Finally, for comparison purposes, we also test our model by switching ELM with a linear classifier (or regressor), to implement the mapping functions γ.

4.3 Results

Figures 3(a)–(f) show the mean prediction accuracy of the ELM network after 10-fold cross-validation (on the partition I) as a function of the number of hidden nodes (error bars represent the 95% confidence intervals (CI) across the 10 folds). A peak in accuracy, combined with small CI, is spotted at *20* nodes for valence and *30* for arousal. For the regression task (Fig. 3(c) and (f), for valence and arousal respectively), we are opting for the smallest RMSE, which is *20* nodes for both valence and arousal.

The results of the prediction on the partition II set are summarized in Table 1 for valence and Table 2 for arousal. For the (multi-class) classification, we report (a) the true positive rate (TP), which corresponds to the number of correct class predictions over the total number of predictions, (b) the F-measure, the harmonic mean of precision and recall, which weights them evenly and (c) the 95% confidence interval of the mean TP over the 10-folds. For regression, we report (a) the RMSE and (b) the 95% CI.

Table 1. Prediction/fitting of the valence of mood Vm

	3-classes (pos./ neut./neg.)			5-classes (SAM)			Regression (AB)	
	TP	F	95% CI	TP	F	95% CI	MRSE	95% CI
ELM	**0.78**	**0.77**	±0.040	**0.68**	**0.62**	±0.026	**0.27**	±0.012
Linear	0.58	0.58	±0.025	0.37	0.4	±0.025	0.32	±0.025
Exp. discount	0.73	0.74	±0.020	0.56	0.59	±0.020	0.30	±0.012

Table 2. Prediction/fitting of the arousal of mood Am

	3-classes (high/med./low)			5-classes (SAM)			Regression (AB)	
	TP	F	95% CI	TP	F	95% CI	MRSE	95% CI
ELM	**0.74**	0.73	±0.028	**0.50**	**0.52**	±0.037	**0.42**	±0.030
Linear	0.57	0.58	±0.018	0.44	0.42	±0.025	0.48	±0.018
Exp. discount	0.73	0.73	±0.025	0.41	0.39	±0.025	0.55	±0.020

ELMs outperform the linear classifier in all learning tasks. This indicates a non-linear function maps better the emotion features into mood. The exponentially discounted average model performs comparably to our best predictor in the qualitative categorization (3-classes), but significantly worse in the other two tasks, indicating the added value of the approach proposed in this paper. Finally, we observe that in all tasks, ELM predicts valence better than arousal, but this is not systematically true for the linear classifier, suggesting that the final result may be predictor-dependent, and not feature-dependent.

5 Conclusions

In this work, we proposed an effective method for estimating the visually expressed mood from a sequence of expressed emotions, as perceived by the same person, during a given timespan. Our model is based on the computation of salient characteristics of the emotional sequence, which are then mapped into an estimation of the underlying mood via a neural model, and specifically the Extreme Learning Machine. With *10* features from the valence and *7* from the arousal signal, we can estimate the valence of mood in a qualitative way (negative/neutral/positive) with accuracy of *76%* and the (low/medium/high) arousal with *74%*, well above chance and significantly better than the exponentially discounted average model. With increased granularity in the prediction (i.e., 5 mood classes corresponding to the SAM scale points) the accuracy, as expected, decreases, although still yielding acceptable results. The same holds for regression, where there is room for improvement, even though the ELM regressor yields error significantly lower than the chance and model baselines. The added value of the proposed model with respect to the simple baseline model is obvious especially in the 5-class classification task, which results in accuracy improvement *21%* for valence and *36%* for arousal, indicating that the computation of salient features captures better the mood underlying the emotional signal.

Of course, the proposed model has been so far validated based on human annotations of emotions, rather than automatically recognized ones. Inaccuracies in automatic emotion recognition may harm the model accuracy, and therefore further validation is required in that sense. In the future, we also aim at further improving our mood prediction accuracy by (1) determining better representation of the emotional signal, and/or (2) by incorporating contextual (non-affective) features, such as the activity performed by the person whose mood needs to be recognized.

References

Bradley, M.M., Peter, J.L.: Measuring emotion: the self-assessment manikin and the semantic differential. J. Behav. Ther. Exp. Psychiatry **25**(1), 49–59 (1994)

Broekens, J., Brinkman, W.P.: AffectButton: towards a standard for dynamic affective user feedback. In: International Conference on Affective Computing & Intelligent Interaction (2009)

Cohen, I., et al.: Facial expression recognition from video sequences: temporal and static modeling. Comput. Vis. Image Underst. **91**(1), 160–187 (2003)

Cowie, R., McKeown, G.: Statistical analysis of data from initial labelled database and recommendations for an economical coding scheme (2006)

Cowie, R., Sawey, M.: GTrace-General trace program from Queen's Belfast (2011)

Douglas-Cowie, E., et al.: The HUMAINE database: addressing the collection and annotation of naturalistic and induced emotional data. In: Paiva, A., Prada, R., Picard, R.W. (eds.) ACII 2007. LNCS, vol. 4738, pp. 488–500. Springer, Heidelberg (2007). doi:10.1007/978-3-540-74889-2_43

Ekman, P.: An argument for basic emotions. Cogn. Emot. **6**(3-4), 169–200 (1992)

Ekman, P.: Basic emotions. Handb. Cogn. Emot. **98**, 45–60 (1999)

Gebhard, P.: ALMA – a layered model of affect. In: International Conference on Artificial Intelligent and Multi-Agent Systems (AAMAS) (2005)

Gunes, H., Piccardi, M.: Bi-modal emotion recognition from expressive face and body gestures. J. Netw. Comput. Appl. **30**, 1334–1345 (2007)

Huang, G.B., Zhu, Q.Y., Siew, C.K.: Extreme learning machine: theory and applications. Neurocomputing **70**(1), 489–501 (2006)

Huang, G.-B., Zhu, Q.-Y., Siew, C.-K.: Extreme learning machine: a new learning scheme of feedforward neural networks. In: IEEE International Joint Conference on Neural Networks (2004)

Jenkins, J.M., Oatley, K., Stein, N.L.: Human Emotions: A Reader. Blackwell, Oxford (1998)

Katsimerou, C., Redi, J.A., Heynderickx, I.: A computational model for mood recognition. In: Dimitrova, V., et al. (eds.) UMAP 2014. LNCS, vol. 8538, pp. 122–133. Springer, Heidelberg (2014). doi:10.1007/978-3-319-08786-3_11

Kleinsmith, A., Bianchi-Berthouze, N.: Affective body expression perception and recognition: a survey. Trans. Affect. Comput. **4**, 15–33 (2013)

Lane, A.M., Terry, P.C.: The nature of mood: development of a conceptual model with a focus on depression. J. Appl. Sport Psychol. **12**(1), 16–33 (2000)

McKeown, G., Valstar, M.F., Cowie, R., Pantic, M.: The SEMAINE corpus of emotionally coloured character interactions. In: IEEE International Conference on Multimedia and Expo (ICME) (2010)

Mehrabian, A.: Pleasure-arousal-dominance: a general framework for describing and measuring individual differences in temperament. Curr. Psychol. **14**, 261–292 (1996)

Metallinou, A., Katsamanis, A., Narayanan, S.: Tracking continuous emotional trends of participants during affective dyadic interactions using body language and speech information. Image Vis. Comput. **31**(2), 137–152 (2013)

Metallinou, A., Narayanan, S.: Annotation and processing of continuous emotional attributes: challenges and opportunities. In: IEEE International Conference and Workshops on Automatic Face and Gesture Recognition (FG) (2013)

Metallinou, A., et al.: Context-sensitive learning for enhanced audiovisual emotion classification. IEEE Trans. Affect. Comput. **3**(2), 184–198 (2012)

Morris, W.N.: Some thoughts about mood and its regulation. Psychol. Inq. **11**, 200–202 (2000)

Nicolaou, M., Gunes, H., Pantic, M.: Continuous prediction of spontaneous affect from multiple cues and modalities in valence-arousal space. IEEE Trans. Affect. Comput. **2**, 92–105 (2011)

Nicolaou, M.A., Pavlovic, V., Pantic, M.: Dynamic probabilistic CCA for analysis of affective behaviour. In: Fitzgibbon, A., Lazebnik, S., Perona, P., Sato, Y., Schmid, C. (eds.) ECCV 2012. LNCS, vol. 7578, pp. 98–111. Springer, Heidelberg (2012). doi:10.1007/978-3-642-33786-4_8

Oatley, K., Johnson-Laird, P.N.: Towards a cognitive theory of emotions. Cogn. Emot. **1**(1), 29–50 (1987)

Rusell, J.: A circumplex model of affect. Pers. Soc. Psychol. **39**, 1161–1178 (1980)

Russell, J.A.: Core affect and the psychological construction of emotion. Psychol. Rev. **110**(1), 145 (2003)

Sigal, L., Fleet, D.J., Troje, N.F., Livne, M.: Human attributes from 3D pose tracking. In: Daniilidis, K., Maragos, P., Paragios, N. (eds.) ECCV 2010. LNCS, vol. 6313, pp. 243–257. Springer, Heidelberg (2010). doi:10.1007/978-3-642-15558-1_18

Thayer, R.E.: The Origin of Everyday Moods: Managing Energy, Tension, and Stress. Oxford University Press, Oxford (1996)

Thrasher, M., Zwaag, M.D., Bianchi-Berthouze, N., Westerink, J.H.D.M.: Mood recognition based on upper body posture and movement features. In: D'Mello, S., Graesser, A., Schuller, B., Martin, J.-C. (eds.) ACII 2011. LNCS, vol. 6974, pp. 377–386. Springer, Heidelberg (2011). doi:10.1007/978-3-642-24600-5_41

Valstar, M., et al.: AVEC 2013: the continuous audio/visual emotion and depression recognition challenge. In: 3rd ACM International Workshop on Audio/Visual Emotion Challenge (2013)

Västfjäll, D.: Emotion induction through music: a review of the musical mood induction procedure. Music Sci. **5**(1), 173–211 (2002)

A Conversational Agent to Shift Students' Affect State

Ethel Chua Joy Ong[✉] and Zhayne Chong Soriano

Center for Language Technologies, De La Salle University, Manila, Philippines
ethel.ong@delasalle.ph, zcsoriano@gmail.com

Abstract. When a student is feeling negatively while doing some required tasks in a learning environment, in this case, a reading assessment exercise, a conversation with the tutor agent can be initiated to engage the student in an affective text-based dialogue as a means of intervention. Such dialogue can revolve around everyday, commonsense topics that may be related to the reading material or exercise at hand. A semantic ontology populated with commonsense concepts from existing knowledge sources, specifically ConceptNet and SenticNet, provides the conversational agent with the candidate set of topics for discourse. To facilitate the validation of the dialogue system with children, the conversational tutor agent was integrated into a learning environment platform that supports reading of short stories.

Keywords: Conversational tutor agent · Commonsense ontology · Dialogue generation · Learning environment

1 Introduction

Over the past decade, tutor agents embedded in intelligent learning environments (ILE) have evolved in their teaching strategies. Early ILEs employed a simple tutor agent that presents static content and canned tutorial responses in the delivery of the lessons. The use of natural language processing techniques gave way to tutor agents who can provide dynamically generated text-based tutorial responses to students. This capability was later supplemented with the use of speech processing techniques. Empathic computing further provided the tutor agents with the ability to recognize student emotions and to generate affective responses accordingly. These virtual and sometimes embodied conversational agents can engage a student using text, speech, hand gestures, facial expressions, eye gaze and other kinds of body language.

Previous ILEs have been designed to adapt only to the students' cognitive states. However, studies have shown that the affect state of a student has an effect on his/her performance in learning. Findings from the works of [1–3] further argued that being attuned to the student's emotional state plays an important role to the future of research in ILEs. Consequently, systems like AutoTutor [4] and ITSPOKE [5] have been enhanced with the capability to identify the student's affect states during a learning session and to adapt the tutor's pedagogical strategies in order to provide better remediation by scaffolding the learner through a sequence of emotions.

© Springer International Publishing Switzerland 2016
M. Baldoni et al. (Eds.): IWEC 2014/IWEC 2015/CMNA 2015, LNAI 9935, pp. 86–97, 2016.
DOI: 10.1007/978-3-319-46218-9_7

There are many ways to provide interventions that focus on the student's emotional state. One approach is for the tutor agent to engage the student in affective conversation. Dialogue systems model the natural conversations between humans to provide a conversational interface between man and machine that can be text-based, speech-based, or multimodal (incorporating graphics and body language aside from text and speech). While early dialogue systems have been used mostly for information-seeking applications, for learning environments, the interaction has been designed to be entertaining to increase the engagement and motivation of the student [6].

This paper presents the method employed to embody a tutor agent with the ability to converse with a Filipino student between 8–10 years old in a text-based dialogue when the latter is feeling negatively while performing a reading assessment exercise. Section 2 presents an overview of the learning environment used to host the conversational tutor agent. Section 3 describes the semantic ontology that provides the conversational agent with a knowledge source for its possible topics of discourse. This is followed by a discussion of the process in generating the text-based dialogue.

Through the generation of affective text that is attuned to the student's current emotional state, we hypothesize that the student's negative affect state can be disrupted and shifted to a more positive one. A positive affect sets up a learning environment where the student can be motivated to continue with his/her learning activities. Test results and findings that affirm or contradict this hypothesis are presented in Sect. 4. The paper ends with a discussion of issues and recommendations to improve the generation of dialogue to enable a tutor agent to better motivate the student in completing his/her learning activities.

2 The Learning Environment

The learning environment has three modes of operation, namely the story reading mode, the assessment mode, and the conversation mode.

After finishing a story, the student must answer a set of reading assessment exercises, as shown in Fig. 1. Currently, the student has to do a personal evaluation of his/her affect state and make this known to the tutor agent through the options at the bottom of the page: *happy* denotes a positive affect while *sad* denotes a negative one.

When the student reports a negative affect, the tutor agent will try to disrupt this state by engaging the student in a conversational dialogue. Initially, the focus of the topics of discourse may be related to the reading selection. Subsequently, the discourse is guided by the topics that the student may be interested in based on the latter's choices. As shown in Fig. 2, the conversation is currently in a text-based question-answer format. The approach used in identifying the possible topics of discourse, as well as dialogue planning and generation are discussed in Sect. 3.

Again, at the bottom of each dialogue turn are two options for the student to declare his/her current affect. This is used by the tutor agent to determine if it has been able to disrupt the student's negative affect. Once a positive affect has been reported, the student can resume the learning task that was previously interrupted.

It should be noted that there are two learning activities present in the system, namely, the reading task and the reading assessment exercise. However, for this

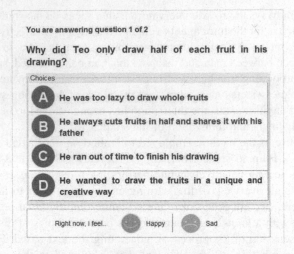

Fig. 1. Sample reading assessment exercise

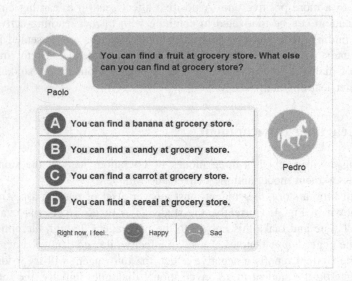

Fig. 2. Sample dialogue turn

research, it was decided that the tutor agent can disrupt and engage the student in a conversation only during an assessment activity, and not during a reading session.

3 Dialogue Generation

The conversation follows a turn-based format. At every given turn, the content of the tutor agent's dialogue is determined by the dialogue planner using a plan-based approach while utilizing the available knowledge in the semantic ontology.

3.1   Semantic Ontology

For the tutor agent to appear engaging to its human user, its dialogue must reflect its role of a conversational peer. Thus, the agent is limited to topics that the student is currently reading and may be interested in. A semantic ontology of commonsense knowledge that young children are familiar with has been utilized to provide the dialogue planner with the possible topics of discourse.

Commonsense knowledge encompasses everyday concepts and their relationships that people intuitively possess, and which allow them to understand and interact with one another. A primary source of commonsense knowledge is ConceptNet [7]. It is a large semantic graph of concepts represented as nodes that are linked with binary semantic relations, such as *isA, partOf, madeOf, subEvent, hasProperty* and *usedFor*.

A separate semantic ontology was constructed to support the task of the dialogue planner. This ontology contains relevant concepts and relations that are extracted from ConceptNet and are supplemented by manually-populated concepts and relations. A number of issues have made it necessary to construct this ontology. First, much of the knowledge described in ConceptNet is unfamiliar (e.g. *Causes(eat, heartburn), IsA (breakfast club, film)*) to and in some cases, inappropriate (i.e. *drugs, alcohol, sex, death,* and *violence*) for the intended users. Secondly, ConceptNet consists of knowledge that is only applicable to certain cultures (e.g. *PartOf(chimney, house)*) and may not be relevant to the target Filipino students. The work of Yu and Ong [8] made a similar approach of combining manually-created resources to supplement the knowledge extracted from ConceptNet in order to generate stories.

Finally, ConceptNet has no knowledge to describe a concept's affective information. Such information is needed as a heuristic in identifying the candidate topics of discourse to be used in the generation of affective text that the tutor agent can use during its conversation with the student.

In the semantic ontology, each concept is defined by a unique identifier, the free text of the word or phrase that the concept represents, and the corresponding polarity value pc derived from SenticNet [9]. SenticNet is a collection of commonsense concepts, each associated with a polarity value that describes how positive or negative is the affect being expressed by a given concept. The polarity value is represented as a float $pc \ \varepsilon \ [-1.0, +1.0]$, wherein a concept that expresses positive affect (e.g., *birthday party*) has a polarity value $pc \approx +1.0$. Conversely, a concept that expresses negative affect (e.g., *homework*) is associated with a polarity value $pc \approx -1.0$. Concepts with neutral or almost neutral polarity values have been excluded from SenticNet; these concepts are associated with a neutral polarity value $pc = 0$ in the semantic ontology.

The semantic ontology is populated with knowledge extracted from ConceptNet 5.1 [10]. In particular, the content of the semantic ontology is limited to concepts and assertions that are familiar to and age-appropriate for the intended users, and applicable in the context of Filipino culture. Most of these concepts and assertions are in the English language. However, a small number of Filipino concepts from ConceptNet 5.1, such as *buko* (coconut) and *halo halo* (Filipino dessert with a mixture of various ingredients, milk and shaved ice), have also been included. As an example, the partial sub-ontology of the keyword '*fruit*' is illustrated in Fig. 3.

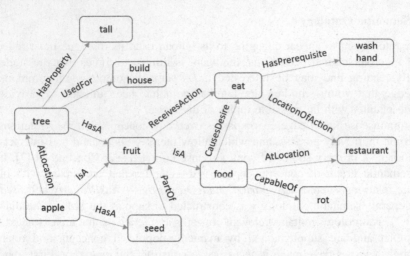

Fig. 3. Partial sub-ontology of the keyword "*fruit*"

3.2 Dialogue Planner

The conversational dialogue framework between the tutor agent and the student is shown in Listing 1.

Listing 1. Conversational dialogue framework: text-based turn-taking

```
1. Tutor gives a statement expressing some commonsense
   thought.
           You can find a fruit at grocery store.
2. Tutor poses an open-ended question related to the
   statement
           What else can you find at grocery store?
3. Tutor presents a list of textual responses
4. Learner selects a response
5. Process is repeated until Learner reports a "positive"
   affect
```

The dialogue begins with the tutor uttering a statement expressing some commonsense thought (e.g., *You can find a fruit at grocery store.*), followed with a question related to the statement (e.g., *What else can you find at grocery store?*). Most questions are open-ended and can be answered with a response from a list of textual responses. This list is provided to ensure that the conversation stays within the contents of the semantic ontology by preventing the student from jumping to a different topic where the tutor agent may have no knowledge to generate an appropriate response. Regardless of the question however, the list of responses will always include an option to change the topic of discourse, and to end the conversation prematurely and resume the learning activity.

Table 1. Sample reading assessment exercise question

1. *Mateo drew his five favorite fruits for his Arts class. Which of these fruits did Mateo draw?*	
a. Guava	c. Mango
b. Banana	d. Buko

When a conversation commences, the dialogue planner uses themes and concepts related to the current reading assessment exercise the student is working on as the initial topic of discourse. These themes and concepts have been pre-determined when the exercises were formulated. A list of keywords *Ke* describing these themes and concepts is associated with each exercise *e*. For example, the reading assessment exercise question in Table 1 is associated with *K1 = {fruit, draw, art class}*.

It is important to minimize the time between the student's reply and the tutor agent's next dialogue turn. Thus, in lieu of accessing the semantic ontology at every turn, the dialogue planner uses the knowledge in the sub-ontologies to determine the content of the affective text. The sub-ontologies also serve to limit the knowledge that the dialogue planner has access to, therefore preventing the dialogue from straying too far from the initial topic of discourse.

To determine the topic that the tutor agent and the student will initially talk about, the tutor agent presents the student with the list of keywords *Ke*, and asks him/her to choose his/her preference. Accordingly, the sub-ontology of the chosen topic is used during the conversation. However, the sub-ontologies of the other topic choices may still be used within the same conversation if the dialogue planner has exhausted all the concepts in the sub-ontology of the selected topic, and the student still feels negatively; or, the student decides he/she wants to talk about something else.

A partial transcript of a conversation is found in Listing 2. *TA-Tn* represents the *n*th turn of the tutor agent, while *USR-Tn* represents the *n*th turn of the student.

Listing 2. A 5-turn conversation between a Tutor Agent and the Student.

```
[TA-T1]:   A meat is delicious. What else do you know
           about meat?
[USR-T1]:  You can eat a meat.
[TA-T2]:   A fruit is good for you. What else is good for you?
[USR-T2]:  An exercise is good for you.
[TA-T3]:   An apple is good for you. How else can you
           describe an apple?
[USR-T3]:  An apple is good to eat.
[TA-T4]:   You can find an apple hang from tree. Where
           else can you find an apple?
[USR-T4]:  You can find an apple in tree.
[TA-T5]:   An apple is red. How else can you describe an
           apple?
[USR-T5]:  An apple is round.
```

Tests were conducted to count the number of dialogue turns that can be generated before all the assertions in the current sub-ontology are exhausted. Replies were selected randomly from the list of possible responses. From these tests, it was determined that the current sub-ontology can provide enough knowledge to sustain a conversation for at least 25 turns. Given this, it is imperative that the semantic ontology consists of a substantial amount of knowledge, in both depth and breadth.

In terms of content, the generated dialogue usually center on the following:

(1) The physical (i.e., color, shape, taste, smell) and non-physical (e.g., *"fun"*, *"beautiful"*, *"tiring"*) descriptions of the current topic of the conversation, as seen in conversation turns [TA–T5] and [TA–T1, TA–T2], respectively;
(2) The location in which the topic may be found (i.e., *you can find food in refrigerator*) [TA–T3] or can be performed (i.e., *you can play at playground*);
(3) The specific variety or examples of the topic (i.e., *a ball is a toy, a carrot is a kind of vegetable*);
(4) The topic's uses (i.e., *you can use pencil to draw*).

Dialogue on events involving the selected topic is likewise generated; however, such dialogue is rare.

It was also observed that the transition between topics is not always smooth, as shown in the sample dialogue in Listing 2. This is especially pronounced when the dialogue planner goes back to a previous topic after exhausting the current one (i.e., *"meat"*, the grandchild node of *"fruit"* → *"food"*). The result is that the dialogue seems to be jumping from the current topic to another topic. The use of transitional devices (i.e., *"also"*), and statements explicitly informing the user of a change in topic (i.e., *"going back to..."*, *"let's talk about..."*) may improve this.

4   Test Results

The current iteration of the semantic ontology consists of approximately 200 commonsense concepts in the domains of everyday objects and activities at home and school, and about food and sports. These domains were selected to complement the reading assessment exercises that follow a reading selection. The semantic ontology was populated by recursively querying the ConceptNet 5.1 web API for assertions whose nodes (i.e. start node or end node) represent the concept describing a search key, and whose lemmas (i.e. start lemma or end lemma) contain the key. Keywords describing relevant themes and concepts in these exercises were enumerated and used as the initial concepts for the recursive queries. From the query results, assertions that are familiar, appropriate and applicable for the intended students were selected and added to the semantic ontology. Finally, the polarity values of the concepts populating the semantic ontology were obtained by querying the SenticNet API.

The test participants are composed of 17 students, age 8–10 years old and studying in private co-ed primary schools. The students are proficient in the English language and are computer literate. The latter two requirements are important to avoid communication problems related to language, and usability problems related to the student's ability to use a computer-based software.

The system currently contains only one (1) story. Each participant was allowed to use the system as long as he/she needs to finish reading the story and to work on the assessment exercise. A survey form with a Yes/Maybe/No format was then used during the debriefing session with each of the students to determine their individual experience in conversing with the tutor agent using two main criteria, namely dialogue content and learning experience. Table 2 shows the evaluation results.

Out of the 17 students, 4 (33.3%) were not able to meet the tutor agent; that is, these students never reported experiencing the "sad" affect while doing the reading assessment exercise. Of the remaining 13, 7 (53.8%) were partially interested in pursuing a conversation with the tutor (Table 2 item #1). A couple of older kids engaged the tutor agent in a conversation for the sake of exploration without actually needing its help since the students had a positive disposition throughout the reading assessment activity.

Table 2. Evaluation results for the *Dialogue Content* criterion (Participants = 13)

Questions	Yes	Maybe	No
1. Were you interested in pursuing a conversation with the tutor?	6 (46.2%)	7 (53.8%)	-
2. Did you understand the tutor?	9 (69.2%)	4 (30.8%)	-
3. Did the tutor provide choices that make sense?	6 (46.2%)	7 (53.8%)	-
4. Did the conversation with the tutor motivate you to continue with the learning activity?	3 (23.1%)	8 (61.5%)	2 (15.4%)
5. Was the tutor able to change your sad feeling?	2 (15.4%)	1 (7.7%)	10 (76.9%)

In terms of understandability (Table 2 item #2), 9 (69.2%) out of the 13 students had no trouble understanding the words used by the tutor, while 4 (30.8%) students partially understood the tutor. This means that the manual process of populating the semantic ontology by selecting concepts from ConceptNet, and the creation of templates used for generating the dialogue were done correctly.

In terms of the appropriateness of the dialogue content (Table 2 item #3), specifically the list of responses, 7 (53.8%) students encountered some concerns with the choices. They found some of the choices to be amusing and do not make sense. The same group of students also found that not all words used are appropriate. There are repetitive choices, e.g., "*you can find a food at a refrigerator*", and "*flower in the park*" vs "*flower at a park*", which varied only in the prepositions that were used. Some of the templates used to generate a conversation turn also contained incorrect words, such as "*a fast food is a kind of food*" and "*a leftover is a kind of food*". Redundant statements also appear, as in "*you need an ice cream so you can eat an ice cream*". While the students were using the system, they react and vividly express their emotions, with statements such as "*Duh?*" when the tutor seemed to ask "dumb" questions, or "*What is this?*" when the questions posed by the tutor are ambiguous.

In terms of the tutor's ability to motivate the students (Table 2 item #4), 8 (61.5%) out of the 13 test participants were unsure if their conversation with the tutor has motivated them to continue with the learning task, while only 3 (23.1%) students felt happy when they conversed with the agent. 2 (15.4%) students were not motivated at all by their conversation with the tutor. One student also claimed that the tutor helped him/her regain interest in the activity, but eventually got bored when the same conversation turned redundant and boring.

10 (76.9%) of the 13 students claimed that their negative affect was not shifted despite engaging the tutor in a conversation (Table 2 item #5). However, it should be emphasized that the study was not able to determine the affect of the students prior to using the system. This means it is possible that some or all of the 10 students did not need the help of the tutor to shift their affect if they were not sad in the first place.

In a study conducted by Wik and Hjalmarsson [6], they found out that the longer the conversation takes requiring more dialogue turns between the tutor agent and the student, the better the interaction. Thus, while the students were using the system, the number of reading assessment questions until the student initiates a dialogue with the tutor (by reporting a "sad" feeling), and the number of turns until the dialogue with the tutor was terminated by the student (by reporting a "happy" feeling) were also tracked. It took an average of 4.09 reading assessment questions before the dialogue between the student and the tutor is initiated. It took an average of 7.125 dialogue turns between the tutor and each of the students before the latter went back to resume his/her learning activity.

Separate system testing showed that, given the current size of the knowledge base, the tutor can engage a student in a 20-turn dialogue (20 dialogue questions), though a number of the questions were already repeating, similar to the experience as reported by some of the students. 1 (7.7%) student completed the whole dialogue before returning to the required learning activity. This same student was very patient while engaging the tutor in a conversation, sometimes laughing when he/she found something amusing with the way the tutor presented its question and list of responses.

The seeming disinterest of the students with the system in general and the tutor in particular may be attributed to a number of factors. The first factor is the lengthy reading material with minimal pictures that was used. Though none of the students explicitly stated that the story itself is boring, 7 (41.2%) out of the total 17 participants gave a neutral answer to the question "*Is the story interesting?*". 5 (29.4%) of the participants showed interest in using the system again provided that the selection of stories is changed and more interesting stories are added. While the remaining 4 (23.5%) students did not fully understand the story, one student, the youngest, did not understand the story at all.

The second factor is the tutor agent. During debriefing, a number of students claimed that they did not understand the rationale behind the need for a tutor agent. The concept of a tutor agent in a reading environment is new to them. This may be related to the third factor, the non-facial appearance of the tutor agent. The current research was focused only on the dialogue rather than the tutor's animated facial features. Contrary to the findings of Graesser and his colleagues [11] that "the effects of the media are either subtle or non-existent", and that the message of the dialogue facilitates learning among college students, for young students, the dialogue alone is not sufficient to catch and hold their attention to the learning activity. Furthermore, educational software that utilize games to teach young students about basic concepts in math and language may sometimes employ the use of familiar animated characters to deliver lessons and instructions, such as those seen in [12].

Despite the mostly negative feedback, the students did like a few things about the system, specifically the colorful interface and the use of avatars to represent their individual profiles. The latter was observed when the students took so much time in creating their accounts and selecting an avatar.

5 Conclusion and Further Work

When a student is feeling negatively while performing the required activities in an ILE, he/she may encounter difficulties concentrating and grasping the lessons. In this research, a tutor agent has been designed to assume the role of a conversational peer who can initiate an affective dialogue with the student as a means of intervention. Specifically, such dialogue revolves around everyday, commonsense topics. A semantic ontology of commonsense concepts extracted from ConceptNet 5.1, combined with their corresponding affect-based polarity values sourced from SenticNet, has been constructed to provide the dialogue planner with the topics of discourse.

Tests conducted among a limited population of Filipino students who are between 8 to 10 years old produced mixed results, similar to the findings reported by [13] where neither positive nor negative effects on the student's motivation in the learning tasks were evident with the use of conversational agents. Though 9 out of the 13 participants (69.2%) are able to understand the contents of the text-based dialogue presented by the tutor agent, 7 (53.8%) students were not interested in pursuing further conversation with the tutor as they find the dialogue tend to become redundant and at times boring. These issues with the dialogue made the tutor agent ineffective in motivating the students to resume their learning activity. 10 (76.9%) of the 13 participants also claimed that the tutor has not been able to change their negative affect state.

It was also observed that the negative affect of the students was primarily caused by the available story currently present in the system. Younger kids discontinued reading the story as soon as they found it boring. The older kids finished the story but gave their negative opinions and pointed out the need for more interesting stories to be added. This behavior highlights the potential role that a particular story may play in the learning experience of a student. On the other hand, the use of good stories or stories that are familiar to young children may question the need for a conversational tutor agent. Future work can focus on determining if the student's bias towards the story may have affected his/her attitude towards the tutor agent and the latter's attempt at intervention. Tests should also be conducted to determine the relationship between the features of the stories (i.e., genre, lexile, popularity or familiarity) and the need for a conversational tutor agent to motivate the completion of the required reading and/or assessment tasks. Findings from these tests may be used to address the concern regarding the novelty of using computer-based tutor agents in the delivery of teaching instructions, as experienced by some of the test participants.

In the area of text processing, it is worth exploring the combined use of both the affect state and the age of the student as heuristics in the generation of text-based dialogue that is adaptive to the individual needs of the students, to determine if this may improve the student's attitude towards the conversational peer. Younger students (8 years old) may find the repetitive nature of the conversation with the tutor to be more helpful. Older kids, on the other hand, may appreciate a more mature conversation with the tutor agent.

Furthermore, the tutor agent currently provides conversation-based interventions only during a reading assessment task, when the student appears to be getting demotivated in completing the required learning activity. But the tutor agent should be capable of initiating dialogues at various points in the learning process, depending on the specific learning goals. Dialogues can be generated as a form of feedback to student responses to scaffold him/her towards the correct answer, or to guide the student towards understanding the problem.

To achieve these, other types of dialogue that have been identified in [14], which include inquiry, persuasion, negotiation, deliberation and eristic dialogues, should be explored to provide variances to the information-seeking dialogues currently generated in this research. Future research should also weigh the possible consequences of disrupting a student during a reading session when difficulties in reading are encountered to provide some form of dialogue-based interventions. For instance, persuasive dialogue can be used by the tutor agent to motivate the student towards some behavioral or emotional change, i.e., the desire to complete the learning task. Deliberation dialogue, on the other hand, can be used by the tutor to engage the student in a collaborative discussion of the reading material through simplifying or rephrasing complex sentences or story subplots, or exploring the characters' actions surrounding the events in the story.

References

1. Zakharov, K., Mitrovic, A., Johnston, L.: Towards emotionally-intelligent pedagogical agents. In: Woolf, B.P., Aïmeur, E., Nkambou, R., Lajoie, S. (eds.) ITS 2008. LNCS, vol. 5091, pp. 19–28. Springer, Heidelberg (2008). doi:10.1007/978-3-540-69132-7_7
2. Pekrun, R.: Emotions as drivers of learning and cognitive development. In: Calvo, R., D'Mello, S. (eds.) New Perspectives on Affect and Learning Technologies, vol. 3, pp. 23–39. Springer, New York (2011)
3. D'Mello, S.K., Graesser, A.: Dynamics of affective states during complex learning. Learn. Instr. 22, 145–157 (2012)
4. D'Mello, S., Picard, R.W., Graesser, A.: Towards an affect-sensitive AutoTutor. IEEE Intell. Syst. 22(4), 53–61 (2007). IEEE
5. Forbes-Riley, K., Litman, D.J.: Adapting to student uncertainty improves tutoring dialogues. In: Proceedings of 14th International Conference on Artificial Intelligence in Education (2009)
6. Wik, P., Hjalmarsson, A.: Embodied conversational agents in computer assisted language learning. Speech Commun. 51(10), 1024–1037 (2009). Elsevier Science Publishers
7. Liu, H., Singh, P.: Commonsense reasoning in and over natural language. In: Negoita, M.Gh., Howlett, Robert, J., Jain, Lakhmi, C. (eds.) KES 2004. LNCS (LNAI), vol. 3215, pp. 293–306. Springer, Heidelberg (2004). doi:10.1007/978-3-540-30134-9_40

8. Yu, S., Ong, E.: Using common-sense knowledge in generating stories. In: Anthony, P., Ishizuka, M., Lukose, D. (eds.) PRICAI 2012. LNCS (LNAI), vol. 7458, pp. 838–843. Springer, Heidelberg (2012). doi:10.1007/978-3-642-32695-0_82
9. Cambria, E., Speer, R., Havasi, C., Hussain, A.: SenticNet: a publicly available semantic resource for opinion mining. In: Proceedings of 2010 AAAI Fall Symposium Series on Common Sense Knowledge, pp. 14–18. Association for the Advancement of Artificial Intelligence (2010)
10. Speer, R., Havasi, C.: Representing General Relational Knowledge in ConceptNet 5. In: Proceedings of 8th International Conference on Language Resources and Evaluation (LREC 2012), pp. 3679–3686. European Language Resource Association (2012)
11. Graesser, A., Moreno, K., Marineau, J., Adcock, A., Olney, A., Person, N.: AutoTutor improves deep learning of computer literacy: is it the dialog or the talking head? Artif. Intell. Educ.: Shaping Future Learn. Intell. Technol. **97**, 47–54 (2003). IOS Press
12. Jumpstart Fun Games for Kids. http://www.jumpstart.com
13. Miksatko, J., Kipp, K.H., Kipp, M.: The persona zero-effect: evaluating virtual character benefits on a learning task with repeated interactions. In: Allbeck, J., Badler, N., Bickmore, T., Pelachaud, C., Safonova, A. (eds.) IVA 2010. LNCS (LNAI), vol. 6356, pp. 475–481. Springer, Heidelberg (2010). doi:10.1007/978-3-642-15892-6_51
14. Walton, D., Krabbe, E.C.W.: Commitment in Dialogue. SUNY Press, Albany (1995)

Comparing Affect Recognition in Peaks and Onset of Laughter

Faramarz Ataollahi[(✉)] and Merlin Teodosia Suarez

College of Computer Studies, De La Salle University,
2401 Taft Avenue, 1004 Manila, Philippines
f_ataollahi@yahoo.com, merlin.suarez@delasalle.ph

Abstract. Laughter is an important social signal that conveys different emotions like happiness, sadness, anger, fear, surprise, and disgust. Therefore, detecting emotions in the laughter is useful for estimating the emotional state of the user. This paper presents work that detects the emotions in Iranian laughter by using audio features and running four machine learning algorithms, namely, Sequential Minimal Optimization (SMO), Multilayer Perceptron (MLP), Logistic, and Radial Basis Function Network (RBFNetwork). We extracted features such as intensity (minimum, maximum, mean, and standard deviation), energy, power, first 3 formants, and the first thirteen Mel Frequency Cepstral Coefficients. Two datasets are used: one that contains segments of full laughter episodes and one that contains only laughter onsets. Results indicate that MLP algorithm produce the highest rate of accuracy which is 86.1372% for first dataset and 85.0123% for second dataset. Besides, using the combination of MFCC and prosodic features led to better results. This means that recognition of emotions is possible at the start of laughter, which is useful for real-time applications.

Keywords: Laughter · Emotion recognition · Audio signal

1 Introduction

Laughter is an important signal in human interactions and conveys different kind of emotions like happiness, sadness, anger, surprise, fear, and disgust [7].

Different methods with different performances are used in several researches to recognize emotion in speech and laughter [4, 6, 7, 12]. Most researches use machine learning approaches to build affect models, which are essentially data-driven. Various emotion corpora have been created, with some containing acted [4, 6] and spontaneous data [3, 12]. The AVLaughterCycle database [14] consists of both acted and spontaneous laughter. Some studies use audio signals [7, 9, 11] while the others use audio-visual signals [1, 2].

There are several features which can be extracted from audio signals to detect emotions. Galvan et al. [2] used minimum, maximum, mean and standard deviation of pitch and intensity, as well as energy, pitch contours, the first three formants and the thirteen Mel Frequency Cepstral Coefficients (MFCC). Kudiri et al. [6] used different features such as Relative Bin Frequency Coefficient (RBFC) that lead to 72.01% accuracy rate by using SVM classifying algorithm.

© Springer International Publishing Switzerland 2016
M. Baldoni et al. (Eds.): IWEC 2014/IWEC 2015/CMNA 2015, LNAI 9935, pp. 98–107, 2016.
DOI: 10.1007/978-3-319-46218-9_8

Laughter and speech signals carry different emotions like happiness, anger, sadness [4]. Kudiri et al. [6] showed that laughter can convey emotions such as disgust, fear, happiness, boredom, neutral, sadness, and anger. Emotions are usually dependent on culture. There exist few works that focused on local or culture dependent emotions; two of these presented efforts [7, 9] tried to detect different kind of emotions in Filipino laughter using audio signals.

In this study we use Iranian laughter and extract acoustic and MFCCs features, and then we fed the extracted features into WEKA in order to do classification.

2 Related Works

Some of the published papers in the field of emotion recognition used audio or audiovisual signals. For example Truong and Leeuwen [12] presented detecting emotions in laughter and speech. They used perceptual linear prediction, pitch, and energy as features, Gaussian Mixture Model (GMM) as the classifier, and they reached an accuracy rate of 20%.

In another study, Iliev et al. [4] presented their research in the field of detecting emotions in speech. They tried to detect 3 different emotions, namely, happiness, anger, and sadness. Mean, standard deviation, minimum, average of both pitch and energy conjunction with Tone and Break Tiers (TOBI) features were extracted. Finally they used GMM as the classifier and reached an accuracy rate of 75%.

A study done by Hamidi and Mansoorizade [3] on emotions in Persian speech were detected. They used MLP as the classifier and the minimum, maximum, mean of energy and pitch, as well as the amount of 13 MFCC coefficients as the features to reach the accuracy rate of 78%. Emotions in Filipino laughter was detected in study of Miranda et al. [7]. They tried to detect 5 kinds of emotions, namely, happiness, giddiness, eagerness, embarrassment, and suffering by using two classifying algorithm.

In our study we have detected three kinds of emotions, namely, happiness, surprise, and irony in Iranian laughter. We used audio files and extracted minimum, maximum, mean, and standard deviation of intensity, energy, power, the first three formants and the first thirteen MFCCs as features. Then we used MLP, SMO, Logistic, and RBFNetwork as classifiers to classify these 3 kind of emotions in laughter.

3 Iranian Emotional Laughter Database

One of the problems in laughter emotion recognition is lack of appropriate laughter databases. Some laughter databases exist [2, 7, 10, 13]. Miranda et al. [7] showed a local Filipino laughter database while Urbain et al. [13] presented an international database which people from different countries participated in that project. Emotions are usually dependent on culture. On the other hand, emotions are social cultural constructs and have a deep relationship with culture. Because of cultural norms, an emotional event can be comprehensible for a certain cultural groups while others may not understand that event [17]. The objective of this research is to identify the emotions in Iranian laughter, and to examine the use of onsets instead of the whole laughter files in emotion recognition. Although there were Persian speech databases [3], there is no Iranian laughter database. For this research, an appropriate Iranian laughter database is needed; therefore, we built an Iranian laughter database as explained below:

3.1 Iranian Laughter

Iranians like other people use laughter to express their emotions and feelings. Several kinds of laughter exist. The various emotions carried by Iranian laughter are as follows: irony, surprise, supremacy, fear, embarrassment, and happiness[1,2,3]. For this paper we use three kinds of Iranian laughter, namely: happy, surprise, and irony. These emotions were most frequently occurring in reality TV programs which were the source of the laughter segments.

3.2 Data Collection

Researchers have used audio data for emotion recognition in laughter [7, 9], and the results showed single modal approaches still work; therefore, we use audio signals in this study. The Iranian laughter database is a spontaneous database. We used Iranian reality TV programs like TV shows, behind scenes, and interviews sourced from YouTube. Reality TV programs were chosen because these contain clips of spontaneous laughter. In addition, the clips are easily available on YouTube. We watched different programs and chose the samples. Both male and female laughter were used. The database contains three kinds of laughter, namely, happy laughter, surprised laughter, and irony laughter. It contains 1,975 laughter episodes with 466 happy, 1,093 surprise and 417 irony episodes. Ten (10) Iranian dentistry students who lived in Manila annotated the laughter episodes. The episodes are fixed-length ones and the length of each episode is 240 ms. We examined different lengths shorter than 200 ms, but most of extracted features of episodes shorter than 200 ms had undefined value. By increasing the length of episodes and watching the values of extracted features, we chose 240 ms as the length of episodes. We segmented the audio files manually by using Audacity[4].

3.3 Pre-processing

The laughter files contain noise and some unwanted signals. Therefore, noise removing is necessary to make sure that extracted features contain the minimal noise [7]. Miranda et al. [7] and Galvan et al. [2] used Jaudio for noise cleaning. In this study we used Audacity, which is free software for audio editing and noise removal (See footnote 4).

---

[1] http://www.irangrand.ir.

[2] http://www.seemorgh.com.

[3] http://tandorosti.hmg.ir.

[4] http://manual.audacityteam.org/o/man/noise_removal.html.

In removing the noise, the audio file that contains noise was opened in Audacity and the Get Noise Profile function was selected. Then the noisy audio file was selected and the Noise Removal function was applied. We used the default value of Audacity in noise removal which is 24 dB noise reduction, 0 dB sensitivity, 150 Hz frequency smoothing and 0.15 s attack/decay time. Figure 1 represents an audio signal with noise while Fig. 2 shows the cleaned signal.

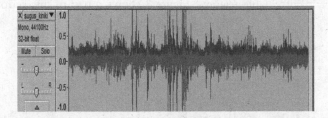

Fig. 1. Noisy audio signal

Fig. 2. Audio signal after noise removal

3.4 Data Segmentation

After noise removal, we segmented clean audio files manually by using Audacity (See footnote 4). The number of original audio files is 104, with 34 happy laughter files, 45 surprise laughter, and 25 irony laughter files. These audio files have different lengths between 1 s to 14.35 s. We examined different segment lengths, but most of extracted features of segments shorter than 200 ms had undefined value. For example, all mfcc values are undefined. By increasing the length of segments and watching the values of extracted features, we chose 240 ms as the length of segments. First each single audio file of these original files was segmented to equal length instances with the length of 240 ms, and then this segmentation process was repeated for the same original file with 50% overlap. Audacity (See footnote 1) can automatically cut audio files to equal length segments. No overlapping laughter, laughter produced by more than one person simultaneously, is considered. After segmentation the total number of episodes is 1,975, which the number of happy episodes is 466, the number of surprised episodes is 1,093, and the number of irony episodes is 417. The database was balanced by using Undersampling method because classifying algorithms work well when the dataset is balanced [16]. We removed some of the surprised samples randomly, so the number of surprised instances after balancing dataset is 502.

4 Feature Extraction

PRAAT[5] was used to extract features. A PRAAT script was written to create 3 tables of features, namely, acoustic_table, mfcc_table, and combination_able. Acoustic_table contains minimum, maximum, mean, and standard deviation of intensity, energy, power, and first three formants (F0, F1, F2). The mfcc_table contains the first thirteen MFCCs, and combination_table contains all features in the last two table; acoustic_table features and mfcc_table features. Figure 3 shows a part of this script.

```
Create Table with column names... acoustic_table 1385 pmin
Create Table with column names... combination_table 1385 pi

for i from 1 to 417
 select Sound ir'i'
 To Intensity... 100 0 yes
 select Sound ir'i'
 To Formant (burg)... 0 5 5500 0.025 50
endfor

for i from 1 to 502
 select Sound sur'i'
 To Intensity... 100 0 yes
 select Sound sur'i'
 To Formant (burg)... 0 5 5500 0.025 50
endfor
```

Fig. 3. PRAAT script for extracting features

In general, the Maximum, Minimum, Mean, and Standard deviation of intensity, the first three formants (F0, F1, and F2), energy, power, and the first thirteen Mel Frequency Cepstral Coefficient (MFCC) are extracted.

Intensity is the rate of sound per unit area, and it is one of the prosodic features that commonly used in emotion recognition [7]. The Formant shows the human vocal tract resonance and demonstrates the acoustic energy around a frequency in audio signal [7, 9].

The Mel Frequency Cepstral Coefficients are coefficients for making MFC. This feature is also used commonly for emotion detection. Although Kennedy and Ellis [5] presented using the first 6 MFCCs resulted a good performance in laughter recognition, in this work we extracted the first 13 MFCCs.

After extracting features and creating Tables, we save the tables as comma-separated files (CSV). These files will be used for emotion classification.

5 Classification

For classification, we used WEKA[6] (Waikato Environment for Knowledge Analysis), which is a free software developed at the University of Waikato, New Zealand.

---

[5] http://web.stanford.edu/dept/linguistics/corpora/material/PRAAT_workshop_manual_v421.pdf.

[6] http://www.cs.waikato.ac.nz/ml/weka.

We fed the three CSV files (acoustic_table.csv, mfcc_table.csv and combination_table.csv) into WEKA and run 4 machine Learning algorithms on these tables. These algorithms are MLP (Multilayer Perception), SMO (Sequential Minimal Optimization), Logistic Regression, and Radial Basis Function Network (RBFNetwork).

MLP is a feed forward neural network, which can map input data to a set of appropriate output data and is able to do tasks regarding to the training input data. It has multiple layers of nodes, which make a directed graph. It is able to do tasks regarding to the training input data. MLP is a modification of the standard linear perception [7].

SMO (Sequential Minimal Optimization) is a SVM (Support Vector Machines) implementation in WEKA. This algorithm use linear model for implementing non linear class boundaries [15]. SVM is a linear classifier that creates optimal hyperplane, which is an N-dimensional hyperplan for doing classifications [7]. It is a learning model that has algorithms for analyzing data and recognizing different patterns.

Logistic Regression is a special case of generalized linear model. This model measures the relationship between the categorical dependent variable and independent variables[7].

RBFNetwork (Redial Basis Function Network) is an artificial neural network with several distinctive features. This model has 3 layers and uses radial basis functions. The reaction of this network to a given input is determined by the activation functions in hidden layer [8].

6   Results and Analysis

We conducted several experiments to train classifiers with different sets of features. First we applied four machine learning algorithms, namely, MLP, SMO, Logistic, and RBFNetwork for all instances of balanced dataset, using 10-fold cross validation. The balanced dataset contains 466 happy laughter episodes, 502 surprised laughter episodes, and 417 irony laughter episodes, which the total number of episodes is 1,385. PRAAT used to extract features of these audio files. In total, 22 features are extracted and saved in three different tables by a PRAAT script. The acoustic_table contains 9 features, namely, Maximum, Minimum, Mean, and Standard deviation of intensity, the first three formants (F0, F1, and F2), energy, and power. The mfcc_table contains the first thirteen Mel Frequency Cepstral Coefficients (MFCC) features. The combination_table contains the features of acoustic_table and mfcc_table. On the other hand, the combination_table contains Maximum, Minimum, Mean, and Standard deviation of intensity, the first three formants (F0, F1, and F2), energy, power, and the first thirteen MFCCs. We saved these tables as comma separated value (CSV) files and fed them to WEKA. Table 1 shows the results of running classification algorithms on different set of features.

As can be shown in Table 1, the best results were achieved when MLP was used on all 22 features. In this case, the correctly classified instance (CCI) or accuracy rate is 86.13%, while the incorrectly classified instance (ICI) rate is 13.86%, and the Kappa

---

7 http://cs229.stanford.edu/notes/cs229-notes1.pdf.

Table 1. Results of experiments conducted on balanced dataset

Algorithm	CCI	ICI	Kappa
MLP (Prosodic)	67.29	32.70	0.50
MLP (MFCC)	84.33	15.66	0.76
MLP (Prosodic + MFCC)	86.13	13.86	0.79
SMO (Prosodic)	56.89	43.10	0.34
SMO (MFCC)	70.97	29.02	0.56
SMO (Prosodic + MFCC)	74.87	25.12	0.61
Logistic (Prosodic)	57.25	42.74	0.35
Logistic (MFCC)	72.63	27.36	0.58
Logistic (Prosodic + MFCC)	76.89	23.10	0.65
RBF Network (Prosodic)	57.54	42.45	0.36
RBF Network (MFCC)	72.56	27.43	0.58
RBF Network (Prosodic + MFCC)	68.15	31.84	0.52

statistics value is 0.79. The high value of Kappa shows that the dataset is good for building a model. Although the combination of MFCC features and other features led to the best accuracy rate for all algorithms, MFCC features are good enough for classifying the laughter episodes. As it is shown in Table 1, the accuracy rate and Kappa statistics value for MFCC features are close to the values of all features.

Table 1 shows that the MLP outperformed the other algorithms in detecting emotions in laughter. The Table 2 shows the Confusion Matrix of MLP algorithm for all 22 features. If we take a closer look at this Confusion Matrix, the MLP succeeded to classify correctly 356 out of 417 for irony, 449 out of 502 for surprised, and 388 out of 466 for happy. In total, 23 + 33 instances are incorrectly classified as irony, 19 + 45 instances are incorrectly classified as surprised, and 42 + 30 instances are incorrectly classified as happy.

Table 2. Confusion matrix of MLP algorithm

Confusion matrix			
	Irony	Surprise	Happy
Irony	**356**	19	42
Surprise	23	**449**	30
Happy	33	45	**388**

Miranda et al. [7] did emotion recognition in Filipino laughter by using audio files. In that study, the database contains 27 acted laughter episodes. Actors were acting 5 emotional states: natutuwa (happiness), kinikilig (giddiness), nasasabik (excitement), nahihiya (shyness), and mapanakit (shaudenfraude). The extracted features are the Minimum, Maximum, and Mean values for Pitch and Intensity, the first three formants (F0, F1, F2), and the first thirteen Mel-frequency Cepstral Coefficients (MFCC). Two algorithms, namely, MLP and SVM are used for emotion classification. The best results of that study are shown in Table 3.

Table 3. Results using prosodic features [7]

Algorithm	CCI	ICI
MLP	44.44	55.55
SVM	18.51	81.48

As Table 3 shows, the best accuracy rate in this study is 44.44, which is produced by running MLP on prosodic features. In comparison with this study, our study has a higher accuracy which is 86.13. The reason of big difference is that we gathered spontaneous laughter, and also our database contains more episodes. Moreover, removing the noise and unwanted signals from audio files induced a synergistic effect.

The second group of our experiments is related to onset classification. After segmenting each laughter file, we considered the first 25% of episodes of the laughter file as the onset of that file. For the balanced dataset, the number of happy onsets is 138, the number of surprised onsets is 149, and the number of irony onsets is 120. Onsets are fixed length episodes with 240 ms length. For classifying these new dataset, we used the same process for balanced dataset. The 22 features, namely, Maximum, Minimum, Mean, and Standard deviation of intensity, the first three formants (F0, F1, and F2), energy, power, and the first thirteen MFCCs are extracted and saved in three tables (acoustic_table, mfcc_table, combination_table). Four classifiers, MLP, SMO, Logistic, and RBFNetwork are used to classify onsets by using these tables. Table 4 shows the results of onset classification.

Our motivation of doing onset classification is to design a real-time emotion recognition system on laughter. We are studying and planning to build a real-time system that can automatically detect emotions in Iranian laughter; therefore, we did onset emotion classification.

Comparing Tables 1 and 4 shows that the results are very close. For example, in the best case in Table 1, the Correctly Classified Instances (CCI) is 86.13 with a Kappa value of 0.79. For the same case in Table 4, the CCI is 85.01 and a Kappa value of 0.7; hence, the results of our experiments shows that we can probably use onsets instead of

Table 4. Results of onset classification

Algorithm	CCI	ICI	Kappa
MLP (Prosodic)	69.28	30.71	0.53
MLP (MFCC)	81.08	18.91	0.71
MLP (Prosodic + MFCC)	85.01	14.98	0.7
SMO (Prosodic)	61.17	38.82	0.41
SMO (MFCC)	71.99	28.00	0.57
SMO (Prosodic + MFCC)	75.43	24.57	0.62
Logistic (Prosodic)	61.42	38.57	0.41
Logistic (MFCC)	77.39	22.60	0.65
Logistic (Prosodic + MFCC)	79.60	20.39	0.69
RBF networks (Prosodic)	64.86	35.13	0.47
RBF networks (MFCC)	79.11	20.88	0.68
RBF networks (Prosodic + MFCC)	72.23	27.76	0.58

the whole laughter file for emotion classification to decrease the response time of the real-time emotion recognition systems.

7 Conclusion and Future Works

Based on our results, audio signals are good enough for emotion recognition in laughter. Using the combination of MFCCs and prosodic features led to better results than using MFCC features only. MLP in comparison with other algorithms (SMO, Logistic, and RBFNetwork) has higher accuracy rate, which is 86.13 while the accuracy rate of SMO is 74.87, the accuracy rate of Logistic is 76.89, and the accuracy rate of RBFNetwork is 72.56. We also developed a model based on onsets of laughter files. The results show that it is possible to use onsets instead of the whole laughter files in real-time laughter emotion recognition systems to lessen the response time, which is a significant factor. For future research, it is possible to extend this study in different ways. One significant extension can be adding more emotions. The other extension can be adding visual data, which probably improve the performance of the model. Finally, it is possible to use this study results in designing real-time emotion recognition systems.

References

1. Eyben, F., Petridis, S., Schuller, B., Tzimiropoulos, G.: Audiovisual classification of vocal outbursts in human conversation using long-short-term memory networks. In: 2011 IEEE International Conference on Acoustics, Speech and Signal Processing (ICASSP), pp. 5844–5847. IEEE, Prague (2001)
2. Galvan, C., Manangan, D., Sanchez, M., Wong, J., Cu, J.: Audiovisual affect recognition in spontaneous filipino laughter. In: 2011 3rd International Conference on Knowledge and Systems Engineering (KSE), pp. 266–271. IEEE, Hanoi (2011)
3. Hamidi, M., Mansoorizade, M.: Emotion recognition from persian speech with neural network. Int. J. Artif. Intell. Appl. **5**, 107–112 (2012)
4. Iliev, A.I., Zhang, Y., Scordilis, M.S.: Spoken emotion classification using ToBI features and GMM. In: 14th International Workshop on 2007 and 6th EURASIP Conference Focused on Speech and Image Processing, Multimedia Communications and Services, Systems, Signals and Image Processing, pp. 495–498. IEEE, Maribor (2007)
5. Kennedy, L.S., Ellis, D. P.: Laughter detection in meetings. In: NIST ICASSP (2004)
6. Kudiri, K.M., Verma, G.K., Gohel, B.: Relative amplitude based features for emotion detection from speech. In: 2010 International Conference on Signal and Image Processing (ICSIP), pp. 301–304. IEEE, Chennai (2010)
7. Miranda, M., Alonzo, J. A., Campita, J., Lucila, S., Suarez, M.: Discovering emotions in Filipino laughter using audio features. In: 2010 3rd International Conference on Human-Centric Computing (HumanCom), pp. 1–6. IEEE, Cebu (2010)
8. Oyang, Y.-J., Hwang, W., Ou, Y.-Y., Chen, C.-Y., Chen, Z.-W.: Data classification with radial basis function networks based on a novel kernel density estimation algorithm. IEEE Trans. Neural Netw. **16**, 225–236 (2005). IEEE

9. Rodriguez, R.L., Ataollahi, F., Cabredo, R.: Modelling and detecting emotions of Filipino laughter using audio signal. In: 14th Philippine Computing Science Congress, pp. 168–174. Computing Society of the Philippines (2014)
10. Szameitat, D.P., Alter, K., Szameitat, A.J., Wildgruber, D., Sterr, A., Darwin, C.J.: Acoustic profiles of distinct emotional expressions in laughter. J. Acoust. Soc. Am. **126**, 354–366 (2009)
11. Tanaka, H., Campbell, N.: Acoustic features of four types of laughter in natural conversational speech. In: ICPHS XVII, Hong Kong, pp. 1958–1961 (2011)
12. Truong, K.P., Van Leeuwen, D.A.: Automatic detection of laughter. In: INTERSPEECH, pp. 485–488 (2005)
13. Urbain, J., Bevacqua, E., Dutoit, T., Moinet, A., Niewiadomski, R.: The AVLaughterCycle database. In: LREC 2010, Malta, pp. 2996–3001 (2010)
14. Urbain, J., Niewiadomski, R., Bevacqua, E., Dutoit, T., Moinet, A.: The AVLaughterCycle. Multimodal User Interfaces **4**, 47–58 (2010). Springer
15. Witten, I.H., Frank, E.: Data Mining – Practical Machine Learning Tools and Techniques, 3rd edn. Morgan Kaufmann, Burlington (2011)
16. Yap, B.W., Rani, K.A., Rahman, H.A.A., Fong, S., Khairudin, Z., Abdullah, N.N.: An application of oversampling, undersampling, bagging and boosting in handling imbalanced datasets. In: 1st International Conference on Advanced Data and Information Engineering (DaEng-2013), vol. 285, pp. 13–22. Springer, Singapore (2013)
17. Zare, S.: Home and away: blogging emotions in a Persian virtual Dowreh: a thesis presented in fulfilment of the requirements for the degree of Doctor of Philosophy in Linguistics and Second Language Teaching at Massey University. Massey University, Palmerston North (2011)

Modeling Work Stress Using Heart Rate and Stress Coping Profiles

Juan Lorenzo Hagad[✉], Koichi Moriyama, Kenichi Fukui,
and Masayuki Numao

Department of Architecture for Intelligence,
8-1 Mihogaoka, Ibaraki, Osaka 567-0047, Japan
{hagad,koichi,fukui,numao}@ai.sanken.osaka-u.ac.jp

Abstract. Automated mental health analysis of stress could lead towards diagnosis tools that can be used in environments such as clinics, schools and corporations. However, attempts at building general models are often limited by the subjectivity of physiological stress responses. This work aims to discover the effects of combining data from physiological signals and psychological context from work activities when building a machine-learned model of mental stress. A software application was built to guide subjects through a monitoring process which allowed pre and post-assessment of psychological context through various stress-related annotation modules including the Cohen Stress Scale and the COPE inventory. Meanwhile, wearable sensors tracked physiological data in the form of heart beats. Tests were performed on this data by building supervised and unsupervised machine-learned models. Results show a general increase in classification performance when psychological context data is integrated into the models. Furthermore, models present similar performance using either questionnaire answers or coping profile scores.

Keywords: Mental stress · Stress recognition · Decision support systems · Physiological signals · Psychological profiles · Stress coping

1 Introduction

Long-term exposure to stressful environments has been shown to be a major risk factor in the development of major depressive disorder (MDD) [10], a disorder that affects an estimated 350 million people across the world [11]. The two most dominant locations where working adults are exposed to stress are the home and the workplace [18]. In the case of the workplace, it has been found that a number of factors such as workload, work hours, job security, and corporate structure can affect the depressive tendencies of employees. This tendency and the typically large number of individuals present in work environments makes it difficult to impose traditional forms of patient monitoring. In response to this and various other limitations, we have witnessed a recent surge in the development of ambient intelligences for the purpose of mental health monitoring [1].

© Springer International Publishing Switzerland 2016
M. Baldoni et al. (Eds.): IWEC 2014/IWEC 2015/CMNA 2015, LNAI 9935, pp. 108–118, 2016.
DOI: 10.1007/978-3-319-46218-9_9

This work focuses on automated monitoring of stress signals in work environments. Such systems fall under a class of systems called decision support systems (DSS), a branch of works under ambient intelligence. DSS are frequently used to assist healthcare professionals with data analysis and decision-making tasks. As noted by a survey by [1], a number of systems have been used to provide medical diagnosis suggestions based on patient data. A growing number of these works leverage technologies such as wearable sensors [16,17,19] and signal processing algorithms [5,8] to extract psychological states from physiological signals. These, coupled with machine learning techniques allows investigators to model the intangible signs related to stress.

However, a major hurdle towards the creation of reliable models is the subjectivity of each individual's physiological responses to stressors. It has been shown that persons may vary in terms of how they deal with emotional stressors [4] and that this could impact how they respond to stressful situations. We posit that by parameterizing this subjective responsiveness and including it in the model, we can augment the purely physiological models.

To test the above-mentioned hypothesis, this work investigates machine-learned models of mental stress using a combination of data from physiological signals and from psychological context in work activities. Specifically, we build models utilizing data from heart rate and psychological coping profiles. By building a monitoring and annotation system, and using research-grade wearable physiological sensors, we observe subjects as they perform work-related activities at a personal computer. Additionally, we measure their stress coping habits using standardized profiling tools used in psychology. Finally, we use machine learning algorithms to model the relationships between these features while using self-reported stress annotations as ground truth.

2 Related Works

2.1 Machine Modeling Stress

Stress analysis has garnered increased attention in recent years with the bulk of the work focusing on physiological signals such as galvanic skin response (GSR) [16,17,19], heart rate (HR) [14–17,19], facial expressions [5] and vocal tone [8]. In this work, we focus primarily on HR since it is autonomic, easy to analyze, and more immediate than GSR. In addition, [15] has shown that some HR features may even reflect long-term effects stress. Values extrapolated from HR signals have often been used as components in creating various general and user-specific models of stress.

[16] makes a comparison between general and personalized models of stress. In their study, data was acquired from subjects performing stressful acts such as public speaking, mental arithmetic, and doing a cold pressor test. GSR, HRV and skin temperature sensors were used to measure physiological stress responses. Support Vector Machines (SVM) were used for classification and performance was evaluated using leave-one-subject-out cross validation. From the results, it

was found that personalized models performed significantly better than standard generic ones. Theses results supported their initial hypothesis that adding personalized features into model improves discrimination ability. However, it should be noted that the personalized approach featured in the aforementioned work involved modifying the SVMS to enable modeling statistical differences between subjects. Instead of calculating these variances and requiring modifications to existing machine-learning techniques, the current work attempts to use psychology-based profiling tools as a form of personalized features utilizing psychology-domain knowledge.

Another work [17] presented a method for increasing the flexibility of HRV-GSR stress models by adding contextual information in the form of user activity. Using accelerometer data, activities such as sitting, standing, and walking were detected. SVMs were then applied for the classification task. Based on their results, it was found that the addition of activity context led to an increase in the accuracy of the models. However, they also noted that physiological signals and the resulting models remained heavily user-dependent, limiting the reliability of large general models. Similar to this approach, the goal of the current work is to improve model flexibility by introducing contextual information. However, here we introduce psychological context through psychological stress tests and other self-annotations.

2.2 Gathering Stress Data

In past works on stress analysis it was common practice to use of artificial scenarios to elicit the desired stress responses. While these may be able to evoke clear stress responses, many of these responses may not necessarily mirror the subtle responses seen in authentic scenarios. Studies have shown the merits of using naturalistic datasets in building affective models [13], and it may be time that we move towards using more authentic datasets. Building such datasets involves gathering data from subjects involved in actual, or at the very least close to real-world scenarios.

In a an effort to study the use of ECG as an indicator of real-life stress conditions, [14] studied ECG data from students on two different occasions: while undergoing a university examination and after holidays. Through this work, they were able to study the correlations between non-linear HRV features and stress. Using a variety of non-linear analysis measurements on the data, they built a Linear Discriminant Analysis (LDA) classifier. Analysis showed a significant reduction in HRV features during the stress sessions, and the generated LDA was able to perform with a 90% accuracy. Their work shows that HRV can be a reliable indicator of stress even in naturalistic scenarios. However, in [14] the discrimination task involved two very different experiences and environments (exams vs. holiday) and is therefore expected to be more unambiguous.

In a similar yet less constrained study, [15] showed that stress may show long-term effects on some HRV features. Subjects answered a Stress Response Inventory to measure their emotional, somatic, cognitive and behavioural responses to stress. Using K-means clustering analysis, subjects were divided into low and high stress groups. In the current work, we are interested in detecting short-term stress in a fixed working environment involving a broader spectrum of scenarios while testing both supervised and cluster-based approaches.

2.3 Coping Strategies and Stress

A study by [4] investigated psychological stress in 148 university students from Malaysia. They found that psychological stress did not seem to be affected by personality. Instead, high levels of psychological stress were linked to certain types of coping strategies namely, *avoidant* and *socially supported* coping. These findings were consistent with previous studies which noted that certain stress coping responses such as venting may be maladaptive and unable to resolve stress. The underlying reason behind this may be that these responses tend to foster avoidant reactions. On the other hand, coping strategies such as planning, acceptance, reinterpretation and growth are more likely to lead to addressing the source of the issues, resulting in reduced levels of psychological distress. By including these factors into our machine-learned model, we hope to be able to reduce the ambiguity of stress features relative to each subject.

3 Methodology

In this work, we design and build an automatic work stress monitoring and assessment system that tracks physiological signals from heart rate and psychological coping profiles in order to build a flexible model of stress.

3.1 Monitoring Software

A monitoring and annotation tool was built and used to track subjects' personal profiles and work activities. The monitoring software was based on *Sidekick* [9], a tool designed for tracking and analysing student learning behaviours. This scheme was chosen because it featured a self-regulated workflow that allowed subjects to perform natural tasks with limited input from the experimenter. Meanwhile, the system could record data silently in the background. Modifications and additions were made to switch the focus towards parameters related to mental stress. These changes include additional psychological profiles, video recording, and a different set of annotation labels. For this initial work, volunteers from among the students of Osaka University were used as research subjects.

3.2 Procedures

As mentioned in the preceding section, subjects are guided through the experimental procedure by the system. This allows experimentation and data gathering with minimal influence from the experimenter. The advantage of such an approach is two-fold. First, it minimizes the interaction and therefore the biases that can be relayed from experimenter to subject. And second, it makes it easier to extend the process beyond the experimental environment, allowing for potential large-scale expansion. The following modules are currently supported: profile creation, work activity planning, data tracking and observation, and lastly self-reported annotation.

Profile Creation. Upon first joining the experiment, subjects are instructed to install the monitoring software on their work PCs and to create a personal account. As is common with such studies, they must first agree to a confidentially agreement. They are then presented with a set of psychology questionnaires that will consist their personal profile.

The first questionnaire is the COPE Inventory [3], a tool developed to assess coping responses in response to stressful situations. It determines a person's inclination towards exhibiting responses that are expected to be either functional or dysfunctional. Those with dysfunctional coping mechanisms are expected to be more prone to the negative effects of stress.

Another questionnaire used is the Toronto Alexythimia Scale (TAS-20) [2], a tool designed to measure and diagnose Alexythimia. People with this condition generally have difficulty identifying their own emotions and instead minimize emotional experiences. Subjects with high enough scores may be excluded from the experiments. In general, the scores may also be used to measure subjective sensitivity to stressors and emotions. For the current work, these questionnaires were designed to only be filled out once for the duration of the study. The tasks that follow are iterated throughout multiple sessions.

Work Activity. At the beginning of each data gathering session, subjects create a work activity plan. The work plan consisted of a general description of the current task as well as a list of goals which must be achieved by the end of the session. For this experiment, each activity was limited to approximately 1 h. This was done to regulate the time and effort it took to review and annotate the sessions afterwards. Subjects are also asked to answer a few questions about their current stress state using the short version of Cohen's Stress Scale, as well as provide details about their regard towards the task such as the perceived importance and effort required to complete the task. This task also doubled as a habitation period where participants could get used to the wearable sensors and experimental setup.

Annotation. Self-reported stress annotations are made immediately after the hour-long work session. Using webcam and desktop recordings as reference, subjects are able to review and select time segments in the recorded video where they performed certain work tasks. For each task, they also labelled the level of stress they felt, the primary stressor, and the importance of the tasks towards achieving the goal. A finite list of work task categories and stressors are provided by the UI, and a 4-point Likert-scale is used for the stress and importance ratings (1 = Very low, 4 = Very high).

3.3 Physiological Signals

Participant heart rates were measured using the Imec wearable ECG sensor, a wireless, wearable device that continuously measures user heart rate. Data from the sensor was aligned to timestamp labels in the monitoring software to build the feature vectors. As noted in [14], features of heart rate are influenced by various environmental factors such as body position, activity level, verbalization and breathing. In order to minimize the effect of these factors, environmental setup and time-of-day conditions were kept similar throughout all sessions. Furthermore, a 15 min adaptation period was allotted at the beginning of each session to allow subjects to adjust to the experimental conditions.

Of the many values extracted from HR, the most commonly linked to stress is *heart rate variability* (HRV). HRV is a feature that is used by most related literature, and even medical research [14] has linked HRV to the activity of the autonomic nervous system in response to stress. So, for each session the following HRV metrics were calculated: Average of NN intervals (AVNN), Standard deviation of NN intervals (SDNN), root-mean-squared differences between adjacent NN intervals (rMSSD), percentage of differences between adjacent NN intervals greater than 50 ms (pNN50), spectral power measures of NN intervals of varying frequencies (ULF, VLF, LF, HF) and the ratio of low to high frequency power (LF/HF).

HRV analysis was performed over the HR recordings at the task level. RR interval time series was extracted using the PhysioNet library's [7] QRS detector (WQRS). The WQRS detector uses a length transform algorithm to detect nonlinearly scaled ECG curve length features. Based on previous literature [14], this algorithm is capable of attaining a NN/RR ratio of over 90%, indicating a high level of data reliability for "normal" heart beats. No additional cleaning was performed on the raw ECG data.

3.4 Machine Learners

The following supervised and unsupervised machine learning techniques were used to build the tested stress models: Support Vector Machines (SVM), Multilayer Perceptrons (MLP), and K-means Clustering. SVMs were selected due to their popular use in related works [16,17,19]. They also have the advantage of being able to employ kernels to fit different types of data and classification problems. MLPs are a direct competitor to SVMS and are also notably used in related works [6,12]. Lastly, K-means clustering was included in order to benchmark and compare the performance of unsupervised techniques for stress classification. In this work, a majority-labeling scheme was used to compare clustering performance with classification accuracy.

4   Experiments and Results

Data was gathered from 4 healthy male subjects, aged 20 to 32. Each subject used the monitoring application to perform work activities for about a 1 h duration each. They then made self-reported annotations for the entire session. None of the subjects were excluded from the experiment based on their Alexythimia scores. A total of 18 work sessions were recorded, which were further divided into 150 individual task segments. Of these task segments, only 146 had usable HRV data and were used to build the models. The length of each task segment ranges from 5 to 30 min, depending on the annotation of the subject. HRV statistics were extracted for each task segment.

4.1 Data Preparation and Evaluation

To test the effect of coping profiles, a number of feature vectors were built based on combinations of the HRV metrics discussed in Sect. 3.3, the coping profile data discussed in Sect. 3.2, and the task segment annotation data. Three variations of feature organization were tested. The base feature vector, *hrv*, contains only the HRV data. The second set, *with_answers*, combines the base features with the questionnaire answers from the 60-item COPE inventory. The third set, *with_scores*, similarly contains the base features but combines it with the psychological coping profile scores for each of the 15 coping methods as measured by the COPE inventory. These three sets of data were used to train the models discussed in 3.4. The resulting models were then evaluated using 10-fold cross validation and their classification performance was compared using paired t-tests. The performance results are presented in the following Tables 1 and 2:

Table 1. SVM classification results

a. Multiclass results				b. Binary results		
Data	Accuracy	F-measure		Data	Accuracy	F-measure
hrv	39.3103	0.225		hrv	73.6842	0.625
with_answer	42.069	0.416		with_answer	84.2105	0.846
with_score	42.069	0.416		with_score	78.9474	0.789

Table 2. MLP classification results

a. Multiclass results				b. Binary results		
Data	Accuracy	F-measure		Data	Accuracy	F-measure
hrv	48.9655	0.482		hrv	86.8421	0.87
with_answer	51.0345	0.503		with_answer	89.4737	0.895
with_score	52.4138	0.516		with_score	86.8421	0.87

For the multiclass models, the raw 4-point stress labels (Very low to Very high) were used as ground truth. Based on the results, all the models performed better than random. We observe the weakest performance from the HRV-only

Table 3. Clustering results

Data	Multiclass accuracy	Binary accuracy
hrv	47.5862	71.0526
with_answer	45.5172	78.9474
with_score	45.5172	76.3158

SVM model at 39.31% accuracy and a F-measure of 0.255. The low F-measure indicates that performance may not have been equal across all classes. This can be attributed to an imbalance in samples, with majority of data samples given a stress rating of 2. Still, using the same dataset the MLP was able to perform better at 48.97% accuracy and 0.482 F-measure.

Looking at the performance of the profile-inclusive models, we observed an increase in performance across all of the classifiers. 4-class SVM performance increased from 39.31% to as much as 42.07% ($p < 0.1$), while MLP performance increased from 48.97% to 52.41% ($p < 0.05$). Binary classifier performance shows similar improvements at 73.68% to 84.21% ($p < 0.01$) for SVMs, and 86.84% to 89.47% ($p < 0.05$) for MLPs. In short, the hybrid models consistently outperformed the purely physiological models. Furthermore, among the supervised models, MLPs proved to be more suitable for the task than SVMs.

We were also interested in seeing whether unsupervised models are also able to disambiguate between different stress levels. Based on the results in Table 3, all K-means models performed better than random for both the multiclass (>45%) and binary class models (>71%). In fact, the multiclass clustering models performed better than the SVM classifiers across all datasets. Next, when comparing multiclass cluster-based models we see that the model trained using only HRV data outperformed those that included profile data, contradicting the pattern observed from the supervised models. On the other hand, the binary models showed a similar pattern to the classifier models where the profile-incusive models outperformed the base model. Overall, the cluster-based models performed on par with or better than the worst classifier models.

5   Discussion

This paper presented a method for creating stress models from authentic work-related activities, and compared the performance of purely physiological and profile-inclusive models. Data was gathered through a monitoring software that was installed in participants' work PCs. These were used to gather their psychological profiles with the aid of the COPE inventory and TAS-20. During work activities, physiological data was monitored through the Imec wearable ECG sensor. The current dataset was gathered from the daily work activities and self-reported annotations of students from Osaka University. The initial hypothesis was that stress models that include psychological profiles would lead to better performance. To test this hypothesis, a combination of extracted HRV features and psychological profiles from COPE were used to train a number of machine learned models. These models were evaluated through cross-validation, and their performance was compared.

Based on the supervised classifier results, we saw that including psychological profiles into the data vectors generally led to a significant increase in performance ($\alpha < 0.05$). We saw the largest gains in the binary SVM models where performance increased from 73.68% to 84.21% ($p < 0.01$) when the raw profile answers were included. This could mean that coping profiles could be used as contextual information for improving existing stress classifiers. We also noted that MLPs performed better than SVMs, gaining an additional 9% for the multiclass models, and up to 13% for the binary models. This could be because either the MLP is better able to deal with the high-dimensional data, or the SVM parameters needed further optimization (Grid Search is not exhaustive). In any case, the results show promise for future investigations of other forms of psychological profile.

The clustering results were less promising, with the purely physiological HRV cluster-based model performing better ($+ 2\%$, $p > 0.1$) than the profile-inclusive models for the multiclass problem. This could be due to a number of reasons, however it could be that additional complexity introduced by the additional data resulted in classes that were not easily separable. Since we only used the most basic form of K-means without any kernels, it is possible that the increased dimensions, leading to insignificant performance gains. Therefore, it may be necessary to investigate the usefulness of certain features for the clustering problem. On the other hand, binary clustering for the profile-inclusive models performed better ($+ 7\%$) than the base model. Whichever the case, the clustering results were comparable to some of the supervised models, showing that the features used hold good potential for stress modeling.

In future works, we plan to continue adding more samples to the dataset and to make a comparison of user-specific and general models. Furthermore, we plan to test the relative importance of our data features in order to discover insights regarding the role of coping profiles in regulating stress. We may also investigate other modalities such as skin conductance, video, and activity information. Lastly, we plan to apply hierarchical machine learning algorithms to build models that take into account the interactions between different physiological modalities and contextual information.

References

1. Acampora, G., Cook, D., Rashidi, P., Vasilakos, A.: A survey on ambient intelligence in healthcare. Proc. IEEE **101**(12), 2470–2494 (2013)
2. Bagby, R.M., Parker, J.D., Taylor, G.J.: The twenty-item toronto alexithymia scale—I. Item selection and cross-validation of the factor structure. J. Psychosom. Res. **38**(1), 23–32 (1994)

3. Carver, C.S., Scheier, M.F., Weintraub, J.K.: Assessing coping strategies: a theoretically based approach. J. Pers. Soc. Psychol. **56**(2), 267–283 (1989)
4. Chai, M.S., Low, C.S.: Personality, coping and stress among university students. Am. J. Appl. Psychol. **4**(3–1), 33–38 (2015)
5. Dinges, D., Rider, R., Dorrian, J., McGlinchey, E.L., Rogers, N.L., Cizman, Z., Goldenstein, S., Vogler, C., Venkataraman, S.: Optical computer recognition of facial expressions associated with stress induced by performance demands. Aviat Space Environ. Med. **76**, B172–B182 (2005)
6. Gaggioli, A., Pioggia, G., Tartarisco, G., Baldus, G., Ferro, M., Cipresso, P., Serino, S., Popleteev, A., Gabrielli, S., Maimone, R., Riva, G.: A system for automatic detection of momentary stress in naturalistic settings. In: Cybertherapy, Brussels, August 2012
7. Goldberger, A.L., Amaral, L.A.N., Glass, L., Hausdorff, J.M., Ivanov, P.C., Mark, R.G., Mietus, J.E., Moody, G.B., Peng, C.K., Stanley, H.E.: PhysioBank, physiotoolkit, and physionet: components of a new research resource for complex physiologic signals. Circulation **101**(23), e215–e220 (2000)
8. Hernandez, J., Morris, R.R., Picard, R.W.: Call center stress recognition with person-specific models. In: D'Mello, S., Graesser, A., Schuller, B., Martin, J.-C. (eds.) ACII 2011. LNCS, vol. 6974, pp. 125–134. Springer, Heidelberg (2011). doi:10.1007/978-3-642-24600-5_16
9. Inventado, P.S., Legaspi, R., Moriyama, K., Fukui, K.I., Numao, M.: Sidekick: a tool for helping students manage behavior in self-initiated learning scenarios. Int. J. Distance Educ. Technol. (IJDET) **12**(4), 32–54 (2014)
10. Magalhaes, A.C., Holmes, K.D., Dale, L.B., Comps-Agrar, L., Lee, D., Yadav, P.N., Drysdale, L., Poulter, M.O., Roth, B.L., Pin, J.P., Anisman, H., Ferguson, S.S.G.: CRF receptor 1 regulates anxiety behavior via sensitization of 5-HT2 receptor signaling. Nature Neurosci. **13**(5), 622–629 (2010)
11. Marcus, M., Yasamy, M., van Ommeren, M., Chisholm, D.: Depression: a global public health concern. World Health Organization, Technical report (2012)
12. Martinez, H., Bengio, Y., Yannakakis, G.: Learning deep physiological models of affect. IEEE Comput. Intell. Mag. **8**(2), 20–33 (2013)
13. McDuff, D., el Kaliouby, R., Senechal, T., Amr, M., Cohn, J.F., Picard, R.: Affectiva-mit facial expression dataset (am-fed): naturalistic and spontaneous facial expressions collected "in-the-wild". In: Proceedings of the 2013 IEEE Conference on Computer Vision and Pattern Recognition Workshops, CVPRW 2013, pp. 881–888. IEEE Computer Society, Washington, DC (2013)
14. Melillo, P., Bracale, M., Pecchia, L.: Nonlinear heart rate variability features for real-life stress detection. Case study: students under stress due to university examination. BioMed. Eng. Online **10**(1), 1 (2011)
15. Salahuddin, L., Jeong, M.G., Kim, D., Lim, S.K., Won, K., Woo, J.M.: Dependence of heart rate variability on stress factors of stress response inventory. In: 2007 9th International Conference on e-Health Networking, Application and Services, pp. 236–239, June 2007
16. Shi, Y., Nguyen, M.H., Blitz, P., French, B., Fisk, S., De la Torre, F., Smailagic, A., Siewiorek, D.P., alAbsi, M., Ertin, E., et al.: Personalized stress detection from physiological measurements. In: International Symposium on Quality of Life Technology, pp. 28–29 (2010)

17. Sun, F.-T., Kuo, C., Cheng, H.-T., Buthpitiya, S., Collins, P., Griss, M.: Activity-aware mental stress detection using physiological sensors. In: Gris, M., Yang, G. (eds.) MobiCASE 2010. LNICSSITE, vol. 76, pp. 211–230. Springer, Heidelberg (2012). doi:10.1007/978-3-642-29336-8_12
18. Tennant, C.: Work-related stress and depressive disorders. J. Psychosom. Res. **51**(5), 697–704 (2001)
19. Zhai, J., Barreto, A.: Stress detection in computer users based on digital signal processing of noninvasive physiological variables. In: 28th Annual International Conference of the IEEE Engineering in Medicine and Biology Society, EMBS 2006, pp. 1355–1358, August 2006

Wizard-of-Oz Support Using a Portable Dialogue Corpus

Masashi Inoue[✉] and Hiroshi Ueno

Yamagata University, 3-16, 4 Jyonan, Yonezawa, Yamagata, Japan
masash.inoue@gmail.com, m.inoue@acm.org

Abstract. This paper presents a Wizard of Oz (WOZ) data collection method that uses dialogue examples (or utterances) from one domain for use in a target domain. Providing a text-based dialogue system with empathy requires providing the system with a wide range of expressions, with expressions corresponding best to users. However, there are few dialogue examples available and the variation of utterances is limited. We have to collect wider range of example utterances. A typical method to collect dialogue data is the WOZ method. The use of WOZ for dialogue data collection often requires substantial cognitive load for participating wizards. To alleviate this problem, an utterance suggestion mechanism using a portable corpus is introduced. We investigated differences in the response times of a wizard when utterance suggestions from a portable corpus are offered. We also evaluated the ratio of utterance suggestions selected versus free utterances. The experimental results indicate that using a portable dialogue corpus to suggest utterances for wizards has a potential to be helpful in data collection.

1   Introduction

Providing a text-based dialogue system with empathy requires a wide range of expressions corresponding best to users. However, in most dialogue scenarios or domains, there are currently few dialogue corpora for obtaining utterance variations in constructing example-based dialogue models. Dialogue samples (or utterances) must be collected from either human-to-human or human-to-machine interactions. The Wizard-of-Oz (WOZ) method is often used for such data collection in human-to-machine situation [1]. In this method, a participant, or a wizard, simulates the behaviour of the dialogue system being developed and interacts with the users through utterances. A problem with the use of this method is that the cognitive load of a wizard is often considerably high, when composing and typing utterances in text-based dialogue systems. In addition, it is required to collect diverse interactions to create the dialogue corpus suitable for training data of statistical dialogue systems. If a wizard is not the system designer, it might be difficult to predict what dialogue would benefit a future system. As a result, wizards may find it difficult to generate appropriate utterances. On the wizards' cognitive load problem, user interfaces for wizards have been improved to mitigate the cognitive load [8]. In addition to the interface,

M. Baldoni et al. (Eds.): IWEC 2014/IWEC 2015/CMNA 2015, LNAI 9935, pp. 119–128, 2016.
DOI: 10.1007/978-3-319-46218-9_10

we further consider dialogue content to overcome the cognitive load problem by preparing utterance suggestions, or candidates. By selecting and clicking one of the candidates, wizards can bypass the process of generating utterances and preparing textual output. The problem is then how to prepare the collected utterance candidates. The size of utterance candidates may still significantly large to be created manually and dialogue samples must been collected automatically.

To create an utterance candidate set automatically, in this paper, we propose a method for importing a corpus that has been developed in a domain other than the current target domain. The imported corpus after modification is called a portable corpus. We experimentally compared the effectiveness of using the portable corpus as the source of utterance candidates during the WOZ data collection. We found that role-play became easier for wizards with utterances suggested from the portable corpus.

2   Corpus Insufficiency

2.1   Corpus Porting

The scarcity of dialogue corpora has been an issue in the field of dialogue understanding in which systems have been developed by using large-scale training data. There have been several attempts to mitigate corpus insufficiency. For example, domain and language portability were sought by using machine translation and concept mapping [5]. In contrast to the dialogue understanding task, in which it is important to handle what is said, in the dialogue generation task, in which it is important how to say something, the portability needs to be carried out by preserving expressions rather than by skimming the statistical essence of the original corpora [4]. By focusing on the exact phrases used in one domain, researchers have investigated the utility of cue phrases in one domain for classifying the dialogue acts in another domain [9].

2.2   Alternative Dialogue Corpus

Considering the scarcity of recorded dialogue data, other types of language resources have been investigated for alternative dialogue corpora. For example, twitter conversation has been considered as the corpus. In reality, there are few direct interactions between tweets. Therefore, a pseudo conversation has been investigated. Two tweets that are similar in content are considered a pseudo conversation [2]. Another approach is the use of gamification. Crowdsourcing has been combined with gamification to obtain dialogue data for non task-oriented dialogue [3]. The game used was the dialogue skill test in which participants got higher score if they select typical utterances than unusual ones. These methods were used for generic chitchat. In this study, we investigate another approach that incorporates actual dialogue samples in different domains for example-based utterance generation for specific dialogue tasks.

3   Dialogue Corpus

3.1   Target Corpus

We consider three kinds of corpora: source corpus, target corpus, and portable corpus. First, we describe the target corpus that consists of dialogue samples relevant to the dialogue systems being developed. Our target corpus is the collection of dialogues for the LAST MINUTE task [7]. In this task, users were asked to pack travel items into a suitcase during summer break. The travel was planned without prior appointment, and a taxi had been called to pick the users up in approximately a half hour. Through the interaction with a dialogue system, the users had to complete packing their items in a limited time. The items were grouped in several categories. There are multimodal dialogues for the task collected by using the WOZ method. The original corpus consists of three dialogues in German, and we translated one dialogue into Japanese. We use the translated dialogue as an example from the target corpus. Most of the utterances in the example are to progress the task such as "Next category". Part of the dialogue that is translated into English is shown in Table 5.

3.2   Source Corpus

We use the NICT Kyoto tour dialogue corpus [6] as the source corpus. This corpus contains the dialogues exchanged between simulated travellers and a professional tour guide for determining a one-day sightseeing plan in the city of Kyoto. They talked about where to visit and which means of transportation should be used. The corpus is a large-scale dataset and consists of 100 dialogues each of which contains 300–700 utterances. A total of 42,673 utterances were available and used in our experiment. All participants were native speakers of Japanese. An example dialogue from this source corpus is shown in Table 6.

3.3   Portable Corpus

The portable dialogue corpus is derived from a source dialogue corpus by removing domain-dependent or task-dependent expressions from the utterances. The process of converting a source corpus into a target corpus is called porting. Given an utterance $\mathbf{u} = \{w_1, w_2, \ldots, w_m \ldots, w_M\}$ where w_m represents a word or morpheme in the utterance, and assuming that each word has its domain dependency score s_m, we remove all the utterances that contain w_m with $s_m \geq t$ where t denotes a threshold value. In the following experiment, we set $s_m = 1$ when w_m is either a proper noun or a numeral; otherwise, $s_m = 0$. The threshold value t was set to 0. For example, assume that the following three utterances are in the source corpus: (1) 'Do you want to go to Tenryuji temple?', (2) 'Yes, how long does it take?', (3) 'It takes about 30 minutes.' The first utterance contains the proper noun w_7 'Tenryuji' with $s_7 = 1$ and deleted. Similarly, the third utterance includes a number w_4 '30' with $s_4 = 1$ and removed. Then, the remaining second utterance is stored in the portable corpus. As the result of processing the entire target corpus, we obtained 5, 868 utterances for the portable corpus. Although the LAST MINUTE task focuses on the items for travelling while the NICT Kyoto tour dialogue task focuses on the schedule, there are some expressions that are commonly used in both settings. Example utterances in the portable corpus are shown in Table 7. Note that the utterances in portable corpora are sampled and used independently; they do not appear in the original order when used in the experiment.

3.4   Difference Between the Corpora

The difference between source and target corpora can be characterized in the following two aspects. The first aspect is the expected use of the corpora. The source corpus was created for the development of a statistical dialogue system, and a large number of dialogues of human-to-human communication in a face-to-face setting were collected. Different tourists have different preferences, and their destinations may vary. The target corpus was created to understand the user behaviour when interacting with dialogue systems. The task is designed for collecting emotionally elicited multimodal reactions by users under stress. The dialogues proceed according to a fixed procedure toward the completion of the task. Therefore, it is relatively easier to collect dialogue samples of similar content from diverse participants than a free-structured dialogue. This allows the designers to explore the nature of multimodal emotional reactions of different users.

The second aspect is the type of interaction. Both source and target corpora are created from task-oriented dialogue records, and are related to travel situations. The dialogue task in the source corpus involved planning a schedule through human-to-human communication in a face-to-face setting. On the other hand, the dialogue task with the system in the target corpus is concise and operational. Therefore, although the tasks are related to the travel preparations in both source and target corpora, the characteristic of utterances are not similar except the ones used as portable corpora.

4   WOZ System

4.1   System Overview

The WOZ dialogue system consists of user input window, wizard input window, utterance candidate window, and task progress assist window. The task progress assist window is similar to the utterance candidate window but contains pre-defined utterance candidates for making topic shift toward the task goal. Users and wizards interact through user input text and wizard input text. The current dialogue logs are shown to both wizards and users. Utterance candidates and progress assist list are shown to wizards only. Progress assist list consists of utterances aligned in line with the progress of LAST MINUTE packing task. Wizards can select utterances from the list at any point to move the dialogue to the next stages.

4.2 Utterance Candidates

To reduce the load for wizards in the WOZ data collection process, wizards can select utterances from the list rather than composing utterances by themselves. The utterance candidates are generated by using a ranking model that is statistically trained by using dialogue samples. For the rank-learning algorithm to find relevant responses from the samples, the ListNet algorithm was used [10]. Five highest ranked utterances were presented to wizards as the response candidates. The candidates were taken from the portable corpus, not from the target corpus. If the data collection process continues, we can add utterances from the collected target dialogues to enrich sample utterances.

5 Experiment

5.1 Experimental Conditions

We conducted a WOZ task in the LAST MINUTE scenario described in Sect. 3.1 for the purpose of evaluation, measuring the degree of cognitive load. The progress of the dialogue task was supported by the system. The subjects or wizards were ten students majoring in computer science, most with limited travel experience. Note that the wizards, not the users of the system, were the subjects of the experiments. The person playing the role of a user of the dialogue system was fixed and proceeded with the dialogue in the same manner as in the example dialogue in the corpus, independently of the participating wizards. Therefore, even though the user knew that the counterpart was wizards and not automatic dialogue system, it did not influence the interaction. We provided information on the dialogue, and asked the wizards to utter freely with the person playing the role of the user. When the user uttered, the system selected five utterance candidates for the wizards from the portable corpus based on the trained language model. The subject can select a relevant utterance as the system utterance from the five candidates shown. If none were relevant, the wizard composed a system utterance. The dialogues ended when time ran out, or when the packing task was completed. The number of candidate utterances was determined based on usability, which depended on the window size.

We estimate the degree of a wizard's load reduction in terms of response time and the ratio of utterances taken from the candidates. The response time was the sum of the user time (a subject was selecting or editing responses) and the system time (the WOZ system was retrieving utterance candidates). We had an assumption that the content of the utterances are not influenced by the use of candidates.

5.2 First Experiment

In the first experiment, the user was the system designer, and the wizard was a volunteer student. The LAST MINUTE task was performed using a text-based dialogue interface. In the system, the wizard had three options to input utterances:

Table 1. Median response time measured from the end of previous utterance.

Candidate unused	80.24 s
Candidate used	41.72 s

Table 2. Ratio of candidate usage at each dialogue phase (%).

Introduction	14.29
Packing	6.45
Closing	25.00

editing text freely, selecting utterances from the candidates and modifying them if needed, and selecting task progression utterances to move to the next topic. The user followed as similar path as that of the example dialogue from the target corpus. All participants were native speakers of Japanese and used Japanese as their language of communication. The response time result is summarized in Table 1 and the candidate usage result is summarized in Table 2. From Table 1, it can be concluded that the utterances using candidates were generated quicker than the manually edited utterances. Moreover, utterance candidates were used more often during the beginning and ending phrases of the dialogue as shown in Table 2. In those phases, there were greetings and informational utterances about users themselves. The wizard used candidate utterances more in those introduction and closing stages to diversify the interaction because the users could not develop the topic if the system responded with simple back-channelling. During the packing task in the middle of the dialogue, if the system responded with simple back-channelling, the user did not have to respond but could proceed with the task. This characteristic led to a lower rate of candidate usage.

5.3 Second Experiment

The entire LAST MINUTE session lasts about an hour and is expensive. Therefore, we conducted a shorter experiment by using the first introduction phase of the session. The user uttered dialogues freely to interact with the wizards. As in the first experiment, the user was fixed and eight wizards participated. The closing utterance was pre-defined as in the previous experiment, but other interactions were conducted freely. We found that the use of candidates varied among participants as shown in Table 3. Some participants used only the candidate utterances as the wizards while other participants did not use the candidates at all. Two wizards, 4 and 5, used both utterance candidates and their own utterances. We compared their median response times in both conditions as shown in Table 4. Although the absolute response time differed among wizards, we could observe that the use of candidates reduced their response time.

Table 3. Ratio of candidate usage (%).

Participant index	1	2	3	4	5	6	7	8
Usage ratio	100	100	100	71.43	75	0	100	0

Table 4. Median response time measured from the end of previous utterance.

Participant index	4	5
Candidate unused	46.6 s	38.0 s
Candidate used	31.9 s	24.1 s

6   Conclusion

The WOZ method is often used for collecting realistic dialogue data between users and the dialogue system in a particular domain. In WOZ, however, a wizard may find it troublesome to generate and input appropriate utterances for data collection purpose. In this study, we investigated a method to suggest utterances taken from a dialogue corpus in order to reduce the burden of the wizards. Since large dialogue corpora usually do not exist in the target domain, we modified an existing dialogue corpus from another domain (source corpus) into a reusable form (portable corpus). The utterance candidates were then suggested from the portable corpus. In the experiment using a text-based dialogue interface with the utterance suggestion functionality, the utterance candidates were frequently used during the WOZ data collection process. In addition, we found that the utterance input time was reduced by suggesting utterances. These results suggest the utility of utterance candidates taken from the portable dialogue corpus.

To increase confidence in the above mentioned benefits of the proposed method, we need to conduct a further experiment. In this study, we fixed a user and varied wizards for the purpose of comparison. If we compare multiple users, we can examine the influence of different interaction styles. Also, the dialogue experience of users were not quantitatively evaluated. With multiple users, we can measure the quality of the utterances generated by the wizards. That is, we can test that the decrease of cognitive loads of the wizards did not degrade their response quality.

A possible improvement to the proposed method would be to create a more sophisticated porting procedure for creating the portable corpus. Another direction of improvement is the combination of several source corpora to build a larger portable corpus. In this study, we used quantitative evaluation measure: usage ratio of utterance candidates and response time. Qualitative evaluation such as protocol analysis may help understanding the utterances selection criteria used by the wizards.

Acknowledgements. This research was partially supported by Grant-in-Aid for Scientific Research 24500321. The initial WOZ system was developed by Takahiro Sekino. Part of the experiment was conducted by Kodai Takahashi.

Appendix

Table 5. Dialogue example derived from the LAST MINUTE corpus. W and U indicate the wizard and user utterances, respectively. The transcripts here were translated from Japanese. The Japanese transcripts were translated from German.

	Utterance
W	A taxi will arrive in a few minutes.
W	Next, you can select reading materials.
U	I'll take a newspaper with me.
W	Newspaper has been added.
U	Next category.
W	In this category, you can choose devices.
U	Audio player.
W	Audio player has been added.
U	Adapter.
W	Adapter has been added.
U	And, a camera.
W	Maximum weight has been exceeded and the camera has not been added.
U	I'll take out the adapter.
W	Adapter has been removed.

Table 6. Dialogue example derived from the Kyoto sightseeing speech corpus. G and U indicate the guide and user utterances, respectively. The transcripts here were translated from Japanese.

	Utterance
U	Excuse me. The entrance fee for Tenryuji temple is ...
G	The entrance fee is 500 yen, yes.
U	500 yen, I see.
G	Yes. Or it will be around noon then.
U	Yes, it will almost be time.
G	Uh, you can have lunch then.
U	Yes.

Table 7. Example utterances from the portable corpus. These are independent and not a series of utterances.

Yes, how long does it take?
Thank you very much.
Where do you recommend?
Then, it will be evening, yes.
Well, I will finish here.
Uh, that's correct.
So, I cannot make it, yes.
Yes, yes, yes.

References

1. Dahlbäck, N., Jönsson, A., Ahrenberg, L.: Wizard of Oz studies - why and how. Knowl.-Based Syst. **6**(4), 258–266 (1993)
2. Higashinaka, R., Kawamae, N., Sadamitsu, K., Minami, Y., Meguro, T., Dohsaka, K., Inagaki, H.: Building a conversational model from two-tweets. In: IEEE Workshop on Automatic Speech Recognition and Understanding, Waikoloa, HI, pp. 330–335 (2011)
3. Inaba, M., Iwata, N., Toriumi, F., Hirayama, T., Enokibori, Y., Takahashi, K., Mase, K.: Constructing a non-task-oriented dialogue agent using statistical response method and gamification. In: 7th International Conference on Agents and Artificial Intelligence (ICAART 2014), pp. 14–21 (2014)
4. Inoue, M., Matsuda, T., Yokoyama, S.: Web resource selection for dialogue system generating natural responses. In: Stephanidis, C. (ed.) HCI 2011. CCIS, vol. 173, pp. 571–575. Springer, Heidelberg (2011). doi:10.1007/978-3-642-22098-2_114
5. Mostefa, L.F., Besacier, D., Esteve, L., Quignard, Y.M., Camelin, N., et al.: Leveraging study of robustness and portability of spoken language understanding systems across languages and domains: the PORTMEDIA corpora. In: Proceedings of 8th International Conference on Language Resources and Evaluation (LREC 2012), Istanbul, Turkey (2012)
6. Ohtake, K., Misu, T., Hori, C., Kashioka, H., Nakamura, S.: Dialogue acts annotation for NICT Kyoto tour dialogue corpus to construct statistical dialogue systems. In: Proceedings of 7th International Conference on Language Resources and Evaluation (LREC 2010), Valetta, Malta (2010)
7. Rösner, D., Frommer, J., Friesen, R., Haase, M., Lange, J., Otto, M.: LAST MINUTE: a multimodal corpus of speech-based user-companion interactions. In: Proceedings of 8th International Conference on Language Resources and Evaluation (LREC 2012), Istanbul, Turkey (2012)
8. Schlögl, S., Schneider, A., Luz, S., Doherty, G.: Supporting the wizard: interface improvements in Wizard of Oz studies. In: BCS-HCI 2011 Proceedings of 25th BCS Conference on Human-Computer Interaction, Swinton, UK, pp. 509–514 (2011)

9. Webb, N., Liu, T.: Investigating the portability of corpus-derived cue phrases for dialogue act classification. In: The 22nd International Conference on Computational Linguistics (Coling 2008), Manchester, UK, pp. 977–984 (2008)
10. Cao, Z., Qin, T., Liu, T.Y., Tsai, M.F., Li, H.: Learning to rank: from pairwise approach to listwise approach. In: Proceedings of 24th International Conference on Machine Learning, ICML 2007, pp. 129–136 (2007)

Identifying Significant Task-Based Predictors of Emotion in Learning

Najlaa Sadiq Mokhtar and Syaheerah Lebai Lutfi[(✉)]

School of Computer Sciences, Universiti Sains Malaysia,
11800 Minden, Pulau Pinang, Malaysia
najlaa89@gmail.com, syaheerah@usm.my

Abstract. Emphatic computing is concerned with enabling a system to recognize a user's current state and then providing the appropriate response to the user with the intention to support the user emotionally. However, in order to do so, the system must first identify the state of the user. Studies in computer-based tutoring are increasingly investigating ways to incorporate synthetic tutors that are equipped with computational models of empathy – in which these agents are trained to understand learners' emotions and respond based on the detected learner state. However, cultural differences affect the way people express and detect emotions. This paper attempts to identify the task-based features that could discriminate the learner's emotions in a Malaysian context. By studying several existing task-based features from literature, and combining them with new features, this study attempts to detect four frequent emotions that accompanies learning, namely, frustration, *boredom, uncertainty and neutral.* A user study is conducted with 33 students and results revealed that certain features can be used as predictors for the abovementioned emotions. Interestingly, results also showed that there is a tendency for students to choose synthetic tutors of the same race.

Keywords: Empathy · Intelligent tutoring system · Task-based features · Emotions

1 Introduction

Studies in human-computer interaction has demonstrated much concern in social-psychological development, especially empathy [1, 2]. In particular, researches in this area often incorporate synthetic agents (as tutors) that are equipped with computational models of empathy - in which these agents are trained to understand learners' emotions and response based on the detected emotion. In short, emphatic computing is concerned with enabling a system to recognize a user's current state and then providing the appropriate response to the user with the intention to support the user emotionally [3].

Generally, computer-based tutoring system is less engaging compared to human tutoring due to their "insensitiveness" to learners' affect. A truly intelligent tutoring system will take into consideration the learner's state, and adapts to that state before providing an appropriate learning content or feedback [4] to improve learning. To have

© Springer International Publishing Switzerland 2016
M. Baldoni et al. (Eds.): IWEC 2014/IWEC 2015/CMNA 2015, LNAI 9935, pp. 129–142, 2016.
DOI: 10.1007/978-3-319-46218-9_11

an appropriate feedback, an ideal intelligent tutoring system (ITS) needs to first be able to detect the learner's state. One of the straightforward ways to detect learners' states is through capturing task-based interactions – which are to systematically log the inter-actional features between the students and the system such as the time taken and responses to questions [5]. The present paper reports a similar study within a Malaysian context.

[6] asserted that individual differences such as gender, academic and culture background will affect their learning style. Malaysia is unique in the sense that she is Asia's melting pot of cultures, with people from all sorts of background and races - Malaysia is made up of three biggest races – Malay, Chinese and Indian. Cultural differences may influence the way people detect and express emotions [7] and this in turn influences the cognitive process of learning, leading to differences in learning styles. There can also be an eastern/western divide in learning, whereby the underlying models of emotions for learning in the West may not work if reused in a Malaysian context. This paper attempts to identify the task-based features that could discriminate the learner's emotions in a Malaysian context. By studying several existing task-based features from literature, and combining them with new features, this study attempts to detect four frequent emotions that accompanies learning, namely, frustration, boredom, uncertainty and neutral. Although the intent of the study is towards automatic pre-diction of those abovementioned emotions, this paper only focuses on the identification of the task-based features that are significant discriminators of those emotions. A user study is conducted using a web-based e-tutorial platform that was developed especially for this study, with 33 undergraduates of the School of Computer Sciences students from Universiti Sains Malaysia (USM).

The following section presents the state-of-the-art of studies from similar area. Section 3 describes the methodology in this study. Section 4 presents the user study and the results obtained and finally, in Sect. 5, we conclude the study and share the future directions of this study.

2 Literature Review

The relationship between affect and engagement towards students' performances in learning system is pivotal [8]. Several researches in neurosciences and psychologies demonstrated that emotions are widely related to cognition. [9] stated that emotions exert influences in various behavioral and cognitive processes such as concentration, decision-making, and long-term memorizing and hence, learning itself is influenced by the learner's emotional state. In a computer-based learning context, [9] revealed that people who have negative attitudes toward computers will lead to less self-efficacy on using the computer and reduce their chances of performing computer-related tasks considerably compared to those who have positive attitudes toward computers.

Negative attitude towards computer-based learning may be due to the system demonstrating lack of affect, and hence failing to tailor to learners' needs and leading to disengagement.

2.1 Intelligent Tutoring System (ITS)

Most ITS have been developed with various systematic strategies to attract the learners and promote interactive learning environment [4]. Some strategies include error identification and correction, learner's cognitive states and student modelling [10]. A more recent strategy is to improve the ITS to make it an affect responsive system by including learner models [5]. By integrating affect, ITS is given the ability to recognize learner's affective state and become more effective, user friendly and also to provide an interactive learning environment. Many studies in emotion modelling in ITS focus on predicting student frustration (see [5, 11, 12]), perhaps because frustration is reported at a higher rate in a learning environment (further explained in the next section). However it is also important to detect other negative states such as boredom, and uncertainty, as attempted in this paper.

2.2 Emotions that Accompany Learning

Several studies has strongly proven that emotion plays an important role in learning, which use self-annotation methods to report students emotions (see [9, 13]). There are four frequent emotions that are attached to learning, namely; frustration, boredom, uncertainty and neutral [4, 14–17]. [4] revealed that boredom and frustration have been reported at a higher rate in the relationship between affect and learning. In a similar vein, [5] have also found that frustration have been reported at higher percentage in learning. Apart from the above, [14, 18] showed that uncertainty plays an important role in learning process because it is the state that is the main interest in the domain of dialogue-based tutoring. Meanwhile [19] reported that highly negative experience suffered by students such as boredom and frustrations are expected to persist and may disengage them from the learning task.

2.3 Empathetic Synthetic Tutor

Empathy is defined as the awareness of the empathizer of the difficulties faced by the other person that generates an affective state in the empathizer which reflects their own situation to a greater extends [20]. Empathy demonstrates the emergence of emotional computing [21, 22]. In several studies within Affective Computing (see [23–25], empathy is being investigated is a technique that has been automated for recognizing user's affect.

For example, the technology that leverages virtual reality that incorporates empathy such as a synthetic tutor could overcome the emotional limitation of the user. This is done by combining visual and logical thinking characterized by immersion, interaction, and imagination to provide new learning methods [26]. According to [27], a synthetic tutor could help remote students to enhance their understanding of the learning content when it is emotive. Moreover, [13] proved that this tendency has been showed in the development of a graphical surrounding that operates as a synthetic tutor or teacher that is able to interact with students to achieve communication.

Besides that, to enhance the communication between tutors and remote students in some degree, intelligent synthetic tutors are required because they can perceive, adapt to the environment and make proper decisions in an automated way [27]. [26] argued that several modes of learning such as collaborative learning, explorative learning and learning group discussions can be practiced by virtual reality to promote all-round developed students. Furthermore, in order to offer the best elements of enhanced learning, intelligent tutors have proved their efficacy by adapting to the behavior of students – that is, by intervening in an interactive environment [28]. In a similar vein, [27] demonstrated that intelligent synthetic tutors are deemed important in learning since they could recognize learners' input information and make proper actions.

3   User Study

Figure 1 shows the high level methodological framework that encompasses this study. As mentioned earlier, this study focused in identifying the task-based features to predict emotions that occur frequently in learning; boredom, frustration, uncertainty and neutral, towards developing a computational model of emotion in learning.

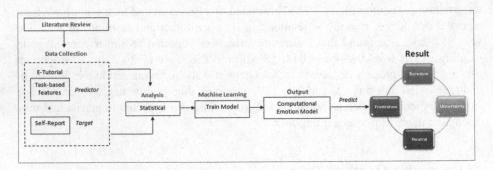

Fig. 1. High level research framework.

The data collection phase involved a user study with 33 students of Year 1 and Year 2 undergraduates in Computer Science from USM. Based on race, there were 13 Malay and 20 Chinese students who participated. There were no Indian students (USM has quite low number of Indian students in comparison to other races). Each student was asked to use the E-Tutorial Programming system that was developed especially for this study. There are two tutorials, Tutorial 1 and 2, and each tutorial contains 30 questions each in total, and is split into 10 questions for each session – which are: beginner (10 questions), intermediate (10 questions) and advanced (10 questions). The questions are appear in a random order. It is compulsory to answer all questions. For each of the tutorial, subjects get 30 min, totaling to 1 h for both tutorial session. The experiment was held in a laboratory in the School of Computer Science and is observed by the researcher from a distance. The subjects were not aware that they are being observed. A pair of subjects are let in per experiment and placed in a distance from each other. At the end of the experiment, subjects were given a token in the form of cash. Figure 2 shows the screenshots of the interfaces of both Tutorial 1 and 2 of the E-Tutorial Programming system.

As mentioned earlier, there were two (2) tutorials that the students are required to complete. The main difference between Tutorial 1 and Tutorial 2 is that Tutorial 1 has no e-tutor while in Tutorial 2 there are three built-in non-adaptive standard e-tutors and students can choose their preferred e-tutor – this will be further explained in Sect. 3.4. Task-based data was extracted and logged automatically offline in the system through objective and subjective metrics. The next section provides further details on the metrics used.

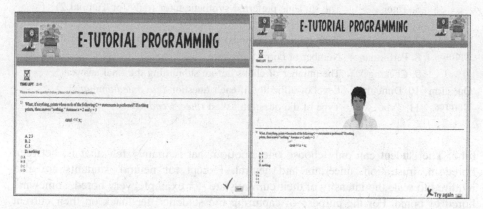

Fig. 2. E-Tutorial Programming system interfaces. Tutorial 2 displays e-tutor on the screen (right).

3.1 Objective Metric: Task-Based Features

There are 11 objective features that were grouped into three parts, student, question, and tutorial-based features, as shown in Table 1. The features were inspired by previous work, but some new features were decided motivated by the context of the learning in Malaysia, for example, race and preferred tutor. These objective features were automatically collected and kept in a log during the student-system interaction. The significant objective features mined from the interaction will be fed as predictors in training the model in a supervised learning. Student related features are those elements that are related to students' personal data, experience and choices such as gender, races, personality etc. Similarly, tutorial and question related features are such as number of clicks and difficulty of question respectively.

3.2 Subjective Metric: Self-reported Student State

While the objective metrics provide the possible predictive features, the self-report is collected to provide the target (emotional state). At the end of each session (after 10 questions), the system will ask the student about how he or she feels at the particular

Table 1. Task-based features and their descriptions

Type	Features	Description
Student features	1. Gender	Gender of the student
	2. Races	Races of the student *(Malay/Chinese/Indian)*
	3. Experience	Student experience using computer *(not familiar/familiar/very familiar)*
	4. Interest	Student interest with the subject in the tutorial *(Strongly Agree/Agree/Neutral/Disagree/Strongly Disagree)*
	5. Personality	Personality of the students *(Openness/Conscientiousness/Extravert/Agreeableness/Neurotic)*
	6. Tutor chosen	The students preferred synthetic tutor (only for Tutorial 2)
Tutorial features	7. Time taken	Time taken (in seconds) to answer each question in the tutorial
	8. Performance	Number of correct answer
	9. Clicking	The number of clicks before submitting the final answer
Question features	10. Difficulty	Level of difficulty of each question *(easy/medium/hard)*
	11. Type	Type of the question asked *(theory/coding)*

time. The student can only choose one emotion that is mainly felt, that is, between boredom, frustration, uncertain and neutral. Except for neutral, students are also required to scale the intensity of their current state - or example, very bored, somewhat bored or bored. For the purpose of capturing the students' feedback on their current feelings, a virtual questionnaire is used as shown in Fig. 3. This questionnaire popped up only three times in total for each tutorial – precisely in the initial, middle and end phases of the tutorial. This is to avoid students getting annoyed from having to report their states frequently.

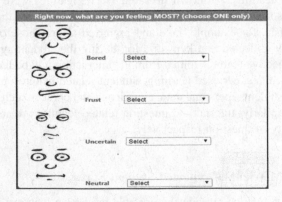

Fig. 3. The self-report screen

3.3 Subjective Metric: Student Feedback on the Tutorials

At the end of each tutorial session (or when the 30 min time given is up), another virtual questionnaire pops up for the students to evaluate each tutorial – the content of the questionnaire is shown in Table 2. Tutorial 2 has one additional question which is the PREFERENCE of the student. Precisely, they were asked to choose the preferred tutorial. For question 1–6, students were required to rate their answers in a 7-point scale - between the scale of +3 (Excellent) to −3 (Very Poor). The main reason to use the 7-point scale is to enable the students to better distinguish between positive category and negative category. For instance, +1 to +3 as positive and vice versa. This will provide reliable feedback [29] in the Tutorial 2, it has one additional question which is asked which tutorial that student more preferred either Tutorial 1 or Tutorial 2.

Table 2. Feedback from the students questionaire

Questionnaire on students' experience
1. I did learn something from this tutorial session | LEARN
2. I will try more online tutorials like this in the future | CONTINUANCE
3. I prefer tutorial session such as this compared to going to class | PREFERENCE
4. I would recommend this tutorial session to other friend | RECOMMENDATION
5. I think this tutorial session is exciting | EXCITEMENT
6. Overall, I am satisfied with this tutorial session | SATISFACTION
7. I prefer… | PREFERENCE *

* Only asked in Tutorial 2

3.4 Tutor Preference

As mentioned earlier, there is a difference between Tutorial 1 and Tutorial 2. In Tutorial 2, students were able to choose their preferred synthetic tutor, which is not available in the Tutorial 1. Figure 4 showed the synthetic tutors that were featured in Tutorial 2. These synthetic tutors are specially designed to reflect Malaysian races. Students were not told which tutor represents which race and were not conditioned to choose their preferred tutors.

Fig. 4. Synthetic tutors. From left to right: perceived Malay, Chinese and Indian tutors.

4 Results and Discussion

This section summarizes the results obtained from the experiment mentioned above. Using 33 numbers of subjects × 30 numbers of questions, 990 data were obtained and analyzed. Table 3 shows the summary of the subjective metrics result. The average time taken to complete all questions for Tutorial 1 is 18.32 min and 18.56 for Tutorial 2. All subjects managed to complete the experiment.

Table 3. Self-reported states from Tutorial 1 and Tutorial 2.

Emotion	T1.S1	T1.S2	T1.S3	T2.S1	T2.S2	T2.S3
Boredom	1	0	5	6	5	8
Uncertainty	11	13	18	9	10	11
Frustration	4	7	1	6	7	6
Neutral	17	13	9	12	11	8

T1: Tutorial 1, T2: Tutorial 2, L1: Session 1, L2: Session 2, L3: Session 3

4.1 Statistically Significant Features

Statistical Package Social Sciences (SPSS) were used to analyze the data. Pearson correlation analyses were first conducted on the data that was obtained from both tutorials to inspect the significant features. Since there were too many results obtained from the analysis, we present only the significantly features that are correlated to those four emotions (boredom, frustration, uncertainty and neutral). Table 4 summarizes the statistically significant correlations between the task-based features and the emotions for both Tutorial 1 and 2.

Table 4. Significant features for predict emotions in each tutorial.

Features	Affective states							
	Boredom		Frustration		Uncertainty		Neutral	
	T1	T2	T1	T2	T1	T2	T1	T2
Races						−		
Interest				−			+	
Question type	−		−					
Question difficulty	−							
Time taken		+	+	+	+			
Performance		+		−	−		+	+
Clicking	+	+	+	+	+			

T1: Tutorial 1, T2: Tutorial 2.
+/− indicates that the feature is a positive or negative correlation with the emotions at $p < .05$ significance level.
Empty cells indicate that the feature was not statistically significantly correlated with the respective emotion.

The relationship between the various features and affective states described above was generally intuitive and in the expected directions. Of particular interest are the features that predict uncertainty. Most of the Malay students feel more uncertain in Tutorial 2 compared to the Chinese students. Further discussion follows:

- Boredom

For Tutorial 1, boredom has been shown to be negatively correlated with the question level difficulty and question type. This suggests that easy questions will lead students to feel bored during learning. According to [30], students that often select problems that are too easy or too hard will end either feeling discouraged or bored. Meanwhile, the number of clicking showed positive correlation - when students started to feel bored, the clicking increased in the attempt to answer the questions. On the contrary, for Tutorial 2, boredom was significantly correlated with two other features, which are all positively correlated, which are, time taken and performance. Longer time taken indicates that students are bored. Students might not know the answer to certain questions and take more time. Consequently, boredom would still occur although the students could perform better.

- Frustration

In Tutorial 1, frustration showed both positive significant correlation with number of clicking and time taken. This result suggested that the highest number of clicking and longer time to answer certain questions was probably due to uncertainty that eventually led to frustration. Another factor leading to frustration was lack of interest in programming. According to [31], frustration happens to students who suffer from lack of confidence. This will also cause the students to take a long time to answer questions. In Tutorial 2, frustration showed five significantly correlated features. Time taken and number of clicking showed significant positive correlation, while the other three features; interest with the subject, type of question and the performance of students showed significant negative correlation, which is rather intuitive. It is good to note that interest with the subject is one factor that contributes to frustration. Students who like the programming subject tended to be less frustrated compared to those who are not interested.

- Uncertainty

For Tutorial 1, uncertainty showed significant positive correlation with the number of clicking and time taken. Meanwhile, there is a substantial significant negative correlation with students' performance ($r = .448$, $p = .001$). Students that feel uncertain during learning session tended to achieve low performances. Many researchers [16, 32–34] have agreed that negative emotions such as uncertainty will reduce the achievement of students. In the second tutorial only races of students showed significant negative correlation with uncertainty. Surprisingly, the result revealed that Malay students tended to feel uncertain during learning session compared to Chinese students but did not particularly reflect a significant result in low performance. Chinese students do tend to get better results in programming subject in USM, although to date, this has not been studied empirically. The closest study by [35] showed that Malay students have zero confidence in Mathematics class compared to Chinese students.

- Neutral

As neutral show the absence of the other three negative emotions, it was considered as positive emotion in this study. In Tutorial 1, the result showed that neutral emotion have a positive correlation for both performance and interest of subject features. Note that students may not really feel neutral, but rather, they might not have felt any of the three negative emotions. According to the studies done by [34, 36], there is a link between positive emotions and achievement. However, for Tutorial 2, there was only one feature that showed significant correlation with neutral, which is performance. Similar as the result obtained in Tutorial 1, we can conclude that students who perform better would feel more neutral.

4.2   Comparisons of Students Feedback of Tutorial 1 and Tutorial 2

Dependent T-test was used to analyze the data obtained from the subjective questions, as shown in Table 5. Based on the test, we found out that students are more likely to recommend the e-tutorial (Tutorial 1) to other students compared with Tutorial 2. Results from the interview indicated that most students gave good response towards the E-Tutorial Programming system. Most of them enjoyed interacting with Tutorial 1, and found it to be simple and user-friendly.

Table 5. Significant features for predict emotions in each tutorial

Subjective metric		Sig. (2-tailed)
Pair 1	LEARN.T1 – LEARN.T2	.744
Pair 2	CONTINUANCE.T1 – CONTINUANCE.T2	.059
Pair 3	**PREFERENCE.T1 – PREFERENCE.T2**	**.050**
Pair 4	**RECOMMENDATION.T1 – RECOMMENDATION.T2**	**.018**
Pair 5	EXCITEMENT.T1 – EXCITEMENT.T2	.525
Pair 6	SATISFACTION.T1 – SATISFACTION.T2	.070

T1: Tutorial 1, T2: Tutorial 2.
Bolded value show the statistically significant result at p < .05 (2-tailed).

4.3   Tutorial Preferred

In summary, we discovered that Tutorial 1 is significantly preferred by the students. Table 6 shows the summarized result 22 out of 33 students representing 66.7% of the participants have chosen Tutorial 1 and the other 11 students have chosen Tutorial 2 as their preferred tutorial.

Face to face interview with students revealed that the standard synthetic tutor in Tutorial 2 is rather annoying because tutor does not have the ability to adapt to outcome of the interaction and hence considered not functional. In Tutorial 2, a standard non-adaptive tutor was intentional to check whether synthetic tutors that is not sensitive to students' emotions would still be preferred over the one without a synthetic tutor at all. In the future, we intend to conduct a user study of students using the e-tutoring

Table 6. Percentage of tutorial preferred

	Number of students	Percentage
Tutorial 1	22	66.7%
Tutorial 2	11	33.3%

platform directed by a synthetic tutor that is affect-sensitive and one that is not. This is to investigate whether adaptive, affect-sensitive tutor will improve students' perceptions over the functionality of the tutor.

4.4   Synthetic Tutor Preferred (Tutorial 2)

Although there is no statistically significant correlation between the student race and the tutor chosen, we have obtained some interesting patterns – there was more than half Malay students (7 out of 13–53%) that chose the perceived Malay tutor while 60% (12 out of 20) Chinese students chose the perceived Chinese tutor. This result suggests that students prefer a tutor that is in the same race with them. It is worth to note that there were Malay students who chose Chinese tutor and vice versa, but this may be due to the fact that there were some similar facial features of Chinese and Malay in the tutor and since students were not told which tutor represents which race, they may have perceived that one represents their own race (Fig. 5).

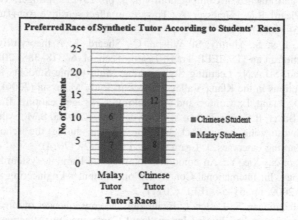

Fig. 5. Preferred race of tutor according to students' races.

5   Conclusion

In this study, the optimum task-based features were successfully identified, towards building a computational model of emotion that would be the underlying model of an affect-sensitive synthetic tutor. The idea is to create an empathetic and more naturalistic environment for computer-based learning. A web-based E-Tutorial Programming system was utilized as a platform to collect data of Malaysian students solving tutorial.

Pearson correlation results indicated that certain features showed that they can be used as predictors for boredom, frustration uncertainty, and the lack of these emotions – neutral.

Other finding is that the students have preferred the tutorial session without a tutor rather than one that has a non-adaptive, standard tutor. Students also showed that there is a tendency of choosing tutors of the same race.

Future directions of this work include building an automatic emotion prediction model using the optimum features as predictors and self-reported emotion as target, towards building an empathetic ITS.

Acknowledgement. The authors would like to thank Universiti Sains Malaysia for the funding of this work from the grant no. 304/PKOMP/6312153.

References

1. Davis, M.H.: Empathy: A Social Psychological Approach. Westview Press, Boulder (1994)
2. Sabourin, J., Mott, B., Lester, J.: Computational models of affect and empathy for pedagogical virtual agents. In: Standards in Emotion Modeling, Lorentz Center International Center for Workshops in the Sciences
3. Aquino, R.J., Battad, J., Ngo, C.F., Uy, G., Trogo, R., Suarez, M.: Towards empathic support provision for computer users. In: Nishizaki, S.-H., Numao, M., Caro, J., Suarez, M.T. (eds.) Theory and Practice of Computation, vol. 5, pp. 15–27. Springer, Tokyo (2012)
4. D'Mello, S., Picard, R.W., Graesser, A.: Toward an affect-sensitive AutoTutor. IEEE Intell. Syst. **22**, 53–61 (2007)
5. Rajendran, R., Iyer, S., Murthy, S., Wilson, C., Sheard, J.: A theory-driven approach to predict frustration in an ITS. IEEE Trans. Learn. Technol. **6**, 378–388 (2013)
6. Syed Mohamad, S.J.A.N.: Learning Style among Multi-Ethnic Students in Four Selected Tertiary Institutions in the Klang Valley. Universiti Putra Malaysia (2006)
7. Matsumoto, D., Juang, L.: Culture and Psychology. Cengage Learning, Boston (2012)
8. Pardos, Z.A., Baker, R.S., San Pedro, M., Gowda, S.M., Gowda, S.M.: Affective states and state tests: investigating how affect and engagement during the school year predict end-of-year learning outcomes. J. Learn. Anal. **1**, 107–128 (2014)
9. Wang, Z., Qiao, X., Xie, Y.: An emotional intelligent e-learning system based on mobile agent technology. In: International Conference on Computer Engineering and Technology, 2009, ICCET 2009, pp. 51–54. IEEE (2011)
10. Robison, J., McQuiggan, S., Lester, J.: Evaluating the consequences of affective feedback in intelligent tutoring systems. In: 3rd International Conference on Affective Computing and Intelligent Interaction and Workshops, pp. 1–6. IEEE (2009)
11. Rodrigo, M.M.T., Baker, R.S.: Coarse-grained detection of student frustration in an introductory programming course. In: Proceedings of the Fifth International Workshop on Computing Education Research Workshop, pp. 75–80. ACM (2009)
12. McQuiggan, S.W., Lester, J.C.: Modeling and evaluating empathy in embodied companion agents. Int. J. Hum.-Comput. Stud. **65**, 348–360 (2007)
13. Daradoumis, T., Arguedas, M., Xhafa, F.: Current trends in emotional e-learning: new perspectives for enhancing emotional intelligence. In: 2013 7th International Conference on Complex, Intelligent, and Software Intensive Systems (CISIS), pp. 34–39. IEEE (2013)

14. D'mello, S.K., Craig, S.D., Witherspoon, A., Mcdaniel, B., Graesser, A.: Automatic detection of learner's affect from conversational cues. User Model. User-Adap. Interact. **18**, 45–80 (2008)
15. Baker, R.S., D'Mello, S.K., Rodrigo, M.M.T., Graesser, A.C.: Better to be frustrated than bored: the incidence, persistence, and impact of learners' cognitive–affective states during interactions with three different computer-based learning environments. Int. J. Hum.-Comput. Stud. **68**, 223–241 (2010)
16. Forbes-Riley, K., Litman, D., Friedberg, H., Drummond, J.: Intrinsic and extrinsic evaluation of an automatic user disengagement detector for an uncertainty-adaptive spoken dialogue system. In: Proceedings of the 2012 Conference of the North American Chapter of the Association for Computational Linguistics: Human Language Technologies, pp. 91–102. Association for Computational Linguistics (2012)
17. Plass, J.L., Heidig, S., Hayward, E.O., Homer, B.D., Um, E.: Emotional design in multimedia learning: effects of shape and color on affect and learning. Learn. Instruct. **29**, 128–140 (2014)
18. Forbes-Riley, K., Litman, D.: Benefits and challenges of real-time uncertainty detection and adaptation in a spoken dialogue computer tutor. Speech Commun. **53**, 1115–1136 (2011)
19. Sabourin, J.L., Lester, J.C.: Affect and engagement in Game-BasedLearning environments. IEEE Trans. Affect. Comput. **5**, 45–56 (2014)
20. McQuiggan, S.W., Robison, J.L., Phillips, R., Lester, J.C.: Modeling parallel and reactive empathy in virtual agents: an inductive approach. In: Proceedings of the 7th International Joint Conference on Autonomous Agents and Multiagent Systems, vol. 1, pp. 167–174. International Foundation for Autonomous Agents and Multiagent Systems (2008)
21. Elliott, C.D.: The affective reasoner: a process model of emotions in a multi-agent system. Ph.D. Northwestern University (1992)
22. Gratch, J., Marsella, S.: A domain-independent framework for modeling emotion. Cogn. Syst. Res. **5**, 269–306 (2004)
23. Picard, R.W., Picard, R.: Affective Computing. MIT Press, Cambridge (1997)
24. Graesser, A., McDaniel, B., Chipman, P., Witherspoon, A., D'Mello, S., Gholson, B.: Detection of emotions during learning with AutoTutor. In: Proceedings of the 28th Annual Meetings of the Cognitive Science Society, pp. 285–290. Citeseer (2006)
25. Kapoor, A., Picard, R.W.: Multimodal affect recognition in learning environments. In: Proceedings of the 13th Annual ACM International Conference on Multimedia, pp. 677–682. ACM (2005)
26. Zhao, H., Sun, B., Hu, X., Zhu, X.: The study of emotional education based on virtual reality in e-learning. In: 1st International Conference on Information Science and Engineering (ICISE), pp. 3540–3543. IEEE (2009)
27. Hu, Y., Zhao, G.: Virtual classroom with intelligent virtual tutor. In: International Conference on e-Education, e-Business, e-Management, and e-Learning, IC4E 2010, pp. 34–38. IEEE (2010)
28. Chaffar, S., Frasson, C.: Using an emotional intelligent agent to improve the learner's performance. In: Proceedings of the Workshop on Social and Emotional Intelligence in Learning Environments in Conjunction with Intelligent Tutoring Systems (2004)
29. Lutfi, S.L., Fernández-Martínez, F., Lorenzo-Trueba, J., Barra-Chicote, R., Montero, J.M.: I feel you: the design and evaluation of a domotic affect-sensitive spoken conversational agent. Sensors **13**, 10519–10538 (2013)
30. Hsiao, I.H., Sosnovsky, S., Brusilovsky, P.: Guiding students to the right questions: adaptive navigation support in an e-learning system for Java programming. J. Comput. Assist. Learn. **26**, 270–283 (2010)

31. Gulzar, S., Yahya, F., Nauman, M., Mir, Z., Mujahid, S.H.: Frustration among University Students in Pakistan (2012)
32. Blair, C.: School readiness: integrating cognition and emotion in a neurobiological conceptualization of children's functioning at school entry. Am. Psychol. **57**, 111 (2002)
33. Pekrun, R., Elliot, A.J., Maier, M.A.: Achievement goals and achievement emotions: testing a model of their joint relations with academic performance. J. Educ. Psychol. **101**, 115 (2009)
34. Valiente, C., Swanson, J., Eisenberg, N.: Linking students' emotions and academic achievement: when and why emotions matter. Child. Dev. Perspect. **6**, 129–135 (2012)
35. Wong, K.Y., Quek, K.S.: Do Chinese and Malay students report different ways of studying mathematics? 1–13 (2007)
36. Pekrun, R., Goetz, T., Perry, R.P., Kramer, K., Hochstadt, M., Molfenter, S.: Beyond test anxiety: development and validation of the test emotions questionnaire (TEQ). Anxiety Stress Coping **17**, 287–316 (2004)

Design of Populations in Symbiotic Evolution to Generate Chord Progression in Consideration of the Entire Music Structure

Noriko Otani[1]([✉]), Shoko Shirakawa[1], and Masayuki Numao[2]

[1] Faculty of Informatics, Tokyo City University,
3-3-1 Ushikubo-nishi, Tsuzuki, Yokohama 224-8551, Japan
otani@tcu.ac.jp
[2] Institute of Scientific and Industrial Research, Osaka University,
8-1 Mihogaoka, Osaka, Ibaraki 567-0047, Japan
numao@sanken.osaka-u.ac.jp

Abstract. Adopting a motif, that is the most basic component of a music, has been proposed for generating a chord progression adapted to personal sensibility in consideration of the entire music structure. Personal sensibility models for the motif and chord progression are induced, and chord progression is generated based on the models using an evolutionary computation. Symbiotic evolution is an evolutionary computation algorithm that is characterized by maintaining a partial solution population and a whole solution population. A whole solution is a combination of some partial solutions. As a musical piece can be considered as a combination of motifs, symbiotic evolution is appropriate for the tasks of generating a chord progression. In this paper, we propose how to design populations in symbiotic evolution to generate chord progression in consideration of the entire music structure. Our experimental results show that musical pieces having the target structure are composed.

Keywords: Symbiotic evolution · Population design · Chord progression · Music composition · Personal sensibility model

1 Introduction

The Constructive Adaptive User Interface (CAUI) aims to compose music that arouses an individual's particular sensibility (Numao 2002). Here, "sensibility" means the ability to cause some emotion by an extrenal stimulus. The kind of sensibility aroused by a stimulus differs according to the individual. The CAUI induces a personal sensibility model by using an individual's emotional impressions of music and composes music based on the model.

It is necessary to consider not only the partial structure but also the entire structure in order to compose high-quality music. Nishikawa (2009) proposed adopting a *motif* in generating a chord progression for CAUI in consideration of the entire music structure. A motif is the most basic component of a musical piece, and consists of two bars. The personal sensibility models for the chord

© Springer International Publishing Switzerland 2016
M. Baldoni et al. (Eds.): IWEC 2014/IWEC 2015/CMNA 2015, LNAI 9935, pp. 143–154, 2016.
DOI: 10.1007/978-3-319-46218-9_12

progression and motif are induced using inductive logic programming (ILP), and a chord progression is generated using a genetic algorithm (GA). The personal sensibility model for the chord progression is represented as a rule for a sequence of chords; for example, "The listener feels tender when a root of a chord progresses in the order of III, III, and VI." On the other hand, the model for the motif is a rule for a structure of two bars. By using personal sensibility models for both chord progression and motif, an individual's sensibility can be reflected in not only the sequences of chords but also the structure of the musical piece.

In this paper, we propose how to design populations in symbiotic evolution (Moriarty 1996) for generating a chord progression in consideration of the entire music structure. Symbiotic evolution is an evolutionary computation algorithm, a particular feature of which is a partial and a whole solution population. A whole solution is a combination of some partial solutions. As a musical piece can be considered as a combination of motifs, symbiotic evolution is appropriate for the tasks of generating a chord progression.

We targetted a structure called *Kishotenketsu*. Japanese students, in general, learn to write essays using the *Kishotenketsu* structure, the origin of which is in Chinese poetry. It consists of four parts: introduction, development, turn, and conclusion. When an individual listens to a musical piece comprising these four parts, he/she may experience the "development" similar to a story.

2   Representation and Composition Procedure of Musical Pieces

This section explains the representation of music and composition flow that were designed in our previous work (Otani 2012). In this study, the musical piece is a sequence of quarter notes, with a 4/4 time signature.

2.1   Representation and Composition Procedure

A musical piece consists of a frame structure, chord progression, melody, and bass part. The frame structure comprises eight components: *key, tonic, tonality, tempo, melody instrument, melody instrument category, chord instrument,* and *chord instrument category.* A chord progression is a sequence of chords. A chord is a set consisting of *root, type,* and *tension. root* is a root of a chord, such as I, ♯I, ♭II, etc. *type* is a chord type, such as M, 7, aug, dim7, etc. *tension* is an extension of a chord, such as the 9th, 11th, 13th, etc. When a previous chord is played in succession, the chord is represented by "–" instead of the set.

The following is the composition procedure.

1. Generate training sets, and induce personal sensibility models for the frame structure, motif, and chord progression using ILP.
2. Generate a frame structure that adapts to the personal sensibility model for the frame structure using a GA.
3. Generate a chord progression that adapts to the personal sensibility model for the motif and chord progression using symbiotic evolution.

4. Generate a bass part and a melody using the chord progression.
5. Combine the frame structure, chord progression, bass part, and melody to develop a tune.

2.2   Generation of Training Sets

We target an individual's specific sensibility for inducing a personal sensibility model and composing a musical piece. Target sensibilities can be located in the direction "positive" or "negative" on the axis of sensibility evaluation. A target sensibility and its opposite sensibility are used together to generate training sets.

The individual listens to and evaluates various musical pieces using a semantic differential method (SDM), and his/her affective perceptions are noted. The individual rates a musical piece on a scale of 1–5 for bipolar affective adjective pairs, namely, *favorable-unfavorable*, *bright-dark*, *happy-sad*, *tender-severe*, and *tranquil-noisy*. The former adjective in each pair expresses a positive affective impression, while the latter expresses a negative one. The individual may provide a high rating for any piece that he/she finds positive. On the other hand, he/she may provide a low rating for any piece that he/she believes to be negative. With the exception of the first pair, all the adjectives were selected from the affective value scale of music (AVSM) (Taniguchi 1995) owing to their simplicity.

Table 1. Individual's ratings for musical pieces in examples

Direction of target sensibility	Training set	Ratings	
		Positive examples	Negative examples
Positive	t_2	5	1–4
	t_1	4, 5	1–3
Negative	t_2	1	2–5
	t_1	1, 2	3–5

Two training sets, t_1 and t_2, are generated using the individual's ratings. Table 1 shows the individual's ratings for positive and negative examples in each training set. When learning a model for a positive impression, pieces with higher ratings are used as positive examples and the remaining pieces are used as negative examples. When learning a model for a negative impression, pieces with lower ratings are used as positive examples and the remaining pieces are used as negative examples.

2.3   Induction of Personal Sensibility Models

Personal sensibilty models for the frame structure, motif, and chord progression are learned by employing FOIL (Quinlan 1990), a top-down ILP system that learns the function-free Horn clause definitions of a target predicate using background predicates. Two models with multiple levels are constructed using two training sets. A personal sensibility model involves a partial structure of music that affects a listener's specific sensibility. The frame structures and chord progressions of musical pieces used for generating training sets are used as background knowledge.

The following three clauses are personal sensibility models for the frame structure, motif, and chord progression, respectively.

```
frame(bright,A):-tempo(A,andante),chord_category(A,piano).
motif(bright,A):-motif(A,bar((iv,major),-,_,-),bar(_,-,-,-)).
chords(bright, A):-has_chord(A,B,C),root(C,vi),type(C,minor),
                   next_to(A,B,D,_),has_chord(A,D,E),root(E,vi).
```

These clauses describe musical features that induce a feeling of brightness in the listener. The first clause indicates that the individual feels bright when listening to music played *andante* on a kind of piano. The second clause is a feature of a motif wherein the first bar consists of a IV major chord and an arbitrary chord, and the second bar consists of four arbitrary chords. The third is a feature of chord progression with two successive chords: VI minor and VI.

3   Generation of Chord Progression Using Symbiotic Evolution

In this section, the method to generate a chord progression consisting of four parts is explained in detail. A chord progression is generated to suit the listener's sensibility model using symbiotic evolution.

3.1   Symbiotic Evolution

The symbiotic evolution algorithm is an evolutionary computation algorithm, and was proposed for forming neural networks (Moriarty 1996). This algorithm results in a fast, efficient search and prevents convergence to suboptimal solutions. It is characterized by maintaining two separate populations: a partial solution population, the individuals of which represent partial solutions, and a whole solution population, the individuals of which are combinations of individuals in the partial solution population and represent whole solutions. In the former population, partial solutions that may be components of the optimal whole solution are generated. In the latter population, combinations of the partial solutions that may be the optimal solution are generated.

A musical piece can be considered as a combination of motifs. Motifs that may be contained in a suitable musical piece should be found, as well as a suitable combination of motifs. Symbiotic evolution is appropriate for the tasks of generating a chord progression because of its characteristics. In the proposed method, a motif is expressed as an individual in the partial solution population, and a chord progression as an individual in the whole solution population.

3.2   Partial Solution Individual

In a chromosome of an individual in the partial solution population, the *root_type* gene and *tension* gene are alternately located in a line. Figure 1 shows an example of a chromosome of a partial solution individual. The *root_type* gene expresses the ID assigned to a combination of *root* and *type*. The integer 0–75 is assigned as an ID to 75 (*root, type*) and "-," which are contained in the existing musical pieces, respectively. The *tension* gene expresses ID 0–7 assigned to *tension*. A combination of the *root_type* gene and *tension* gene is translated to a quarter note in phenotype. Four combinations are translated to a bar, and eight combinations are translated to a motif.

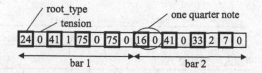

Fig. 1. Partial solution individual

3.3   Whole Solution Individual and Partial Solution Population

When a musical piece consisting of $2N$ bars is generated, a chromosome of an individual in the whole solution population is expressed as a pointer sequence the length of which is N. If the whole solution individual is designed according to a general symbiotic evolution algorithm is applied, only one partial solution population is maintained, and a chromosome of a whole solution individual is expressed as shown in Fig. 2(a). Partial solutions for different parts evolve in the same population. As individuals belonging to the same population tend to converge, it is difficult to generate motifs that have different roles.

In order to reflect the structure of *Kishotenketsu* and generate four types of motifs, three partial solution populations are maintained. These populations correspond to "introduction," "development," and "turn" which are called INTRO, DEVELOP, and TURN, respectively. The chromosome of a whole solution individual is shown in Fig. 2(b). The first $N/4$ pointers in N pointers point to individuals in INTRO. The second and the third $N/4$ pointers point to individuals in DEVELOP and TURN respectively. Partial solutions for different parts evolve in different populations.

Returning to the beginning tone after the large change in "turn" renders the structure more natural. Then, the motifs corresponding to "introduction" are expected to be similar to the motifs corresponding to "conclusion". In addition, the last part of a chord progression should be a harmonic cadence that is a progression of two chords that concludes a musical piece. The last $N/4$ pointers, which correspond to "conclusion", do not point to individuals in any partial

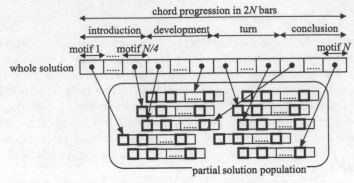

(a) Partial solution population in which individuals for different parts coexist

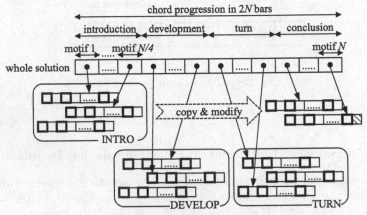

(b) Separate partial solution populations for every different part

Fig. 2. Whole solution individual and partial solution populations

solution population, but to those generated by modifying individuals to which the first $N/4$ pointers pointed. The last part of these individuals was changed to a perfect or a plagal cadence.

3.4 Fitness Value

The fitness value $wfit(W)$ of an individual W in the whole solution population is calculated by the Eq. (1). The partial solution individuals are evaluated using the whole solution individuals, each of which points to the partial solution individual. The fitness value $pfit(P)$ of an individual P in the partial solution population is the largest fitness value of these whole solution individuals, as shown in Eq. (2).

$$wfit(W) = \sum_{P \in W} \{mm(P) + built(P)\} + cm(W) + built(W) + form(W). \quad (1)$$

$$pfit(P) = \max_{P \in W}(wfit(W)). \quad (2)$$

where $P \in W$ means that a partial solution individual P is contained in a whole solution individual W. The partial solution individual receives a higher evaluation when it is pointed to by a better whole solution individual. $built(P)$ and $built(W)$ are penalty functions that penalize a motif or a chord progression when it violates music theory. $form(W)$ is a function that promotes the generation of music with the *Kishotenketsu* structure, and is calculated by Eq. (3).

$$form(W) = form(W, 1) + form'(W, 2) + form'(W, 3) \tag{3}$$

$$form(W, i) = \begin{cases} 20 & \frac{2}{3} \leq rate(W, i) \\ 10 & \frac{1}{2} \leq rate(W, i) < \frac{2}{3} \\ 0 & \text{otherwise} \end{cases} \tag{4}$$

$$form'(W, i) = \begin{cases} 20 & rate(W, i) \leq \frac{1}{3} \\ 10 & \frac{1}{3} < rate(W, i) \leq \frac{1}{2} \\ 0 & \text{otherwise} \end{cases} \tag{5}$$

$$rate(W, i) = \frac{match(W, i)}{note(W, i) \times 3} \tag{6}$$

$match(W, i)$ and $note(W, i)$ are calculated by comparing the corresponding notes in the i-th 1/4 part and the $(i + 1)$-th 1/4 part of the whole solution W. $match(W, i)$ is the number of the same *root*, *type*, and *tension*. $note(W, i)$ is the number of notes, except "-" that means a previous chord is played in succession. $form(W, i)$ is larger for larger $rate(W, i)$ and $form'(W, i)$ is larger for smaller $rate(W, i)$. In other words, if the introduction part of W is similar to the development part, $form(W)$ is larger. When the turn part of W is not similar to the development part and the conclusion part, $form(W)$ is also larger.

$mm(P)$ and $cm(W)$ are functions that indicate the degree of adaptability to the personal sensibility models, and are calculated by Eqs. (7) and (8).

$$mm(P) = \sum_{i=1}^{2}(2i - 1) \cdot \left\{ \sum_{j=1}^{r(M_i)} c(M_i, j) \cdot n(P, M_i, j) - \sum_{j=1}^{r(M_i')} c(M_i', j) \cdot n(P, M_i', j) \right\}. \tag{7}$$

$$cm(W) = \sum_{i=1}^{2}(2i - 1) \cdot \left\{ \sum_{j=1}^{r(C_i)} c(C_i, j) \cdot n(W, C_i, j) - \sum_{j=1}^{r(C_i')} c(C_i', j) \cdot n(W, C_i', j) \right\}. \tag{8}$$

Here, M_i and C_i are the personal sensibility models of motif and chord progression that were generated using training data t_i for the target adjective. M_i' and C_i' are the personal sensibility models of motif and chord progression that were generated using training data t_i for the antonymous adjective. $c(X_i, j)$ is the number of positive examples covered by the j-th clause in the personal sensibility model X_i when the model was learned by ILP. In other words, $c(X_i, j)$ indicates the importance of the j-th rule in the model X_i. $n(Y, X_i, j)$ is the number of parts in Y that satisfy the j-th clause in the personal sensibility model X_i. Therefore, $c(X_i, j) \cdot n(Y, X_i, j)$ means how many and how important rules are contained in Y. $r(X_i)$ is the number of rules contained in the personal sensibility model X_i. The individual that contains the rules for the target adjective that cover a lot of positive examples has the higher value of $mm(P)$ or $cm(W)$. On the other hand, the individual that contains the rules for the antonymous adjective that cover a lot of positive examples has the lower value.

3.5 Procedure

Individuals of both whole and partial solution populations in the next generation are generated using the GA operators: two-point crossover and mutation. The partial solution population is evolved as in (Moriarty 1996). Mutation occurs at rate p, and the note concerned is changed in any of the following four ways.

- Change the *root_type* note to another value randomly.
- Change the *root_type* note to another value that expresses the ID assigned to a combination of the same *type* and different *root* randomly.
- Change the *root_type* note to another value that expresses the ID assigned to a combination of the same *root* and different *type* randomly.
- Change the *tension* note to another value randomly.

The MGG model (Sato 1996), which is an effective evolution strategy for avoiding early convergence, is applied to the whole solution population. Mutation occurs at rate p and the destination of the pointer concerned is changed. The entire sequence of steps is as follows:

1. Generate N_p individuals randomly for three partial solutions respectively, and make them the initial partial solution populations.
2. Generate N_w individuals by selecting one individual from each population randomly, and make them the initial whole solution population.
3. Evaluate whole solution individuals.
4. Evaluate partial solution individuals in three populations.
5. Execute one generation in the three partial solution populations.
6. Execute one generation in the whole solution population.
7. Repeat Steps 3–6 R times.
8. Output the chord progression that is generated from the best whole solution individual that has the maximum fitness value.

4   Experiments

Experiments were conducted in which 17 Japanese university students participated. Thirteen participants were male and four were female, aged between

21 and 23 years. The participants were asked to listen to 53 well-known musical pieces in the MIDI format and to rate each piece in terms of the five impression adjective pairs on a scale of 1–5. The personal sensibility models for each participant were learned on the basis of their individual evaluations.

Subsequently, two musical pieces were composed independently for each participant and each impression. The chord progression of one of the pieces was generated using the same method as general symbiotic evolution. Every partial solution individual was evolved in the same population, and whole solution individuals were represented as shown in Fig. 2(a). The chord progression of the second piece was generated using the proposed method. Partial solution individuals for a different part were evolved in a different population, and whole solution individuals were represented as shown in Fig. 2(b). The former method is called the *coexist* method, and the latter is called the *separate* method. The parameters for generating chord progressions are listed in Table 2.

Table 2. Parameters

Parameter	Value
Mutation rate, p	0.01
Partial solution population size, N_p	480
Whole solution population size, N_w	500
Maximum generation, R	10000

4.1 Examples of Composed Melody

Twenty pieces were composed for each participant, that is, one for each impression adjective and each method. Figure 3 shows the generated musical pieces relating to the adjective *bright* for a certain participant. The score (a) and (b)

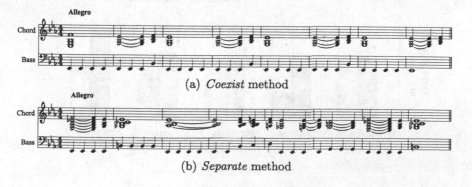

(a) *Coexist* method

(b) *Separate* method

Fig. 3. A composed *bright* musical piece

were generated using the *coexist* and *separate* method, respectively. The piece shown in the score (b) is not harmonious. However the participant rated the piece as 4. On the other hand, the piece shown in the score (a) was rated as 3.

Almost the same chord progressions of two bars are repeated four times in the score (a), whereas the score (b) has an target structure. The *Kishotenketsu* structure can be seen more clearly in the bass part. Each motif corresponds to each part of *Kishotenketsu*. The first three motifs of the bass part are all same in the score (a). On the other hand, the first motif changes a little in the next motif, changes widely in the third motif, and returns to the first motif in the last motif.

4.2 Evaluation of Impression

The participants were asked to rate the pieces composed specifically for them in terms of the five impression adjective pairs on a scale of 1–5. They were not informed that these new pieces would induce specific impressions. Figure 4 shows the average scores that the participants gave for the impression of the musical

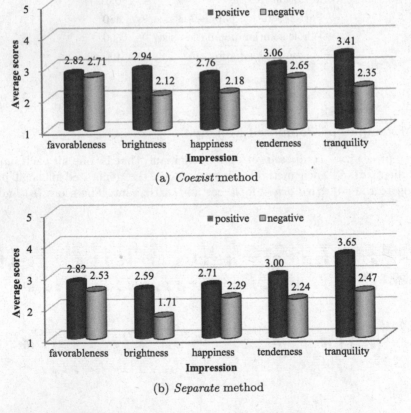

(a) *Coexist* method

(b) *Separate* method

Fig. 4. Evaluation of the impression of the composed musical pieces

pieces composed using the *coexist* and *separate* method. "positive" shows the average score for all the participants' pieces that were composed for the target positive sensibility. "negative" shows the average score for all pieces that were composed for the target negative sensibility. The plausibly acceptable scores would be >3.0 and <3.0 for the positive and negative adjectives, respectively.

It was found that the scores obtained by both methods tended to be low; values exceeding the median 3.0 were acquired only for the positive adjective indicating tenderness and tranquility. However, a right difference between the scores of positive and negative adjectives was obtained for all impressions. A paired t-test at a significance level $\alpha = 0.05$ was conducted to examine the difference in the scores of the pairs of positive and negative adjectives. In the results obtained using the *coexist* method, the values were different for only tranquility. In the results obtained using the *separate* method, significant differences were noted between the values of brightness, tenderness, and tranquility. Therefore, the *separate* method can reflect the positive and negative direction of a personal sensibility to chord progressions better than the *coexist* method.

4.3 Evaluation of Quality

As in the evaluation of impressions, the participants rated the pieces on a scale of 1–5 for four quality criteria: unity, development, fun, and formation. These criteria were shown to them by the following questions.

– Do you feel that the tone of this piece is consistent?
– Do you feel that this piece has the development like a story?
– Do you feel fun when you listen to this piece?
– Do you think that this piece is well-formed?

If the participant felt that the piece met each criterion at a high level, he/she was asked to give a high rating for the piece. Figure 5 shows the average and breakdown of all participants' ratings for the quality of all the musical pieces composed by the *coexist* and *separate* method.

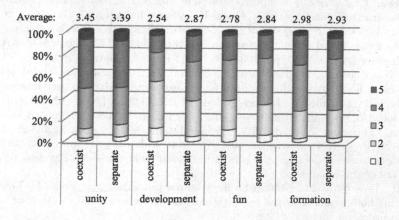

Fig. 5. Evaluation of the quality of the composed musical pieces

Scores exceeding the median 3.0 were acquired only by unity for both methods. It is necessary to improve the other three items. The average and breakdown of the scores for unity, fun, and formation are almost the same in the results obtained by both methods. However, the ratio of 4 and 5 for development in the *separate* method is higher than that in the *coexist* method. According to the paired t-test at a significance level $\alpha = 0.05$, there is a significant difference between the scores of the two methods. The breakdown also indicates that the score obtained by the *separate* method is higher than that obtained by the *coexist* method. This result means that the *separate* method effectively composes musical pieces with the target structure.

5   Conclusion

In this study, we weighed two designs of populations for symbiotic evolution while generating a chord progression in consideration of the *Kishotenketsu* structure. One is maintaining a partial solution population in which individuals for different parts coexist. The other is maintaining three separate partial solution populations for every different part. The experimental results showed that the latter is more effective to reflect the *Kishotenketsu* structure than the former. Although some problems involving quality were found, the experimental results showed that the latter method is more effective for making the structure of a musical piece into the *Kishotenketsu* and reflecting the positive and negative direction of an individual's sensibility to musical pieces than the former method. We had expected that the fun quality also would be increased when the development quality is increased. However, a significant deference for the fun quality was not observed. We should therefore consider another approach for increasing the fun quality of a musical piece.

References

Moriarty, D.E., Miikkulainen, R.: Efficient reinforcement learning through symbiotic evolution. Mach. Learn. **22**, 11–32 (1996)

Nishikawa, T.: Automatic composition system considering both partial and overall music structure. Master's thesis, Osaka University, Japan (2009)

Numao, M., Takagi, S., Nakamura, K.: Constructive adaptive user interfaces - composing music based on human feelings. In: 18th National Conference on Artificial Intelligence (AAAI 2002), pp. 193–198. AAAI Press, California (2002)

Otani, N., Tadokoro, K., Kurihara, S., Numao, M.: Generation of chord progression using harmony search algorithm for a constructive adaptive user interface. In: Anthony, P., Ishizuka, M., Lukose, D. (eds.) PRICAI 2012. LNCS (LNAI), vol. 7458, pp. 400–410. Springer, Heidelberg (2012). doi:10.1007/978-3-642-32695-0_36

Quinlan, J.: Learning logical definitions from relations. Mach. Learn. **5**, 239–266 (1990)

Taniguchi, T.: Construction of an affective value scale of music and examination of relations between the scale and a multiple mood scale. Japan. J. Psychol. **65**, 463–470 (1995). in Japanese

Sato, H., Yamamura, M., Kobayashi, S.: Minimal generation gap model for GAs considering both exploration and exploitation. In: 4th International Conference on Soft Computing, pp. 494–497 (1996)

Item-Based Learning for Music Emotion Prediction Using EEG Data

Peerapon Vateekul[1(✉)], Nattapong Thammasan[2], Koichi Moriyama[2], Ken-ichi Fukui[2], and Masayuki Numao[2]

[1] Department of Computer Engineering, Faculty of Engineering, Chulalongkorn University, Bangkok, Thailand
peerapon.v@chula.ac.th
[2] The Institute of Scientific and Industrial Research, Osaka University, Osaka, Japan
{nattapong,koichi,fukui, numao}@ai.sanken.osaka-u.ac.jp

Abstract. Recently, emotion recognition has gained a lot of attentions particularly in the domain of music recommendation since music can induce emotions. There have been many attempts to predict emotions using Electroencephalograph (EEG) signal, a recording of brain electrical activity. However, almost all of them just employed conventional classification techniques. In this paper, we present a novel emotion prediction algorithm by applying an item-based collaborative filtering (CF). A new EEG-based similarity score is invented to be used in the proposed method. Two-dimensional emotion model is employed, and both valence and arousal levels are discretized into two classes. The experiments were conducted on two data sets: benchmark data and our own collected data. The results show that our method does not only outperform the traditional CF, but also existing classification techniques, i.e., C4.5, SVM, and MLP.

Keywords: Brainwave · Emotion prediction · EEG · Collaborative filtering

1 Introduction

Emotion recognition is an attempt to understand human's emotions, such as sad or happiness, and boring or exciting. Nowadays, it has been realized that there is a strong relationship between emotions and brain activity, which can be recorded from voltage fluctuations in the brain called Electroencephalogram (EEG). There were many prior trials in the emotion prediction using EEG signals [1–8]. However, most of them only focused on the data preprocessing and employed conventional classification approaches, such as support vector machine (SVM), k-nearest neighbors (kNN), multilayer perceptron (MLP), C4.5, Naïve Bayes, etc.

Music recommendation is a trial to suggest a song based on user's preference. One of the selection criteria is user's emotion since music can induce emotions. Collaborative filtering (CF) [9] is a popular approach recommending a song based on the rating history of the system [10, 11]. Item-Based CF is one of the most common CF that

© Springer International Publishing Switzerland 2016
M. Baldoni et al. (Eds.): IWEC 2014/IWEC 2015/CMNA 2015, LNAI 9935, pp. 155–167, 2016.
DOI: 10.1007/978-3-319-46218-9_13

discovers user's interest by utilizing history data of the same song from other users' preferences. A major disadvantage of CF is that it requires a large preference history in order to provide an accurate recommendation. Moreover, newly released songs, which have never been rated by any users, cannot be recommended at all.

In this paper, we focus on the music emotion prediction and aim to propose a novel system that achieves promising prediction accuracy. Our method is called "EEG based collaborative filtering (EEG-CF)". It is an item-based CF that utilizes EEG data to compute its own similarity score based on the assumption that *similar EEG signals should express the same emotion states*". Moreover, the system also includes a mechanism to handle songs (items) that have never been rated by other users. In order to further improve the accuracy, an outlier removal process is proposed to exclude any sample data whose EEG pattern is very different.

Regarding to human emotion representation, one of the famous models to represent human emotion is the arousal-valance emotion model proposed by Russell in 1980 [12]. In this bipolar model (Fig. 1), X-axis is valence showing positive or negative level of emotion, and Y-axis is arousal representing high or low of strength of exci-tation level. Although more dimensions to represent human emotion had been proposed later on, the bipolar model is still widely used in emotion recognition research because basic emotions, such as joy and surprise, can be represented in the dimensional space. Although the model is continuous, we separate arousal levels in to two classes, namely low and high, in the purpose of utilizing categorical classifiers in machine learning. Another advantage is to release the effect of oscillation from one emotion to another emotion within the same quadrant in emotional space, which is expected to have similar pattern of EEG. Valence levels are divided into two classes as well in to positive emotion class and negative emotions class. Base on above-mentioned assumption, we treat exited, happy, and glad emotions as the classes of emotion.

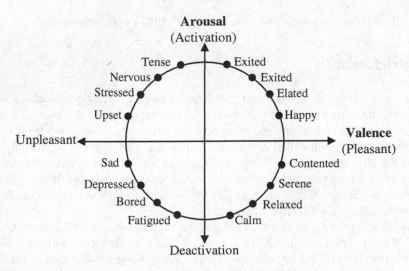

Fig. 1. Two-dimensional Russell's arousal-valence space [12]

There are two music-stimulus data sets in the experiment. The first data set is a standard benchmark called "A Database for Emotion Analysis Using Physiological Signals (DEAP)" [13]. For the second data set, we performed our own experiments to measure EEG signal while subjects are listening to music. The experiments were conducted using 10-fold cross-validation, and the results were compared to 3 existing approaches: C4.5, SVM, and MLP.

In Sect. 2, we present related works: collaborative filtering and performance measures. The proposed method, "EEG-CF," is explained in Sect. 3. Experimental data are summarized in Sect. 4, and the results are reported in Sect. 5.

2 Related Works

2.1 Collaborative Filtering (CF)

CF [9] is a technique that has been widely employed in recommendation systems since it can assist to suggest user's preference based on the rating history. The CF concept can be illustrated via an example in Table 1. Peter's opinion on the movie Titanic can be advised using either his preference on other movies or other users' ratings on Titanic. There are many success case studies of applying CF in the real-world application particularly in e-commerce, e.g., Spotify, Netflix, and Amazon. However, CF has been rarely used in the domain of emotion prediction.

Table 1. An example of predicting Peter's opinion on the movie Titanic

User / Movie	Star Wars	Terminator	Titanic
Joe	5	2	3
John	3	4	5
Peter	5	1	?

CF algorithms can be categorized into two groups including (i) probabilistic and (ii) non-probabilistic algorithms. In this paper, we focus on the non-probabilistic one since it is more commonly used. Also, there are two variants of probabilistic CF: (i) user-based CF and (ii) item-based CF. In the user-based CF, the missing rating of the uth user on the ith item, $r_{u,i}$, can be computed as a weighted sum of the rating by *the same user* on other items as shown in Eq. 1, where j denotes all of items rated by the uth user; $sim(i, j)$ defines the similarity between the two items i and j.

$$r_{u,i} = \frac{\sum_{j \in ratedItemsByUser(u)} sim(i,j) \times r_{u,j}}{\sum_{j \in ratedItemsByUser(u)} sim(i,j)} \tag{1}$$

On the other hand, the item-based CF is a weighted sum of the rating to *the same item* by all other users as shown in Eq. 2, where n denotes all of neighboring users who rate the ith item; $sim(u, n)$ defines the similarity between the two users u and n. From our preliminary experiment, we found that the rating rather depends on the item than the user; therefore, the item-based CF is our option, and it is abbreviated just by "CF" in the remaining of the paper.

$$r_{u,i} = \frac{\sum_{n \subset usersRateToItem(i)} sim(u,n) \times r_{n,i}}{\sum_{n \subset usersRateToItem(i)} sim(u,n)} \tag{2}$$

For the similarity score, there have been many measurement approaches to capture the similarity between two users and also two items. Pearson correlation coefficient, Cosine distance, and Euclidean distance are the most popular approaches to compute similarity. In this paper, Euclidean distance is chosen as our similarity.

2.2 Performance Measure

Given TP: the number of true positive, TN: the number of true negative, FP: the number of false positive, and FN: the number of false negative. F-measure [14] is computed based on two other measures: Precision (Pr): the fraction of positive prediction examples that are relevant (truly positive), and Recall (Rc): the fraction of truly positive examples that are correctly predicted as positive. F_β is a combination between precision and recall in a single formula. A constant $\beta \in [0, \infty)$ controls the trade-off between the precision and recall, as shown in Eq. 3. β is generally set to 1 which lead to Eq. 4.

$$Pr = \frac{TP}{TP + FN} \quad Re = \frac{TP}{TP + FN} \quad F_\beta = \frac{(\beta^2 + 1) \times Pr \times Re}{\beta^2 \times Pr + Re} \tag{3}$$

$$F_1 = \frac{2 \times Pr \times Re}{Pr + Re} \tag{4}$$

In the emotion prediction domain, it is more appropriate to compute F_1 for both positive and negative classes denoted by F_1^+ and F_1^-, respectively. Since the ratio between positive and negative examples can be imbalanced, we follow the method in Weka [14] to compute the overall F_1 (denoted by F_1^*) using a weighted sum as shown in Eq. 5, where n^+ and n^- are the numbers of positive and negative examples, and n is the total number of examples.

$$F_1^* = \frac{(n^+ \times F_1^+) + (n^- \times F_1^-)}{n} \tag{5}$$

3 Proposed Method: EEG-CF

Let us now proceed to describe our proposed methodology based on the item-based collaborative filtering. We invent a method called "EEG-CF," which combines EEG pattern for each subject and music rating information using CF. There are three contributions in EEG-CF comparing to the traditional item-based CF including:

- An EEG-based similarity for the CF equation in Eq. 2,
- A mechanism to handle an item that has never been rated by other users,
- Outlier removal to discard any sample data whose EEG pattern is very different.

In our work, the assumption is that EEG pattern is more appropriate to compute a similarity score than the user-rating information. *"Similar EEG signals should express the same emotion states."* Equation 6 shows our proposed similarity score, where $dist(i, j)_k$ is Euclidean distance between two users i and j on the kth item (song), and $dist_{max,k}$ is the maximum distance among all pairs of the kth sample to other samples. The closer the EEG pattern is, the more the similarity score becomes. Moreover, we also try to improve the similarity score by applying Jaccard coefficient [9] as shown in Eq. 7, where $|S_{i,j}|$ is the number of common song rated by the users i and j, and $|S_i|$ and $|S_j|$ are the numbers of songs rated by users i and j, respectively.

$$sim(i,j)_k = \frac{dist_{max,k}}{dist(i,j)_k} \qquad (6)$$

$$sim(i,j)_k = \frac{|S_{i,j}|}{|S_i| \cup |S_j|} \times \frac{dist_{max,k}}{dist(i,j)_k} \qquad (7)$$

There is an issue of the original item-based CF that it cannot compute the similarity if an item (song) has never been rated. To overcome this issue, *all* examples are included in order to be able to compute a similarity score. Unfortunately, noisy examples are also included when this mechanism is applied.

Outlier is one of the major issues that can affect the prediction accuracy. Different users may have different tastes and show various emotion states on the same song; therefore, we propose to exclude any examples whose EEG pattern is very different from the testing example, or its distance is larger than the threshold, θ. From our preliminary experiment, the best parameter is an average of overall distance plus a standard deviation as shown in the updated similarity equation below (Eq. 8).

$$sim(i,j)_k = \begin{cases} \frac{dist_{max,k}}{dist(i,j)_k}, dist(i,j)_k \leq \theta \\ 0, dist(i,j)_k > \theta \end{cases} \qquad (8)$$

Figure 2 shows the pseudo code, *EEG-CF*, function to predict the rating score for the testing item, *testItem*, assume user i on song k. In the code, there are 4 main steps: (*i*) get a list of users who rate the kth song, (*ii*) calculate the threshold distance, (*iii*) exclude outliers, and (*iv*) compute the item-based CF on the chosen data and return the predicted rating.

```
Function EEG-CF(testItem, testItemEEG, train, trainEEG){
    // Step1: get a user list with the same song on the testing data
    song = getSong(testItem);
    userList = getUserListFromSong( song, train );
    if( size(userList) == 0) userList = train; // use all subjects

    // Step2: calculate threshold distance
    for(i=1; i<size(userList); ++i){
        dist[i] = computeDistance(testItemEEG, trainEEG[ userList[i] ]);
    }
    threshold = mean( dist ) + sd( dist );

    // Step3: exclude outliers
    for(i=1; i<size(dist); ++i){
        if(dist[i] <= threshold) sim[i] = dist[i];
        else sim[i] = 0;
    }
    dist_max = max( sim ); sim = dist_max / dist;

    // Step4: compute the item-based CF and return result
    pred = computeItemCF(sim, userList);
    return pred;
}
```

Fig. 2. Pseudo code of our proposed method, EEG-CF

4 Experimental Data

There are two data sets in the experiment: (*i*) DEAP and (*ii*) our data set, as shown details in Table 2. The first data set is a standard benchmark called "A Database for Emotion Analysis Using Physiological Signals" (DEAP), while the second one is collected by our team.

Although music is a stimulus in both data sets, the main difference is that DEAP's subjects had to listen to all 40 songs, while our subjects chose to listen to 16 songs from overall 40 songs. Hence, they have different data characteristics; the DEAP's matrix, where row is each observation and column represents song, is "dense"; whereas, the matrix of our data set is "sparse".

4.1 DEAP Data Set

In DEAP, there are 32 participants who watched one minute segment videos from 40 YouTube videos. During the experiment, 32 electrode positions were recorded. After the end of each video, participants were rating their tastes level in continuous scale

Table 2. A summary of data acquisition of the experimental data sets: DEAP and our data

Characteristics	DEAP	Our data
#subjects	32	15
#songs	40Youtube videos	16 MIDI songs
Song selection	Subject must listen to all songs	Subject chose their own songs from 40 songs
Rating method	Self-Assessment Manikins (SAM)	Self-assessment manikins (SAM) on 2D space
Rating score	{1,..,9} discrete scale	[−1,1] continuous scale
Emotion state	1 emotion/song	Many emotions/song (converted to 1 emotion/song using the most frequent value)

varying from 1–9 called "Self-Assessment-Manikin (SAM)" scales [15]. For valence, each level is defined as "unhappy or sad" (valence = 1) to "happy or joyful" (valence = 9). For arousal, each level is denoted as "calm or bored" (arousal = 1) to "stimulated or excited" (arousal = 9). In the experiment, the SAM scale is transformed from {1,…, 9} to [−1, 1].

4.2   Our Data Set

In our experiment, there were 15 subjects participated. Ages ranged from 22 to 30 years old. Questionnaires were given to subjects for collecting personal information and musical preferences. Then, subjects were instructed to select 8 familiar songs and 8 unfamiliar songs from 40-song library. Approximately half of all songs were used in previous studies in the emotion-music research, and the remaining songs were relatively recent popular music. Familiarity, rating from one to six, was indexed by subjects to indicate how familiar they were to specific songs. Waveguard™ EEG [16] was prepared for capturing brainwave, with Polymate AP1532 amplifier and APMonitor brainwave recorder software[1]. While listening to 2-minute music clips, 12 selected electrodes, which is shown in Fig. 3, were placed near the frontal lobe according to 10–20 international system and recorded EEG signals. The selected electrodes were selected based on the assumption that the frontal region of brain has high relevance with emotion [17]. Impedances of each electrode were managed to be acceptable values below 20 kΩ. Sampling frequency was set at 250 Hz, and notch filter was off. 16-second pauses were included between each song in order to avoid lasting effects from previous song. Moreover, subjects were asked to minimize their movements as possible and close their eyes while listening to the music to avoid noise that would contaminate EEG data. Total duration in this session was 30–35 min.

To avoid cognitive load due to emotion reporting, we separated EEG signal recording and emotion annotation. After music listening session ended, subjects directly rated their emotion states on the two-dimensional arousal-valence space, while

---

[1] The software is developed for Polymate AP1532 by TEAC Corporation.

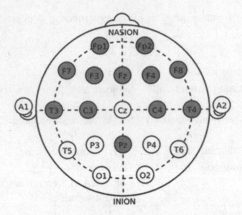

Fig. 3. 12 selected electrodes placement according to 10–20 international system

listening to the same songs from the previous session. The annotation of emotions was performed by clicking on the emotion space shown on the screen. Ranges of arousal and valence values are between −1 and 1. Guidance of arousal-valence emotion model was given and explained to subjects prior to annotate in order that subjects were familiar with this emotion model. After each song's emotion annotation was finished, subjects indicated confidence level of annotated data on the scale of 1 to 3.

Emotion perception in music is quite subjective. Same music can elicit different emotions in different persons [18]. Therefore, self-emotion annotation is necessary in emotion recognition because the technique directly reflects current emotions of listener. We decided to use emotion reported from subject directly as emotion tagging for particular song.

Since subjects were allowed to rate their emotion *many times* in one song, each example represents at the level of *song segments* (not entire song). However, this experiment focuses on the emotion state per subject/song, so the song-segment data for each subject is aggregated by an average. Finally, subject could comment about participated experiment when all of sessions were completed.

4.3 Data Preprocessing

According to annotation results, the average of confidence level of annotation from every subject was 2.358 with standard deviation of 0.67, meaning that we could sufficiently confirm that the emotions reported from subjects were corresponding with real emotions. For the data preprocessing in previous researches, one of the most common feature extraction algorithms is to transform EEG signal from the time domain to the frequency domain. Power Spectral Density (PSD) [19] is our choice of data transformation applying to one-minute temporal window of EEG signals into 5 brain waves. These frequency bands from low to high frequencies, respectively, are called Delta (1–3 Hz), Theta (4–7 Hz), Alpha (8–13 Hz), Beta (14–30 Hz), and Gamma (31–50 Hz). There is also one additional type of feature called "Difference Asymmetry"

Table 3. Statistics of the experimental data sets: DEAP and our data set

Characteristics	DEAP	Our data set
#features	230	90
#examples	1,280	240
%Positive valence examples	63.13%	72.50%
%Positive arousal examples	63.91%	57.50%

(DASM), which is calculated from the difference of feature between a systematic pair of electrodes and previously used in emotion recognition research from EEG [1–3]. Excepted for Fz and Pz, electrodes were paired according to positions in left/right hemisphere of scalp. Fz was paired Pz in the relation of anterior and posterior position. Totally, we obtained 5 features from each 12 electrodes by PSD, and 5 additional features from 6 pairs of electrode. The combinations of these 90 features were used as input for emotion classification and prediction in following steps. Table 3 demonstrates the processed data. Note that the imbalanced ratio is slightly high in DEAP, and there is a severe imbalanced issue in our data set on valence (72.50% positive examples).

5   Experiment

The experiment was conducted on two data sets: DEAP and our data set. Each data set composes of two emotion state values: arousal class and valence class, so there are two separated binary classifiers. To facilitate the evaluation of statistical significance of performance comparisons, all of the experimental results are based on 10-fold cross-validation.

The task of the experiments reported below is threefold. First, we aim to show that our collaborative filtering (EEG-CF) outperforms the traditional one (CF). Second, we want to find out whether or not Jaccard coefficient can improve the performance by comparing between EEG-CF and EEG-CF (JAC). Finally, we illustrate that the proposed method can overcome almost all of the classical classification techniques including: C4.5, SVM, and MLP. Note that there are three SVM variations with different kernels: Support Vector Regression based on universal Pearson VII function based kernel, SVM based on Radial Basis Function kernel, and SVM based on linear kernel [20], which are abbreviated as SMO(puk), SVM(rbf), and SVM(lin), respectively.

5.1   Comparing to the Traditional Collaborative Filtering

In this section, our method (EEG-CF) is compared to the traditional collaborative filtering (CF). The results in Fig. 4 show that, in our data, EEG-CF had better F_1 than CF; there are 27% and 10% F_1-improvements on valence and arousal, respectively. However, there is no significant difference in the DEAP data set.

The reason that the traditional CF performs worse than our method is because, in the sparse data set, there are some items (songs) which have never been rated by users,

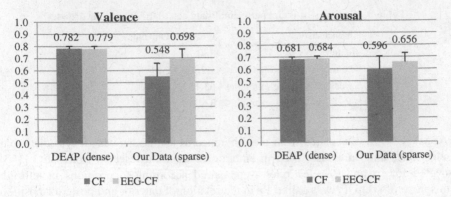

Fig. 4. Comparing of F_1 between CF and EEG-CF on valence (left) and arousal (right)

so there is not enough information for CF to provide accurate prediction. On the other hand, EEG-CF can still perform relatively well in the sparse data set. This infers that our method can correctly predict subjects' emotion state of the new song, which has never been rated.

5.2 Comparing to the Proposed Method with Jaccard Coefficient

There is an attempt to further improve our method by applying Jaccard coefficient as shown in Eq. 7. Unfortunately, the experimental results (Fig. 5) indicate that Jaccard coefficient cannot increase the system performance in terms of F_1. There is no difference in the F_1-results between EEG-CF and EEG-CF (JAC), so EEG-CF is our preferred choice to be compared to the existing works in the next section.

5.3 Comparing to Other Existing Classification Techniques

A new technique is usually deemed useful if its performance compares favorably with that of other techniques. Therefore, we compare here EEG-CF with three classification techniques: C4.5, SVM, and MLP.

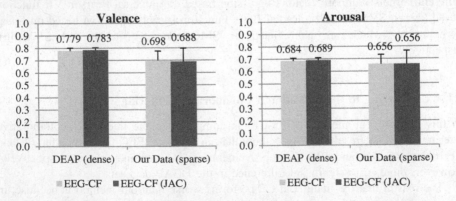

Fig. 5. Comparing of F_1 between EEG-CF and EEG-CF (JAC) on valence (left) and arousal (right)

Figures 6 and 7 demonstrate the results in terms of F_1 on valence and arousal, respectively. Note that the first three bars are baseline cases including (i) AllPos: predicting all examples as positives, (ii) AllNeg: classifying all examples as negatives,

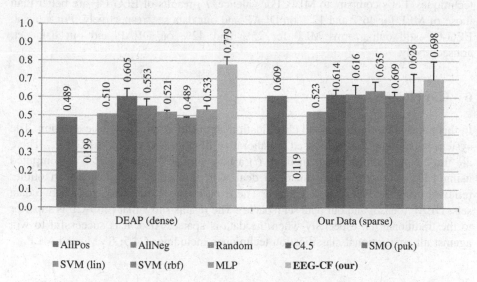

Fig. 6. Comparing F_1 between our method (EEG-CF) in the last bar and other classification techniques on valence. The average and standard deviations are shown. AllPos, AllNeg, and Random (the first three bars).

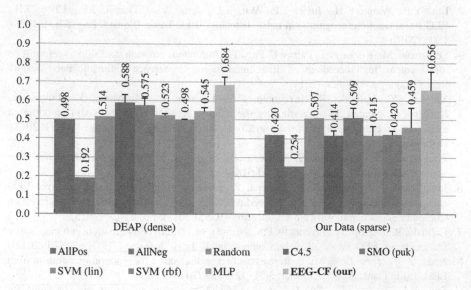

Fig. 7. Comparing F_1 between our method (EEG-CF) and the last bar to other classification techniques on arousal. The average and standard deviations (SD) are shown. Note that there is no SD of AllPos, AllNeg, and Random (the first three bars).

and (*iii*) Random: randomly identifying half of the data as positives and the rest as negatives. The results indicate that EEG-CF outperforms all of the baseline cases on all data sets, while other techniques give the result close to AllPos.

From the result, it shows that our method significantly overcomes all of the existing techniques. Let's compare to MLP. For valence, F_1-results of EEG-CF are better than those of MLP for 46% and 12% on DEAP and our data set, respectively. For arousal, EEG-CF still outperforms MLP for 25% and 42% on DEAP and out data set, consecutively.

6 Conclusion

In this paper, we present a novel classification algorithm to predict music emotion. The system is based on the item-based collaborative filtering and called "EEG-CF." There are three contributions in our method: (*i*) a new similarity score for CF is computed using EEG data, (*ii*) a mechanism to deal with unrated items, and (*iii*) an outlier removal using the EEG-based distance. The experiments were conducted on two data sets: DEAP (dense) and our data set (sparse). The results show that EEG-CF is superior to the traditional CF especially when the data is sparse. Also, it is successful to win against all conventional classification techniques including: C4.5, SVM, and MLP.

References

1. Bos, D.O.: EEG-based emotion recognition. Emotion **57**(7), 1798–1806 (2006)
2. Lin, Y.P., Wang, C.H., Jung, T.P., Wu, T.L., Jeng, S.K., Duann, J.R., Chen, J.H.: EEG-based emotion recognition in music listening. IEEE Trans. Biomed. Eng. **57**(7), 1798–1806 (2010)
3. Soleymani, M., Koelstra, S., Patras, I., Pun, T.: Continuous emotion detection in response to music videos. In: Proceedings of IEEE International Conference Automatic Face Gesture Recognition, pp. 803–808 (2011)
4. Yamano, Y., Cabredo, R., Inventado, P.S., Legaspi, R., Moriyama, K., Fukui, K., Kurihara, S., Numao, M.: Investigating the relation between brainwaves and emotions in music. In: Proceedings of Workshop on Computation: Theory and Practice (WCTP-2012), Philippines (2012)
5. Jatupaiboon, N., Pan-ngum, S., Israsena, P.: Real-time EEG-based happiness detection system. Sci. World J. (2013). Article id 618649
6. Jatupaiboon, N., Pan-ngum, S., Israsena, P.: Emotion classification using minimal EEG channels and frequency bands. In: Proceedings of the 10th International Joint Conference on Computer Science and Software Engineering (JCSSE2013), pp. 21–24 (2013)
7. Cabredo, R., Legaspi, R., Inventado, P.S., Numao, M.: Discovering emotion-inducing music features using EEG signals. J. Adv. Comput. Intell. Intell. Inform. **17**(3), 362–370 (2013)
8. Jenke, R., Peer, A., Buss, M.: Feature extraction and selection for emotion recognition from EEG. IEEE Trans. Affect. Comput. **5**(3), 327–339 (2014)
9. Sun, H.F., Chen, J.L., Yu, G., et al.: JacUOD: a new similarity measurement for collaborative filtering. J. Comput. Sci. Technol. **27**(6), 1252–1260 (2012)

10. Sarwar, B., Karypis, G., Konstan, J., Riedl, J.: Item-based collaborative filtering recommendation algorithms. In: Proceedings of the 10th International Conference on World Wide Web (WWW 2001), pp. 285–295. ACM, New York (2001)
11. Yapriady, B., Uitdenbogerd, A.L.: Combining demographic data with collaborative filtering for automatic music recommendation. In: Khosla, R., Howlett, R.J., Jain, L.C. (eds.) KES 2005. LNCS (LNAI), vol. 3684, pp. 201–207. Springer, Heidelberg (2005). doi:10.1007/11554028_29
12. Russell, J.A.: A circumplex model of affect. J. Pers. Soc. Psychol. 39, 1161–1178 (1980)
13. Koelstra, S., Mühl, C., Soleymani, M., Lee, J.S., Yazdanim, A., Ebrahimi, T., Pun, T., Nijholt, A., Patras, I.: Deap: a database for emotion analysis; using physiological signals. IEEE Trans. Affect. Comput. 3(1), 18–31 (2012)
14. Van Rijsbergen, C.J.: Information retrieval: Butterworths (1979)
15. Bradley, M.M., Lang, P.J.: Measuring emotion: the self-assessment manikin and the semantic differential. J. Behav. Ther. Exp. Psychiatry 25(1), 49–59 (1994)
16. Waveguard. http://www.ant-neuro.com/products/waveguard
17. Schmidt, L.A., Trainor, L.J.: Frontal brain electrical activity (EEG) distinguishes valence and intensity of musical emotions. Cogn. Emot. 15(4), 487–500 (2001)
18. Schubert, E.: Loved music can make a listener feel negative emotions. Musicae Sci. 17(1), 11–26 (2013)
19. Sanei, S., Chambers, J.A.: EEG Signal Processing. Wiley, New Jersey (2007)
20. Üstün, B., Melssen, W.J., Buydens, L.M.C.: Facilitating the application of support vector regression by using a universal Pearson VII function based kernel. Chemometr. Intell. Lab. Syst. 81(1), 29–40 (2006)

Author Index

Printed in the United States
By Bookmasters